A Mile in My Shoes

Cheltenham, MD
www.anointedpresspublishers.com

A Mile in My Shoes

Tammi L. Jackson

A Mile In My Shoes

By: Tammi L. Jackson
www.tammijackson.com

ISBN: 978-0-9843725-4-6
ISBN: 0-9843725-4-7

This book is a work of fiction. Names, characters, places and incidents either are the product of the author's imagination or are used fictitiously, and resemblance to actual persons, living or dead, business establishments, events or locales is entirely coincidental.

To purchase additional books:
www.tammijackson.com

Cover Design:
Michael Caruso

Cover Photo
by: Falko Jaretzky

Published by:
Anointed Press Publishers
(a subsidiary of Anointed Press Graphics, Inc.)
11191 Crain Highway
Cheltenham, MD 20623
301-782-2285

Acknowledgement

To my ***Heavenly Father,*** from whom all blessings flow. Thank you for saving me from myself.

To the ***late Oscar & Ammie Cunningham,*** thank you for showing me love unspeakable.

To my parents ***Kaffie Jackson & Larry Jeter,*** thank you for all you've done.

To my aunts ***Cindy White & Deborah Cunningham,*** there are no words to express how much you truly, truly mean to me.

To ***Saundra Bryant, Melody Tucker, Bobby 'SLLIM' Williams, Janisha Thomas, Trina Moore, William & Shajuana Ross, Lakita Thompson, Charise Clark*** & of course my editor, ***John David Kudrick*** for your unyielding support during this process.

And last but certainly not least…

To ***Vri,*** you make it all worthwhile. Thank you for being so extraordinarily patient with me during this process. May you never have to live the lessons in this book, but I pray you learn the wisdom that comes from having walked A Mile In My Shoes.

Dedication

This book is dedicated to everyone who has ever felt they were drowning in depression, submerged in heartache, or overcome by circumstances.

May the lessons in this book serve as a life preserver.

Foreword

Life is a maze of relationships filled with ambiguities, twists and turns. Everyone wants to be loved, admired, and respected. However, after being hit with some of the harsh and painful experiences of life, a lot of people give up on having these emotions ever becoming fulfilled. Some people even relinquish the yearning to be admired, and they believe that it is futile to think they will be respected. But at the end of the day, if one hasn't received the love, respect, and admiration he or she needs, at our core is still the desire to be acknowledged. There is no better way to know yourself than through relationships. We need relationships for affirmation, interaction, conversation, satisfaction, and self-actualization.

A Mile in My Shoes is a biography of a woman with a fierce determination to redefine relationships and help us make the most of every painful situation. She pulls back the curtain on this often overlooked yet important topic and reveals the guilt, the pain, the sorrow and yes, at times, the joy of trusting. I find her message especially powerful and inspiring when she speaks about the "inner journey"— each relationship gives you an opportunity to see yourself, to stop repeating self-sabotaging patterns, and refine the journey to self-discovery.

Our relationships can be, not merely a source of joy, but the way for us to awaken to God and real love. To find this real love in our relationships, we must go through a profound transformation that will take the form of a journey: a journey from special relationships based on the pursuit of individual interests and specialness, to holy relationships based on the pursuit of a truly common goal.

An excellent portrayal of honesty, the author clearly distinguishes the subtle ways we sabotage our relationships, then sets forth a clear new paradigm of being conscious creators with powerfully conceived steps and commitments, and excellent exercises for transforming oneself and others from victim to victor relationships.

Using a style that draws us into the ongoing inquiry into how intimate relationships work, this book uses mile markers along the way that indicate how far you have travelled and how many miles are remaining for you to build and heal your relationships. This book does more than share the highs and lows of committed relationships. It is not meant to be portrayed in the wrong light. It distills valuable insight that will enable you to see people in a much different light.

This kaleidoscopic writing will provide solace, comfort, guidance and realization that healthy relationship begins with being more aware of self and the impact of your personal beliefs and choices. No one else can define you, or live your life for you, or take away the beauty and uniqueness that is you. They may try, but they won't be successful unless you allow it. An awesome book on building and healing relationships.

~ Dr. Jamal-Harrison Bryant

Introduction

While stalking the life of one woman, **A Mile In My Shoes,** gives a birds eye view account of childhood hurt, that carries over into adult relationships. The author causes the reader to consider the role molestation plays in promiscuity, and further questions the role parental neglect and abandonment plays in neediness and insecurity.

A Mile In My Shoes, takes a look at how the things that happened to us as children shaped us into the adults we've become. Take growing up under the conditions of a "Traditional" household with mom and dad coexisting in a healthy relationship. This affords you a life example or training if you will. However, when you're without the benefit of training, you go into a relationship unqualified, trying to "Helen Keller" your way through it; leaving behind a trail of failed relationships due to unrealistic expectations; lack of training.

Sadly, much like the characters in this book, a lot of women fall victim to their past and find that their unable to have a healthy relationship with a man because they're not looking for a mate, their looking for a daddy; someone to affirm them.

This book depicts the unfortunate; the vicious cycle will continue from relationship to relationship until she stops looking for her daddy and seeks her father.

Who Am I?

She Loves Me, She Loves Me Not

Marcus ran the barrel of the gun from my temple to my jawline, whispering, "You're so beautiful." Although I'd played Tina to his Ike on several occasions, this was the first time he inspired fear in me. The man standing in my living room was crazy. Not the confident, ladies' man I almost married.

I glimpsed over at Damon's motionless body slumped against the wall; he needed me. As I tried to move closer, Marcus wiped the sweat from his brow and yelled, "Stop … moving!" As he paced the floor, he tugged on the bottom of his shirt with his left hand, saying, "Just let me think." He continued pacing and talking to himself.

I asked, "Have you been taking your medicine?"

He didn't respond. Instead, he asked, "Did you ever love me?"

Although my heart was pounding, without hesitation I responded, "Of course."

"Then why you with this fake Al B. Sure-lookin' nigga? He's not who you think he is!" His tone lowered as he said, "*We* should be married with kids by now. We should be having kids!"

In an effort to calm him, I said, "Marcus, you're not thinking clearly." Pointing at Damon, I said, "He needs an ambulance. You don't want murder on your hands. Marc, right now it just looks like a botched robbery. If ... if you just ... just leave ... I-I'll ..."

He yelled, "No!" then went back to pacing the floor, ranting, "I love you! We're s'pose to be together." With the gun at his side, he asked, "Marry me?"

When I didn't respond, he stopped pacing and his face went blank.

From across the room, he pointed the gun in my direction and this time commanded, "Marry me!"
As I shook my head proclaiming I can't, he aimed the gun at my head and said, "IF I CAN'T HAVE YOU ..."

All the nights on the block, with Trey and the boys, I never stared down the barrel of a gun. I took a deep breath and prepared myself for the next moment.

With nothing to lose, I said, "So this is the answer… love me to death?" I walked toward the gun, yelling, "If you gonna do it, do it!"

He didn't flinch.

"It's still all about you, huh, Marcus!" I said. "What you want when you want it. You want somebody to feel sorry for you … 'DeLaina left me.' DeLaina should've left you a long time ago. You wanna blame somebody? YOU did this. You diminished our relationship. For four years, you tried to checker your way through a chess game using hereditary cheating habits as an excuse. You running around here screwing anything with a pulse and I let you because I didn't think I deserved better."

I grew angrier as I flashed back to the purgatory he called love, to the cheating and manipulation. I opened my arms wide and yelled, "WHA-CHU WAITING FOR?"

I was staring at a man that I no longer recognized. He backed up, sat on the love seat, and almost in a whisper said, "You're still the prettiest girl I know."

As a single tear ran down his cheek, he placed the barrel in his mouth.

I realized the reality at the eleventh hour.

As he gripped the trigger, I called his name. "Marcus!"

POP!

Love Determines Family

Let's start from the beginning …

I grew up with hot summers and mild winters in Atlanta, Georgia, long before it became the ATL. I can remember climbing trees and playing stickball in the street from early in the morning until the street lights came on.

While I don't remember much about my mother, Felecia, I do remember she was beautiful. She had big almond-shaped eyes, and long silky jet-black hair like my great-grandmother.

We lived with Felecia's aunt, her husband, and their two sons: Calvin, age nine, and Michael, who was eleven.

I can remember that even my mother called her aunt "Momma." Although I knew that she was my great aunt and he was my great uncle, I can't recall ever calling them anything besides Mommy and Daddy. I don't know if it was because that's what my cousins called them or at age four I already knew the difference between having a child and being a mommy to one.

Mommy had a very close relationship with God and everyone knew it. The phone rang constantly from people she didn't know, asking for prayer as though they could find hope in her voice alone. I didn't know it then but she had the faith for it. Saturday nights, the house would be jam-packed with people who just wanted her to lay her hands on them as if there was promise in her touch.

Now, Sunday was the Lord's Day, make no mistake about it. Everyone in the house that had breath in their body was going to church—except Daddy, as he had a never-expiring get-out-of-church-free card.

***

It was about 8:15 one Sunday morning and Felecia was passed out on the daybed in the den, reeking of cigarettes and gin.

The night before, I sat on the bed and watched my mother get dressed to go out. She put on her short, red dress, the one that hung off one shoulder, and secured her hair to fit underneath her blonde bob wig.

I asked as I always did: "Can I go?"

As she laced up her high heels, wrapping the laces around her calf, she said, "No, not this time, baby."

She never said yes but it was her "No, not this time" that gave me cause to keep asking.

Anyway, Mommy and I got up to cook breakfast as we did every Sunday morning.

Mommy peeped into the den on her way to the kitchen and said, "Get up, party animal. Time to get ready for church."

9:05 …

"Alright, gal! You should've brought ya fass tail in diss house earlier so you could get some sleep. Na, go-on and get up na. Breakfast ready."

After breakfast, Mommy washed me up and dressed me in the pretty pink dress with the bows on the sleeves, laid out a dress for my mother, and checked on my cousins.

Mommy asked my cousin, Michael, "Did dat gal get up yet?"

"No, ma'am."

I saw a storm brewing in her eyes. Mommy marched into the den and said, "Felecia LaNee Richards, if you don't getch-yo tail in dat bathroom and wash da smell of Satan off you! Gal, you betta."

"Alright, Momma, I'm up."

She showered and pulled her hair back into a ponytail in no time flat. She came out of the bathroom with the blue dress on that she wears sometimes on Saturday nights. Mommy didn't like it at all, so she said, "Felecia, I bought you a dress last week. It's hanging on the back of the door in the bathroom."

"Momma, I don't like dat dress; it don't fit me right."

"Oh, wha-chu saying is, it don't show ya behind or ya bosom like that dress der. Let me tell ya something, ya may go out diss house by ya-self looking like a street walker, but ya ain't fit-na go nowhere wit me or diss baby looking like dat."

My mother reached for her robe and said, "Dat's fine, Momma. I ain't feel like goin' to church no-how."

"Heathen, ya going to church but-chu not goin' looking like dat."

I don't know what came over Felecia. Mommy said it was a demon, but whatever it was, it possessed her to put her hand on her hip, roll her eyes, and say, "I'm grown. You can't tell me what to do."

I could hear Michael in the other room whisper, "Is she still drunk?"

Mommy took a step back almost like she didn't trust herself being too close. She balled up her right fist and rested it on her hip, pointed with the other hand,

and said, "Diss here my house. I ain't bring ya into diss world but I'll sho' help ya leave. Listen to me and listen good: as long as ya live in my house, ya gonna abide by my rules. And if ya can't … ya need to have someone else's roof above ya head. Ya hear?"

"Momma, I have a child of my own. You can't talk to me like I'm a lil' kid. I'll come and go as I please."

Michael and Calvin were peeking around the corner, shaking their heads in disbelief.

Mommy grew angrier. "Well, I hope it pleases ya to leave. Let me tell ya something, lil' fass-tail gal … spreading ya legs and making a baby doesn't make ya a woman. When was the last time ya spent time wit dat baby or even told her ya loved her?

All ya care about is partying and running the street. Ya don't care 'bout nobody but ya-self … and since ya don't have respect for me or diss house, I want ya out by tomorrow."

"I don't need you!" my mother said. "Why put off for tomorrow what you can do today? Ain't dat wha-chu always say, Momma?" She snatched the receiver off the hook. I heard her give someone the address and say, "Yes, please. I need one as soon as possible."

As Mommy finished putting the dishes away, I heard her mumbling, "Lord, it's in yo hands now."

I watched my mother storm around the house,

packing, talking to herself. I was almost afraid to ask but I did, dragging each word out as if to prolong the inevitable answer. "Can I go?"

Without looking at me, she mumbled, "No, I'll be back."

I heard a car horn. I ran to the window and saw a yellow cab sitting in the driveway. I was waiting for Mommy to stop her from leaving, to tell her that they'd talk about it after church or something. I remember thinking, *Make her stay*. I watched her pack up everything, including the yellow and white dress with the buttons down the front that she told Mommy she didn't like. She made three trips to the cab, checking and double-checking to ensure she took everything that belonged to her ... except me.

My mother called every Sunday at first ... then only on holidays ... till finally she didn't call at all. Sometimes I think Mommy felt guilty for asking my mother to leave. She loved me just a little bit harder because of it. I could feel it in her touch. Taste it in the plate she'd make just for me. Or maybe I loved her that much.

***

Five years later, things began to forever change. Mommy got everyone up and ready for school as she did every morning—cooked breakfast, made our lunches, and walked me to the bus stop. Everything seemed normal.

Several hours later, I was sitting in Ms. Paginski's reading group, where we were reading a play. I was one of the maidens and my turn was finally coming up when a voice came over the PA system and said, "Ms. Paginski, please dismiss DeLaina Richards. Her father is here to pick her up."

Daddy never picked me up from school before but I didn't question it. I was excited to leave early. I packed my bag in a hurry and skipped to the office. All the ladies in the office were masked with a sad look upon their faces. One came to the doorway, shaking her head, and said, "He's waiting for you outside, sweetie." I stared at her as I walked to the door. I remember wondering why she looked so sad. Through the doors to the outside ...

Daddy was sitting in the car looking down when I hopped in.

"Hi, Daddy!"

He looked up at me with his red eyes. "Hi, Pigtail." That was his pet name for me.

"What's da matter, Daddy? Why you look so sad?"

He filled his lungs with air. "Mommy died this morning."

Not yet understanding death, I asked, "She died?"

"Yeah, she's gone to be with the Lord."

"Is she coming back?"

At age nine, I knew that God was affiliated with the church and we went there to be closer to him, but all the pieces hadn't fallen into place yet. I didn't understand how God was going to help me get dressed in the mornings without Mommy or how he was going to put food on the table for three kids or how he was going to stop Daddy's eyes from being red all the time.

Daddy had never gone to church with us but, after Mommy died, church became his second home. He began to call the Lord's name more often than not—and not because he was mad or cussing like before. I was always Daddy's lil' girl but it seemed we grew even closer after mommy died. He could barely take two steps without me.

Funds were tight but Daddy always seemed to make a way. On my tenth birthday, Daddy cooked my favorite dinner: fresh fish, grits, and buttermilk biscuits from scratch. After dinner, Michael excused himself while Calvin cleared the plates.

Daddy made small talk, saying "You sure are getting old. How old are you today … 30?"

As I laughed, saying "No," the boys came back to the table singing "Happy birthday to you, happy birthday to you…" Calvin carried the cake, while Mike toted a big box with a huge bow on top. After they sang "May God bless you," I closed my eyes tight and wished really hard that Mommy would tuck me in just one more time. But it didn't happen, even though I blew out all the candles.

I didn't want the cake; I wanted to open the gift. But Daddy said, "Eat your cake and ice cream first." In a whiny voice, I said, "DAAAAAADYYYY!"

"A'ight, a'ight."

I ripped the bow off the box and tore into the paper. I opened the box to see a big stuffed teddy bear. He was tan with white paws and feet. When I picked him up, he was almost as big as me. I remember thinking, *He's soft like cotton*. Pointing at the bear, Daddy said, "That was your Mommy's. She had him when she was a little girl. I'm sure she would want you to have him now." Though Daddy had him cleaned and re-stuffed, he still smelled like Mommy.

"What are you gonna name him?" Mike asked.

"Charlie!" I gave Daddy a big hug with Charlie squeezed between us. "Thank you, Daddy."

***

As I got older, I realized that Mommy and Daddy chose me. They could have sent me away at any point but, without a penny from the state or my mother, they nurtured me as though I was one of their very own—proving that blood doesn't determine family ... love does.

Daddy's Girl

Two years later, Michael left for college. The one I wished would leave, stayed. I was twelve and Calvin was turning seventeen in the next week or so. There was something about him; we just could not get along. Every chance he got, he shattered my spirit.

When no one was around, he'd say, "How you get to be so ugly? You're not going to be good for anything but laying on your back, just like yo momma." His words poisoned the well from which I drank for years to come.

Calvin got hooked up with the wrong crowd and started running the streets, selling drugs, determined to screw up his life. He graduated—barely—and not without Daddy constantly hanging a foot up his behind. Once he graduated, he just hung around the house. One morning, I woke up with him in my bed again with his hand down my panties, moving his fingers.

I jumped up yelling, "Stop! I'm gonna tell Daddy!!"

In a devilish tone, he said, "Daddy had to work today … so you know what that means. I get to play with the lil' ugly girl all day. Any … thing … I … want." He smiled with an evil grin.

"NO!"

I grabbed Charlie and ran into Daddy's room, locked the door, pushed the recliner in front of it, and got underneath the bed. It wasn't as easy sliding under there at twelve as it had been at nine. Calvin stood outside the door banging and yelling for me to let him in. He stopped for a while, then in a calm voice, he said, "Come on, Lainee, I was just playin'. It was just a game. I won't do it anymore."

I stayed in that one spot for hours until Daddy got home. Finally, I heard his boots coming up the hallway. Daddy banged on the door.

"Gal, you betta let me in."

I opened the door and jumped in his arms.

"What's wrong?" he asked.

Calvin was standing at Daddy's side, glaring at me.

I started crying. "I was scared, Daddy, and—"

Calvin interrupted. "It's my fault, Dad. I was scaring her. Sorry, Lainee."

Daddy hugged me. "I'm home now. Nobody's gonna scare my baby anymore."

As a result of the things I began to internalize, I started fighting more at school. Daddy didn't care too much at first about the fighting as long as I didn't start it and as long as I won. I remember the first fight I got into ...

Cassidy Wilkerson, a girl in my fourth-grade class, called me ugly because the boy she liked let me borrow a pencil.

"You ugly!" I told her. "You're so ugly, you make onions cry."

That little girl slapped me so hard that she busted my lip and it swoll up like Jimmy Walker's. When I got home, Daddy fussed at me and told me if I didn't beat her butt, he was gonna beat mine. He raised boys, so all he knew to tell me was what he told the boys.

"Now you listen to me, Pigtail, here's what you do ..."

He told me to wait until there were a lot of people around and punch her in the stomach.

"When she doubles over, grab her by the hair, and bang her head on your knee."

He said if I did it right, I wouldn't have to worry about her bothering me again. Sure enough, I never had another issue with her.

***

Sixth-grade classes did nothing for my attention span. In an effort to get to the root of me fighting and causing trouble, they tested me, thinking my mind was underdeveloped. They found it to be the opposite and decided to skip me a grade.

I went into middle school awkward. With money being tight, buying new clothes wasn't an option. I had gotten hand-me-downs from the boys, which I didn't really mind at first, until the name-calling started, then I found myself fighting almost daily.

The person I was in elementary school didn't fit in with the middle-school kids. We were all in the same grade but they had a year more of maturity under their belts.

I just wanted what everyone wanted: someone to talk to. The girls wouldn't let me play with them; they said I wasn't pretty enough, and although most of the boys were too scared of me to say, no, I couldn't play, it's no fun having people be your friend because they're afraid to have you as an enemy. It's these circumstances that made it easy for daddy to become my best friend.

I always knew that he wasn't my biological father, but I couldn't have loved him any more if we had the same blood coursing through our veins. He didn't have to keep me; he chose to. When Mommy died, he could have sent me away. Instead, he poked out his chest and said, "That's my daughter." As I think back now, I don't remember Daddy ever saying "I love you." I remember when he'd tuck me in, I'd say "Night-night, Daddy," then kiss him on the cheek and say "Love you." All he'd say is "Night, baby-girl."

One day, I tried to force his hand. I said, "I love you," out of the clear blue. He didn't respond. So I said it again. "Daddy, I said I love you." Without flinching, he said, "That's good." It didn't really bother me; I didn't know anything else. But I can say that even at that age I knew if I ever forgot my name, I'd still always know Daddy loved me.

He had high blood pressure and high cholesterol but, otherwise he was relatively healthy for his age. The doctor told him to watch his salt intake and to get plenty of exercise. He did ... Daddy walked two miles every morning with or without me.

On the morning of July 17, there was a change. I must have fallen asleep on the couch in the living room. I woke up to Daddy calling my name. I thought he wanted me to come and get something I left in the yard or to go for a walk with him. I didn't feel like doing either so I ignored him. The second time he called, I got up and went out front to see what he wanted. He was sitting on the top step in his blue overalls, holding his chest.

"Go get the neighbor," he said.

I ran to the neighbor's house and banged on the door. Ms. Staples opened the door angrily with her robe and scarf on. Once I told her what was going on, she came right out. I ran back to the house, but when I looked back, I didn't see her. She had gone back into the house. Ten minutes later—it seemed like an hour—she finally came out. She had changed her shirt and put on that long stringy wig she always wears.

I got him down the steps. Ms. Staples came around to the passenger side to help me get him into the front seat. On the way to the hospital, it seemed we caught every red light. Even now I don't understand why she wasn't running them.

He wasn't saying anything. I got scared and called out his name.

"Daddy."

"Hm."

I needed to hear his voice. I think in my fourteen-year-old mind, hearing him respond gave me hope. A couple minutes later, I called out his name again.

"Daddy."

"Hm."

He had on his seat belt but his body began to lean to the left, onto Ms. Staples.

She yelled, "Hold him up! Hold him up!"

I grabbed my life in my arms. I saw his dentures slip out of his mouth onto the seat. I yelled out his name.

"DADDY!"

He didn't respond and suddenly he became heavier. As we pulled in to the emergency room parking lot, Ms. Staples leaned on the horn. Daddy was six-three and 276 pounds. One doctor got in the car in the front seat, an orderly got into the backseat on the driver's side, another was on the passenger side, and still another in the backseat—all trying to get him out of the car. Once they got him out of the car, I went straight to the phones in the waiting area and called my second cousin—Daddy's niece Tilley. I liked her but I never seemed to be one of her favorites. She wasn't home. I left her a message telling her that we were at the hospital. I didn't know Tilley was a nurse before that day. By the time I hung up the phone, she had just gotten off work and was walking through the emergency room. When she saw me from the corner of her eye, she looked around to see who was with me before speaking.

In a startled tone, she asked, "Wha-cha doing here?"

When I didn't reply, she ran to the nurses' station to find out who had been brought in recently, but they didn't have the information yet. With me on her heels, she ran from room to room hoping not to confirm her fears. She found him lying on a table, a nurse to his left with the paddles in her hand and the doctor standing over him saying, "Call it."

Tilley's voice could be heard throughout the waiting room as she screamed "NO!"

The nurses tried to console her. "I'm sorry. You know we did all we could do."

She collapsed onto the floor. Once she came to and realized what had happened, she looked at me and burst into tears. That's when I knew he was gone. I rarely talked to my mother; in fact, I could count on one hand how many times I talked to her in the past two years but I knew her number like I knew my own. I went back to the phone and called her. Angry that I got her answering machine, I hung up. I felt the anger building as I thought of all the things I wanted to say. I called back. The answering machine picked up again. I began tapping my fingers, waiting for the recording to stop, anticipating the beep.

With a cracking voice, I said, "For the first time in my life, I need you, and you're nowhere to be found. I just wanted to tell you my daddy died."

Tilley pulled herself together, grabbed my hand, and said, "Hey na, let's go home."

She took me back to the house to make phone calls. As I walked through the house, I remember thinking, *The house has never sound so quiet, not even at night*. It was almost as though even the house was lamenting. Although everything was exactly where we'd left it that morning, the five-bedroom house seemed so empty.

I went into Daddy's room, straightened up his bed, and folded his pajamas. I put on his robe and rocked in his rocking chair, replaying the morning in my mind. Staring at the picture of he and Mommy on the dresser, I burst into tears.

"I'm sorry! Daddy, I'm sorry!"

Tilley ran into the room grabbed me and held me in her arms. "Your daddy's in a betta place now." With fear tight in my throat, I moaned, "He's all I had.

Don't nobody else want me."

She held me tighter. "God's gonna take care of you."

By this point, I was mad that God had taken both, Mommy and Daddy. He knew I didn't have anyone else and he took them anyway. I shook my head in confusion. Holding on to Tilley for dear life, I could only think, I want my daddy.

As I got older, I found out that Daddy knew he was dying. Apparently, he'd had a conversation with Tilley two days prior. The result of the conversation was him asking her to take care of me should anything ever happen to him. She agreed, thinking she'd never have to hold up her end.

After the funeral, she took me back to my house

and told me to pack up all my clothes—that I was going to live with her. Although there were three empty rooms upstairs in her house, she told me I could have the room in the basement. I didn't mind; I had a bathroom all to myself. Tilley gave me a place to live, but I could tell she didn't want me there.

She was nice to me right after the funeral. Although that quickly dissipated, she acted like I was the daughter she never had when others were around. When her husband—Uncle John-John, as we called him—was around, she acted almost like she was jealous. She never left us alone. I never got an uncomfortable feeling around him, but when he was home, she'd always hover around like she was afraid something would happen.

Once, I was sitting in the living room watching TV when he came in.

"Hi, Uncle John-John."

"That's all? Just 'Hi'? You betta come give me a hug."

I liked him. He always smelled good even when his clothes were filthy.

Still embracing me, he asked, "How've you been?"

"Fine."

He pulled back enough to see my face and gave me a half smile. "The older you get, the more you look like your mother." He laughed. "Same nose." He ran his thumb along the side of my face. "And the same high cheekbones. I see I'm gonna have to get my shotgun."

Out of the corner of my eye, I could see Tilley standing in the doorway. She folded her arms as he kissed me on the forehead. After he went into their bedroom and closed the door, she began fussing at me.

"Didn't I tell you to wash those dishes?"

"No, we haven't even eaten dinner yet."

"Hey na, don't you sass me, lil' girl. Go to your room."

It seemed she treated me worst when he was in town. But for some reason, when he was within earshot, she was attentive. I think she even called me "sweetie" once. Unfortunately, he wasn't around much; he had a tractor-trailer business. He drove those big eighteen-wheelers cross-country. Sometimes he'd be gone for weeks at a time. I heard Tilley tell him once, "You only come home for sex and clean clothes." The walls were thin, so I knew at least one part of that statement was true.

Depression

Life as I knew it had changed. I hated the sun for rising, taunting me, reminding me that it was yet another day without my daddy. I was barely making it minute to minute, contemplating suicide at least twice a day before crying myself to sleep. For some, death is something you just have to deal with. Try explaining that to a fourteen-year-old who not only lost a parent but her whole world.

I couldn't understand how everyone's life was going on while mine was at a standstill. It was six weeks to the day since Daddy had passed, and the pain was riding on me like it happened that morning. I made it until about noon before I decided the pain was more than I could bear. I was the only one in the house. I went into Tilley's bathroom looking for something to stop the tears. I rummaged through her medicine cabinet and found a bottle of sleeping pills. There were only about nine or ten left. I cupped my hand and tossed the pills in my mouth as I threw my head back. I took two big swallows to get them all down and just sat there on the bathroom floor waiting for my pain to go away. I just didn't want to cry anymore. I didn't want it to hurt anymore. I remember sitting there thinking, *Once I finally close my eyes, when I open them, I'll see Mommy and Daddy*. It didn't work out that way.

I woke up in the emergency room to Tilley's voice. She was on the phone asking the person on the other end, "Who's gonna pay this hospital bill? Shoot, I should have left her there. Hum, you should see her, she looks just like no-good mama. She aint gonna be good for nuffin, but laying on her back, just like her. Have to go ... she's waking up."

Standing over me with her arms folded, she let out a sarcastic chuckle. "You can't do anything right."

The ER physician came in. "I think she's going to be just fine but I'd like to admit her to the psychiatric ward on the ninth floor ... just for an evaluation."

Tilley quickly interrupted. "No! I work down at County. I'd like to have one of those doctors take a look at her. Nothing personal."

Daddy had taken out a second mortgage on the

Foster Care

By the New Year, my so-called family had given up hope. They placed me in a foster home in New York with a bunch of bad-behind kids that were a day away from Juvi Hall.

With me riding shotgun, my court-appointed caseworker parked in front of the dilapidated, brick-front, single-family home. I walked inside and stood in the foyer as the caseworker went over the paperwork with the foster mother— Ms. Alisha.

Though she welcomed me with kind words, there was no love in her eyes. It seemed obvious to me that Ms. Alisha's only concern was the monthly foster-care payment she received for each kid. I soon found that my presumption was true. When a new child came into her home, she made them feel special during the caseworker's fourteen-day checkup. After which, each of us were on our own—just another check in the mail and another adult who didn't care.

Circumstance after circumstance forced me to grow up fast.

I shared my room with three other girls. My first night there, I didn't sleep at all. I laid there for hours trying to nod off, and finally got up around 3:30 a.m. and went downstairs to watch TV. I was sitting cuddled up in the corner of the couch when I heard the front door squeak open. I stared at the doorway to see who was creeping in at such an hour.

A girl not much older than me sauntered into the room with her stiletto boots and said, "You must be the new girl." She sat down and grabbed the remote.

"Can't sleep, huh?"

I nodded, looking her up and down. She had on a half pound of makeup, a midriff top, and a skirt that came just below the crease of her hips.

She smelled familiar … like the way my mother use to smell after being out all night.

"So how old are you?" she asked.

My birthday had just passed the day before. It meant about as much to me as it did to everyone else—just another empty, meaningless day. Glaring at her with a bothered look, I mumbled, "Fifteen."

"Cool, you can pass for eighteen easily. I just turned seventeen a couple weeks ago. What's your name again?"

"DeLaina."

"What's your story, DeLaina?"

I snapped. "I'm hungry and ain't no food in this place."

She laughed. "Come with me." She led me through the house and down the back stairs. "By the way, my name is Catherine, but everybody calls me Cat."

She pulled out her keys and unlocked the door to what seemed to be a basement apartment.

"Ms. Alisha know you be down here?"

She laughed, "Yeah, she insisted I have my own space."

It turned out that Ms. Alisha found out that Catherine was working at the strip club and saw dollar signs. Apparently, she was a foster mother itching to turn madam. She tried to bully Cat into prostitution. Although Cat was far from innocent, prostitution wasn't on her to-do list.

Ms. Alisha had gone so far as to tell Cat, "You ain't got no place else to go. Don't nobody want you. Listen to me, there's money to be made. Okay now, there's a john coming over tonight at 10:30. Either you make him feel real good or you betta be gone when I wake up. Have I made myself clear?"

Catherine was very passive and mild mannered. Although she wasn't a fighter, she knew plenty of people who were. She called her cousin Quentin who was some big-time drug dealer on the east side. He was the only family she had left in the city. Although Cat could call him and ask for anything, she was adamant about not living with him … but vague as to the reason why. At the thought of being forced to turn tricks, Cat called Quentin, crying, reiterating Ms. Alisha's pyramid scheme that would put her on top in one way and Cat in another.

Quentin told her, "Pack your things, I'm coming to get you."

"No, I wanna stay here. I just don't wanna do that …"

He told her, "I'm on my way."

When Quentin showed up, Cat answered the door and called for Ms. Alisha. Having never met him, dollar signs danced in her eyes as she looked him over, from his brown gators to the two-carat diamond studs in each ear.

He asked, "Is there somewhere we can talk?"

Thinking he was there to make a date, Ms. Alisha was eager to talk to him. She led him to the basement and said, "What can I do for you?"

As he unbuttoned his jacket, revealing the gun securely tucked in the left side of his pants, he said,

"Lady, you obviously have no idea who I am." Even his tone was intimidating. "I'm Quentin Dyer—Catherine's cousin."

Ms. Alisha stood paralyzed, like someone had just told her she was white.

She began babbling. "Oh, well, uh, you know, we just love Catherine. She's a delight to be around and—"

"Shut up! Cat said someone was trying to make her sell her body. You wouldn't know anything about that, would you?"

"No, uh ... well, uh, maybe she misunderstood a joke I was playing on her."

"Um-hum. I don't like jokes. So this is how it's gonna go down ... You're going to apologize and rescind the offer to make her hoe of the year. And to make up for the ... shall we say ... misunderstanding, she will need her own room, special privileges, and anything else she wants. Am I making myself clear?"

"Crystal."

***

I must have looked as though I was starving. Cat told me to help myself to whatever was in the refrigerator. She and I quickly became friends. For the next couple of months, we hung out on the corner with her friends after school. One evening as I was walking back to the foster home, an ambulance zoom past me.

By the time I got to the house, the police were arriving. I walked in the house to see the paramedics surrounding Ms. Alisha. I followed Cat as she raced through the kitchen. She grabbed all she could and threw it in a hefty bag.

As I watched her packing, I asked, "What happened to Ms. Alisha?"

"Look, I'm not going to another foster home. Social services will be here soon to get all of us."

I, too, was tired of being shipped around. "I don't wanna go anywhere else either, Cat. Where you gonna go?"

"I don't know ... probably my cousin Quentin's house until I get my own place. I can ask him if you can stay if you want, but you gotta hurry up."

I ran upstairs, grabbed my pictures, Charlie, and all the clothes I could fit in one suitcase. I eased downstairs and out the front door, trying not to bring attention to myself. One of the officers standing out front noticed me as I walked by. He stood there with his thumbs in the belt loops of his pants, looking like a black Barney Fife.

"Where are you going, Miss?" he asked.

Cat walked up behind me and said, "Leave her alone, Leonard. She's with me."

He moved aside.

I had to ask. As we walked away, I whispered, "How do you know him?"

"He used to be a regular at the club."

Quentin

We stayed with her cousin Quentin. Everyone called him Dyer. He was okay, but I got a weird feeling when he was around, the same feeling I always got when Calvin was around. When Quentin looked at me, it was like I could feel a draft from the nakedness he created. I made sure I was never alone in the house with him. So, at night when Cat went to the club, I went with her. I'd sit back stage and watch the women change from their clothes and dignity into nothing. For most of them, this was their life; there wasn't anything else—they didn't know anything besides taking their clothes off and shaking their butt.

I watched Pecan, one of the dancers, get dressed. She was very pretty, like my mother. Statuesque with a pretty brown skin tone, big almond-shaped eyes, and full lips. As she warmed up, practicing her squats and splits, I remember thinking about the names that the boys called Cat at school and wondered if men called Pecan names too. I was getting desperate for money. I knew I could do what they were doing, but I hated the way it felt when men undressed me with their eyes. On Pecan's way to the stage, she looked at me and said,

"With the right outfit and a lil' makeup, you can do it too."

When Cat and I got home, Quentin was at the kitchen table counting stacks of money. Tired from the drama of the club, Cat went straight to bed and I plopped down on the couch in the living room to watch TV for a while.

He came and sat beside me. "You know you sexy, right?"

I said what I always said to him: "Boy, leave me alone."

Admittedly, at times my feelings were conflicting. Although there was something about him that made me uneasy, I couldn't help but find myself somewhat flattered. Dyer was a big-time hustler, handsome, well dressed with money and respect. The girls around the way would kill to be in my position, but he was attracted to me—the tomboy, the one that no boy ever looked at twice.

He reached over me for the remote, rubbing his hand up against my thigh. When I pushed him away, he grabbed the remote and turned the TV up. Quentin sucked his bottom lip and said, "Have you ever had oral sex?" He had always come on strong but this time I was uncomfortable.

I got up to go to the bedroom that Cat and I shared when he pushed me down.

"I won't hurt you," he said. "I promise. Just let me get a lil' bit of that."

He was scaring me. I tried desperately not to let him see my fear as I said, "You must be smoking that mess you selling."

As I tried to pull away, he took it out and began stroking it. "Wet it for me. Come on, put it in your mouth."

My heart began pounding. I had never seen one up close before. "Quentin, stop playing." I jerked away from him and proceeded to my room.

He called out, "Okay, okay, I'm sorry. Give me a hug and I'll leave you alone."

He stood there with his belt still buckled while his lower extremity poked through the hole of his unzipped pants, pointing at me. I continued walking toward my room when he ran up, grabbed me, pushed me against the wall, and ripped my shirt open.

"Stop, Quentin! Stop!"

He kept grabbing at my pants, trying to pull them down. When I swung at him and missed, he grabbed my arm. I kept raising my knee upward in hopes of nailing him at least once, but he was too tall for me to hit anything.

He threw me onto the floor and began cursing at me. "Shut up! You been living here free for months. Don't you think you owe me something?"

He sat on top of me, leaned forward, and pinned my wrists down while he licked my breast slowly as if it were an act of passion.

"NO! Quentin, I'll get a job. I'll pay you whatever you want. Please stop! Cat! Cat!"

Cat walked out to the living room, rubbing her eyes. As she got closer, she saw Quentin on top of me with his right hand around my throat and trying to guide himself into me with his left.

She charged at him, knocking him off of me. "What are you doing! She's my friend, Quentin!"

He zipped up his pants. "Awe, man, I was just playing."

Bonnie and Clyde

The next morning, Cat and I left. She had enough saved for us to stay at a motel for a few nights until we could find a place. Cat had this friend that hustled down 28th Avenue. He offered me a spot on his corner and said he'd look out for me. I knew nothing about selling drugs, I had no idea what I was doing, but it was money and it beat sitting in Quentin's crib waiting for him to rape me.

Cat was the only family I had. Although I was scared, I made up in my mind that I'd do whatever I had to—to survive.

So, there I was on the corner for hours every evening after school. Since I was the only female on the block, the guys tried to step on my toes. One night, some dude tried to stick me up for my product and my cash, but luckily Cat's boy, Trey, and his boys, Ricky and Blue, were coming up the block.

Trey yelled, "Yo, get dat nigga!"

The dude took off running. He didn't get far. A few minutes later, I heard three shots—pop, pop, pop. Trey came back to see if I was okay. There were about nine of them that rolled together but only five consistently. There was Ty, short for Tyrone. Walter, Trey's cousin, but everyone called him Blue ... I'll just say he makes Tyrese look light skinned. There's Rick ... pretty Ricky was what they called him. He was one of those El Debarge looking dudes. And then there was Antwan, they called him Big Ant—he was six-four and 340 pounds.

Trey said, "Look, lil' momma, you a sittin' duck out here." He stepped in closer. "You pretty, too, so these dudes think they can take yo stash without repercussions." He reached in his pocket. "Yo, take this. Just keep it, but the rule to the game is, if you pull it on somebody, ya betta be prepared to use it."

I was scared. The game just got REAL.

"I ain't neva shot no gun before, Trey," I said.

"I figured as much. I'll take you to the firing range Saturday."

That night when I got back to the room, I stood in the mirror staring at the young woman I was becoming. I took off the Raiders baseball cap that I never left the house without, took my hair out of the braided ponytail, and fingered the waves to fall around my face. Uncle John-John was right. From what I could remember, I did look like my mother.

I grabbed a handful of my big t-shirt and pulled it tight to show my waist. As I turned to the side looking at the shape my young body had taken, Cat walked past the bathroom door and asked, "What are you doing?"

Embarrassed, I said, "Nothing," and pretended I was getting something off my shirt.

Laughing, she said, "You checking ya self out?"

I looked back in the mirror at the girl that had been looking at me. I asked Cat, "Do you think I'm pretty?"

She walked up behind me and pulled my hair away from my face. "What do you see?" As I shrugged my shoulders, she said, "Girl, you are gorgeous. You know how many girls would kill for your shape, your high cheekbones and chinky eyes? You're beautiful, but what I think doesn't matter—what counts is what you think of yourself."

A couple months later, around midnight, I was leaving the block when a dude ran up behind Trey and put a gun to his head. I backed up against the wall of the corner store. Although I could hear my heart pounding over the commotion of the city, I couldn't stand there and do nothing. Trey had always had my back and never asked for anything in return. I owed him. I pulled out the Smith & Wesson I had tucked in the back of my Gloria Vanderbilts. As I grabbed the piece securely in my right hand, I heard Trey's words in my head—*If you pull it on somebody, ya betta be prepared to use it.* The times we shot at the range didn't prepare me for this moment, but it was now or never. I eased around the side of the building the way I saw it done on TV, shadowed behind two cars, and walked up behind the dude. I jammed the gun in his right side. Scared shiftless, I managed to maintain the façade and played out the role.

I yelled, "Put the gun down!"

"A'ight! A'ight! Be easy. I'm-a put it down …"

He held both hands in the air like he was waiting for his Miranda Rights to be read.

Trey took the gunman's piece and said, "Thanks, lil' momma." He threw me his keys. "Go wait in the car. I got this."

I tucked the piece back in my pants and did as he said. His 5.0 was parked around the corner. By the time I got there, I heard two shots—pop, pop. I quickly got in and sat in the passenger seat, shaking. Moments later, Trey ran up to the car, got in, and sped off. Neither of us said a word for the twenty-three minutes it took to get to my apartment. He pulled into a parking space, turned the car off, and said, "DeLaina! Look, I don't really know what to say. I want to say thank you but it doesn't seem like enough."

"You did the same thing for me."

"Yeah, but you a lil' shorty. I'm s'pose to protect you. Some of the niggas I roll wit wouldn't have done dat, and dat's real."

I felt a feeling inside that I hadn't felt in a very long time. I felt appreciated, but the feeling was quickly taken over by fear that someone would retaliate. Reluctantly, I asked, "Why did he want to kill you?"

"Because he thought I killed his brother."

"Did you, Trey?"

He took a deep breath. "Lil' mama, dar ain't nuffin to be scared of. No one's gonna hurt you."

I believed him the way I had believed Daddy when I cuddled up next to him during a lightning storm and he'd tell me everything's gonna be fine.

I said, "Okay," and got out the car.

He hopped out with one leg still in the car. "Do you want me to stay the night?"

"Please."

We fell asleep on the couch watching a movie Cat rented. The next morning, I woke up in my bed, suddenly recalling the couch and a movie. I looked underneath the covers. I was fully clothed. I went to the living room to find Trey lying on the pullout couch in a wife beater and his boxers.

Puzzled, I asked, "How did I get in my room?"

As he said, "I carried you," I instantly, remembered feeling his lips pressed against my forehead.

Over the course of the next several months is when the pattern of my life took shape. Being with him—living in his world—allowed me to escape the emptiness of my own.

Cat called us the black Bonnie and Clyde. He and Cat were my best friends but my closeness with him was different; we were inseparable. The closer we grew, the more comfortable I became living in his life. He started out as the "big brother." The protector in him reminded me of Mike, which meant if Trey was like a brother, I was having incestrial feelings for him. As hard as I tried to keep them to myself, it became apparent, even to Cat. She kept telling me to talk to him but I was scared. Trey had a reputation for being a dog. He'd meet girls, make them feel irreplaceable, sex them until he got bored, then toss them away like a used tissue.

Cat was right: I was in love with him, but I was afraid of being tossed aside. I was fine with the relationship we had because the bottom line—even without the title and sex—I was his number one girl.

I watched Trey fade in and out of relationships,

secretly wishing it was me. The funny thing is, the biggest issue in his relationships was me—the girls couldn't stand taking a backseat. Whomever came into his life had to understand I was his right hand. By the following year, we were like two peas in a pod.

He had my back like a chiropractor. The more we hung out, the less he wanted me on the corner. One afternoon, Trey noticed some dude posted up across the street, staring in our direction.

He told me, "Diss ain't no place for you, Laina."

"I been out here for a year and a half. Why you buggin? Besides, these dudes ain't got your back. They don't care about you."

"Calm down, ma! I know you'd take a bullet for me long before dees niggas, but I don't want you to. I care about you too much." He kissed me on the lips. "I don't want anything to happen to you."

The next day, neither of us said a word about the kiss, but every time I looked at him, all I could think about was how soft his lips were.

Three days later, Trey and I were on the block. It seemed like any regular day on the corner until we saw that same dude posted across the street. Trey ordered Blue to round up the fellas and told Ricky, "Yo, take Bonnie home and come right back."

I argued, "No! I'm stayin wit you. Besides, we gotta pick up Cat. Remember, she said she needed to talk to us."

"I'll pick up Cat." Trey hugged me and whispered in my ear, "Unless I tell you otherwise, tomorrow I need you to go to my grandma's house and get the silver box underneath my bed. Okay?"

"Yeah, Trey but—" He kissed me on the lips before I could finish my sentence.

"Trust me," he said.

I looked back at Trey as I walked to the car with Ricky. "Something doesn't feel right," I said. "Ricky, what's going on?"

"Nuffin, Bonnie. He just wants his girl off the street."

"His girl?"

I didn't believe him. As we pulled off, I turned around in my seat like a little kid and watched Trey until he was out of sight.

"Go back!"

"Bonnie, Trey wants me to take you home. Relax … you worried for nothing."

Ride or Die

I had never felt that kind of churning in my stomach before. I got home around midnight, tried to watch TV, but something wasn't right and the feeling grew stronger. I had to go back, but my car wasn't working. I strapped up, put the .45 in my ankle holster, then loaded the chamber of the Smith & Wesson and put it in the inside pocket of my Starter jacket. After zipping up, I hopped on Trey's crotch rocket and peeled out of the parking lot, leaving a trail of smoke behind me. I ran the long light at the corner, zoomed through three neighborhoods, and hopped onto the highway, weaving in and out of traffic.

By the time I got back to the city, everyone was gone. The block was silent. Too quiet for a gang- and drug-infested city in New York. I rode around for hours before I remembered that Trey said he'd pick up Cat. I rode past the strip club to see if Cat was still there.

Bruno, the thick-necked bouncer, said "Naw, she left over an hour ago wit some dude."

"Was it Trey?"

"Naw, but I think it was his car … his tags say *DA ONE*, right?"

I was the only one Trey ever trusted enough to drive his car. Things were looking worse and worse by the moment. I rode around for another hour looking for answers to the questions I was afraid to ask. I went home and stretched out on the couch for several hours before I heard a knock at the door. I jumped up and ran to the door, hoping Trey had lost his keys. I looked through the peephole—it was Ricky. As I opened the door, he walked in, never making eye contact.

Before I could say anything, Ricky said, "We found Trey's car out by the junkyard."

I was young but I wasn't dumb. By that point, I had seen too many *Mike Hammer* and *Kojak* episodes with my daddy to not recognize bull when I saw it. Ricky didn't ask me if Trey was home or if I'd heard from him. He automatically assumed or knew he wasn't here.

"Have you seen Cat?" I asked.

"Naw, not since Trey picked her up."

Bruno said that Trey didn't pick her up. I sat on the arm of the sofa trying to piece things together. Interpreting who, what, and when from Ricky's body language.

Needing a moment to collect my thoughts, I asked, "Do you want something to drink?"

"Yeah, some water would be cool."

Once in the kitchen, I peeped around the corner into the living room only to see Ricky popping open the barrel of his gun, checking the bullets. My gut told me he killed Trey—and if I was right, then he had come to kill me, too. Remembering I still had the .45 on me, I took it out of the holster, tucked it in my pants, and grabbed a bottle of water and a Corona from the fridge. As I walked back toward the living room, I noticed him fidgeting on the couch.

I handed him the bottle of water and asked

"What do you think happened to Trey?"

When he said, "Your guess is as good as mine," I took the Corona to his head like I was Cal Ripken, Jr., knocking one out the park. As he fell forward onto the floor, I said, "I doubt it!" I patted him down and removed the pistol from his pants. When I checked his pockets, I found Trey's Gucci watch and the necklace that Cat never took off. It was the only thing that she had of her mother's.

The phone rang and rang but, I didn't have time

to answer it. I ran to the closet and grabbed the duct tape. I pulled Ricky's arms behind him and bound his wrists. Bent his legs back, taped his ankles, and bound them to his wrists. While I waited for him to come to, I put on my Timbs and laced them up tight.

He was still unconscious. After about 45 minutes, I began to worry that I had killed him. I put my index finger underneath his nose; he was still breathing. I got a cup of water and doused it in his face. He opened his eyes and began flipping around. I sat in front of him, straddled a wooden kitchen chair with the .45 in my right hand as he struggled, trying to break free.

"What is this? What's going on, Bonnie?"

"You first! Where's my family?"

"I don't know!"

Trey always told me it ain't what you say, it's how you say it. Ricky rarely came to our apartment because he was afraid of Cat's snake. I grabbed one of the little white mice from the cage and put it down his shirt.

He squirmed around and yelled, "Wha-chu doin!"

I placed the snake on the floor in front of him.

"Let's try this again," I said. "WHERE'S TREY AND CAT?"

I watched thug turn punk in a matter of seconds. As the snake slithered closer, hissing, Ricky began trembling and crying.

He yelled, "Get it! Get it!"

"Did you kill Trey?"

He nodded his head yes. I looked away, fighting back the tears. As the snake slithered over his shoulder, I asked, "Why?"

He laid there sniffling, trembling, and begging. "DeLaina, please! Please get the snake off me. DeLaina, please!"

As I put the snake back in the tank, his pager started going off, then mine began vibrating across the cocktail table. Knowing Trey was dead, there was no one paging me that I wanted to talk to.

I stood there with my arms folded demanding, "Answer me!"

"I owed TJ like ten G's."

I shook my head and sighed. TJ was a hustler on the other side of town who'd been trying to move in on our turf for about six months.

Ricky continued, "I woke up one morning to TJ standing ova me wit a gun to my head askin' bout da money."

He got quiet. I lodged my foot in his side and yelled, "AND?"

"Wh-when I-I said I ain't have it, dat nigga took out all the bullets except one and pulled the trigger like four times. So when he offered me the deal … I took it."

"What deal?"

"He said he'd wipe away my debt if I took out Trey."

I kicked him as hard as I could, attempting to lodge my boot between his ribs. I began cursing. "You stupid! He set you up!" I paced the floor, shaking my head in disbelief.

I finally asked, "Where's Cat?"

His silence answered my question.

"What did she have to do with this?"

"She was there when TJ offered me the deal."

Confused, I asked, "You said they came in the morning. Wait! Why was Cat ... Were you sleeping with her?"

He closed his eyes.

"You son of a ..." I kicked him repeatedly even after the muscles in my thigh tightened.

He let out a faint, "I'm sorry."

"Not yet!"

I gagged him with the bandanna he wore around his wrist and taped his mouth. As I leaned down to place a plastic bag over his head, the front door flew open. It was Blue and Ty. After, fumbling to get to my gun I took aim moving it back and forth between the two.

Blue said, "Put the gun down, Bonnie."

"NO!"

Ty said, "We been calling and paging you all morning tryin' to warn you … Bonnie, we know what Ricky did."

I was scared and didn't know who to trust. "How do I know y'all not in on this with him?"

Blue threw his hands in the air. "DeLaina, we don't have time for this…"

I turned the gun on Ricky. "Not until I finish what I started."

Blue walked toward me and grabbed the gun. "NO! Trey would not want this. Yo, for real, we got this." He looked at Ty, pointed at Ricky, and said, "Help me get this fool. We gotta get up outta here." I watched them drag Ricky out and throw him into the trunk of their car. I felt cheated.

After they left, angry and in a state of despair, I stood in the shower hoping to wash away an ounce of my pain, as the last twenty-four hours replayed in my mind. I should have known something was wrong. I should have been there. Ricky had been acting weird for weeks. Trey and I both noticed it. I knew that punk wasn't his friend. As I began to plot taking out TJ, I remembered what Trey said: Unless I tell you otherwise, tomorrow I need you to go to my grandma's house and get the silver box underneath my bed. I hopped out the shower and strapped up, preparing for a ride through the city. As I pulled into his grandmother's driveway, I was relieved that her car was already gone. I didn't want to have to face her.

He always told me if I ever got into trouble to go to his grandma's house. They kept a spare key underneath the hood of the grill out back. I let myself in. Through the kitchen and downstairs to Trey's room. He lived with his grandmother before he started staying with me and Cat. He'd still stayed there from time to time.

When I opened the door to his room, his scent embraced me. I instantly flashed back to the first time I pressed my nose up against his skin. I flashed back to the night I woke up screaming from a nightmare about Daddy dying. He ran into my room and just held me while I cried hysterically. He never asked what was wrong. He just held me.

If I knew the last time I saw him was the last time I'd see him, I never would have blinked. I wanted to ball up in a corner with the pillow that smelled the most like him and cry, but I didn't go there to cry.

Everything was neat and in place. The box wasn't underneath the bed. His grandma must have cleaned his room. As I searched, I found the metal box in a wooden storage chest at the foot of his bed, buried underneath some sweaters. It was locked. I searched around for the key, on the dresser, in the drawers. No key. I went out back and rummaged through the shed looking for a screwdriver. I found a flathead and a hammer. After forcing the lock off, I sat on his bed and stared at the box resting on my lap. It seemed that time slowed as I reached down to open it. There were stacks of money underneath an envelope addressed to me. It was getting harder to fight back the tears. Chills ran over my body as I realized Trey knew last night was his last night. Trembling, I read the note to myself …

Bonnie,

If you're reading this, it probably means they got me. I knew this day would come. You know the chances we take with the game we play. You and Cat have to get out of town. You can't be out in the street like you're in the wild, wild west with no one at your side. Don't get blood on your hands. Let Ricky and dem cats handle it.

You too smart for this. You got caught up in a world that ain't yours. But you played your part, DeLaina.

I need a favor. There's 80 G's in this box. Take it, move away from here, and go back to school. Start ova without this street life.

I love you.
T
PS: Ricky will look after you, but be careful. Remember what I told you … trust no one, and everyone that befriends you ain't your friend.

Clutching the letter to my chest, I laid on his bed, inhaling him. Trying to figure out where I would go from there. Before I met Trey and Cat, I had nothing to live for. They gave me a reason, but TJ and Ricky stole that. Although I couldn't get it back, I had a .45 that said I could even the score. I popped open the chamber to ensure it was loaded. I grabbed Trey's old backpack and stuffed the money and letter in it.

I sat in the driveway, straddling the motorcycle as I plotted my ride through the city. I twisted my hair up, secured my helmet, and road down TJ's block … twice. No sign of him. But you know what they say: third time's the charm. As I sat at the four-way stop waiting my turn, I saw him coming out of the corner store with some of his boys. Without thinking, I unzipped my jacket enough to slip my hand inside.

As I rode closer, I reached inside my jacket, but before I could pull out my piece, shots rang out from a tan, Ford Taurus with tinted windows sitting at the adjacent corner. I sat there and watched TJ and four of his boys fall to the ground. After the last guy fell, the gun was pulled back into the car and the window went up. I was paralyzed until I heard the sirens racing up the block. The Taurus sped off and I took off in the opposite direction. I ducked behind an abandoned building two blocks away to catch my breath. Gasping for air, I snatched off my helmet and listened to the ambulance rushing to the scene.

I sat there with my helmet tucked under my arm, taking short, deep breaths, all the while mapping out my next move. I knew I could no longer stay in the 718 area code. I wanted to get out of town; I wanted to go somewhere, anywhere. But I had to make a stop first. I went back to the apartment and grabbed some pictures, a couple pairs of jeans, and Charlie. I hopped back onto the highway, heading south, weaving in and out of traffic. Every time I thought about Cat and Trey, I got low and tried to outrun my emotions. After I crossed the New Jersey turnpike, I noticed the needle was near "E."

I pulled up to the pump and took my helmet off. I reached in my front pocket for cash then, patted both back pockets before I remembered the cash in the backpack. I took the backpack off slowly and clutched it in my chest. By the time I filled up the tank and stared at a map contemplating my destination, I was tired. I grabbed a room at the Motel across from the Diner. I fell asleep no sooner than my head hit the pillow … only to relive the whole ordeal in 3-D. I woke up several times throughout the night to my own screams. Finally, I just laid there counting the cracks in the ceiling until I got a call from the front desk reminding me that checkout was at noon. I stayed there three more days … long enough for me to gather my thoughts and come up with a plan. Going back north was out of the question. There wasn't anything there for me anymore. I wanted to call Mike but I didn't want him wrapped up in this mess. I wanted to go someplace where no one knew me.

Reagan

I hopped back on the bike and rode until I saw the "Welcome to Maryland" sign. I didn't know why, but that's where I wanted to be. No one wanted to rent to a seventeen-year-old, but fortunately, I came across the owner of an apartment building who was desperate for money. Initially, she told me no. But when I said I could pay the whole year up front, she handed me a pen and a lease agreement. It definitely wasn't in the best neighborhood; from my living room, I could see the guys hustling on the basketball court.

I contemplated going back to the street to start up my own thing. As I debated, I watched them every day, studying their process, identifying a more effective way of doing business. One afternoon as I was watching their mannerisms, singling out friends from foes, I began to size them up, identifying them with the old gang one by one in my mind: Trey, Blue, and Ricky. As much as I craved that life, I knew it wouldn't be the same without the real Trey. As I formulated a plan in my mind, I kept hearing the words from his letter: go back to school, start a new life without the streets.

A few weeks later, I started my senior year of high school. That's where I met Reagan Mitchell. Rea was a full-figured girl when I met her. I was sitting at a table alone when she walked into the lunch room with two lunches. Like some scene from an after-school special, the kids started in on her.

"That's her problem right dar … two lunches!"

The teacher on duty overheard the kids and said, "Leave her alone. Maybe she has a slow metabolism."

The kid with the big ears rebutted, "Slow? She's Quick Draw McGraw wit a fork."

All the kids laughed but she just brushed it off like it didn't bother her. There was something in her eyes … something familiar about her slow concise steps. Her stride seemed as though she was trying to keep her balance while carrying the burdens of the world on her shoulders.

She reminded me of me, but I was in no place to be anyone's friend. I stayed to myself.

As we moved between classes, someone rushed past and accidentally knocked Reagan's books out of her hands. As she leaned down to pick them up, a group of girls came along and began playing hockey with her history book. As everyone watched and laughed, I was looking to see who the ringleader was. While they were sliding the book back and forth between them, I stepped in and put my foot on top of the book to stop it from sliding.

As I leaned down to pick it up, the ringleader walked toward me. "You shouldn't put your nose where it doesn't belong, newbie. Put the book down!" As I was about to hand Reagan the book, the girl came closer to me, knocked off my Raiders cap, and insisted, "I said, put the book down."

This girl was desperately trying to introduce herself in the wrong way, but I told myself, *Try to be accommodating*. So I put the book down, grabbed the girl by her hair, and smashed her face into the locker repeatedly as I yelled, "Don't. Touch. My. Hat!"

***

A few months later, I noticed that Reagan hadn't been in school for about a week. I heard that her father had passed away. The day she finally returned, she came in late. I excused myself from English class to go to the restroom. As I pushed the bathroom door open, I could hear shuffling. It was Reagan. She was at a mirror trying to compose herself, trying to hide the fact that she'd been crying. Her face was beet red. Still coping with my own issues, I tried to ignore her. I walked past her into a stall, thinking how distraught she appeared, which forced me to revisit my own issues. Standing at the sink washing my hands, I glimpsed up at her in the mirror. She had been crying so much that the redness had diluted the hazel in her eyes. I wanted to leave but something wouldn't let me go.

"I heard your dad passed," I said. "I'm sorry."

She splashed water on her face. "Yeah, me, too."

I knew the pain of losing a parent oh too well. I comforted her to the best of my ability. As it turned out, her pain went deeper than I could have ever imagined.

She had just found out that the man they buried only days prior wasn't her biological father. Apparently, Mrs. Mitchell, her mom, married Leroy King and got pregnant with Reagan. When her mom was eight months pregnant, Leroy beat her within inches of her life and threw her out of a moving car. As Leroy's luck would have it, she was the only girl of eight children. Story was that a passerby found her body on the side of the road. She had lost so much blood that the doctors weren't expecting her or the unborn baby to live. Four of Mrs. Mitchell's brothers and Reagan's grandfather, Bishop Johnson, rushed to the hospital.

They stood around her bed, hands joined, praying to the Almighty—paging Dr. Jesus. When she flatlined, they prayed a little louder, asking him to work a miracle, make a way out of no way. The nurses ran to the room in a panic. Grabbed the paddles, rubbed them together, preparing to shock her heart, but the doctor was already there. Before a nurse could say "Clear," her rhythm reappeared on the monitor. The story is told that the two eldest brothers showed up at the hospital hours later with splatters of blood on their pants and shoes. No one ever saw or heard from Leroy again.

The common ground between Rea and me sparked the development of our friendship. Her family became like a family to me, but I always remembered what Trey said: *Everyone that befriends you ain't your friend*. With that in mind, I kept my past to myself—at least the incriminating parts. I always talked about my best friends, mostly saying that I missed them, but never said their names, like saying their names somehow would tarnish their memory.

College

By the time we left for college, I had discovered makeup and tube tops, and Reagan, well, she had lost over forty pounds and was gaining a whole lot of self-esteem. For the past year she had been referred to as "DeLaina's friend." I think she saw college as an opportunity break away from the shadow.

We met Paige Gibson our freshman year at Hampton University. She was a pretty chocolate girl from a small town in North Carolina that ain't nobody ever heard of. The town where everyone is related in one way or another. She had spent all of her life up until that point working in the family store.

Paige rapidly came into herself. The minute she stepped off the bus, her mentor took her and a couple other freshmen to the local mall for some new clothes and to get their hair done at the cosmetology school just outside of the campus.

Boys began to leer at her in a way she'd never seen. She had never had anyone look at her with a longing look—besides her uncle T-Bone.

She even picked up a nickname. The girls called her "Diva" because every week she was doing something different with her hair: short and black to long and blonde, one extreme to the next. The girls thought it was cute, but the truth of the matter is she changed her hairstyle every week trying to find herself. And because she changed boys the way she changed her hair, the fellas gave her a nickname as well, but it wasn't as becoming as Diva.

Paige desperately longed for that attention. Every guy that told her she was pretty, she thanked him privately. Her naiveté was blatantly obvious. She believed every boy when he said he wanted to be her boyfriend, so she laid with him to consummate their bond. They all probably would have wanted to be her boyfriend if they knew how smart and funny she was, but she only gave them the opportunity to know her body. By the end of sophomore year, she cooled her heels, but not before an STD and two abortions. Reagan and I weren't much better. We were doing pretty much the same things, just never exposed.

Ordinarily, you don't choose your friends. You don't just arbitrarily see a group of people and say, *I'll take the one in the white blouse and the one in the blue shirt,* but I think I chose Paige. I guess because I saw shades of me in her desperation.

Much like Paige, I was confused about sex and love. I thought one begat the other. At least that's the way it was depicted on television. Two people have sex, then someone says, "I love you." So I found myself looking for "I love you's" in the boys dorm. I just want to know somebody cared… at whatever cost.

So, between the frat parties and drunken nights, the next few years flew by. Senior year, Reagan's grandfather got her the motorcycle he'd promised her. Reagan had enjoyed campus life a little too much and almost flunked out of school twice early on. So her grandfather made a deal with her during our sophomore year: if she pulled it together and made it through the first semester of her senior year, he'd buy her a bike. She made it by the skin of her teeth—and not without providing a few favors to her Art Science professor.

On our first official road trip, we rode down to Myrtle Beach for bike week. The only way I can explain it is to say it was like Freaknik on wheels. That's where we met Bria and Sassy. They were a part of a bikers clique that was scouting for new members. After the explosive weekend of jello shots, leather bikini's and drag strip racing, the girls invited us up to Richmond to ride and meet the rest of the gang.

The weekend we decided to go, Paige had to study, but Rea was always down to ride. Rea had gone from 233 pounds to 156 pounds. Although technically, she was still the same person, it seemed her personality changed when she got that bike. Once we began riding with the gang regularly, she became more aggressive and more irrational than usual.

Nonetheless, Rea and I rode up to Richmond. When we got to The Point, a hilltop overlooking the city, we saw bikes lined up and down the strip. Sassy introduced us to everyone, but out of the twenty-four people we met, the only name I remembered was Darrell.

The attraction between us was so strong that he and I pretended not to even notice each other until the night of Bria's birthday party about two months later. He asked me to dance. Naughty by Nature was spinning *hip hop hooray ... ho, ha*. By the time we got to the floor, H-Town was knockin' boots all night long. I could feel the heat from the palm of Darrell's hand on the small of my back. It felt good. After two slow songs, we walked out onto the patio to talk. I could barely hear him talk over my lustful thoughts. As his lips moved, I imagined how soft they'd feel on my collarbone. I wanted him. He offered to take me home. I wanted him to take me wherever there was a room.

He did … again and again.

Twice a week for three months before I finally found out he had a girlfriend—Bria's sister, Angela, who was in school upstate. I stopped seeing him but made sure he saw me. I started riding more often, and it seemed my pants got tighter and my shirts got smaller every week. I wanted him to want me. I did want him, but, looking back, it was for all the wrong reasons. I wanted him more at that point because I couldn't have him.

Angela found out about me and came home for a semester. She of course, started riding with the crew, always with her arms wrapped tight around him. During a ride one Saturday afternoon, we all stopped at the gas station before riding into the city. I hopped off my bike and went inside the store. Angela followed me. Reagan noticed and followed suit. Angela came up behind me and whispered, "I know about you and Relly. I want to make sure you know that it's over."

I stood there for a moment with my back to her, contemplating ramming her head into the wall. She pushed my shoulder and said, "Do you hear me?"
I slowly turned around to find that Reagan had locked her arms inside of Angela's, pinning them back. As I stepped in close, Bria ran inside, yelling, "What's going on?"

Turning to Bria, I said, "Angela was telling me

how intimidating my presence is."

Rea released Angela, giving her a little push.

"Yo," Bria said. "I don't know what just happened, but this is my sister, and if you have a problem with her, you have a problem with me. You understand?"

"Look, Bria," I said. "Your sister put her hands on me." I turned to Angela. "Should that happen again … I will not be responsible for the outcome."

A week or so passed, and Darrell called to apologize for Angela's actions, accepting full responsibility for the situation. By the end of his apology, I invited him over.

I admit it was initially out of revenge, but I can't pretend I didn't care for him.

He eventually broke up with her and took up with me. You couldn't tell me nothing, I thought I had it going on.

A few months after Rell and I started seeing each other seriously, Paige passed on rumors she'd heard about Darrell's temper and the trail of broken hearts he'd left behind.

"It's not my fault that Angela couldn't keep her man."

"And that's really what you think happened … she couldn't keep her man?" Paige asked. "C'mon, you know that ain't what happened. Girl, if he did it to her, he'll do it to you, too."

Her petition for me to abort the relationship fell on deaf ears. I couldn't hear her or anyone else over my desperation. I longed uncontrollably to feel wanted, and Rell made me feel that way.

Besides that, things in my life were looking great! I had finally tracked down my cousin, Michael. We were spending a lot of time together catching up. Apparently, he had moved to Maryland the year before for a job with the Special Forces Unit. And me, I had my man and a job with Brooks & Martin Designs as a junior accountant.

The office sent several of us to Chicago for a three-day training seminar. The original plan was to come back Saturday morning because all the return flights were booked. Anxious to get back home to my man, after my last training class Friday, I decided to go and wait on stand-by. As luck would have it, I was able to get an earlier flight. I came home early, excited to see Darrell ... only to find he was keeping himself busy.

With bags in tow, as I entered the apartment and stepped down into the sunken living room, Darrell jumped up from the floor. "Baby, wha-chu doing back so soon?" he asked.

The big-breasted, half-naked woman he was on top of seemed unfazed. As she put back on her shirt, she cursed him in what sounded like another language mixed with some English. All I could make out was, "Here we go again."

For a moment, I just stood there staring at him. She apologized as she left. I started seeing flashes of red and began walking toward him. He backed away from me, saying, "Calm down, I can explain. It's not what it looks like ...." As he continued backing away, he slipped on the area rug in the hallway and I of course took full advantage of him being down. That was our first official physical altercation.

The Party's Over

I never should have gotten back with Darrell, but what can I say: love has astigmatism. Not exactly sure where the idea came from, but I really thought I could change him … make him do right.

Believe it or not, I think we became conditioned to the fussing and fighting. Honestly, we never really got back on track after that whole half naked chick in my apartment thing. Most times, it felt like he didn't like me, much less love me. He certainly didn't say it. I think he was just used to me, and since I was traveling so much, it made our relationship bearable.

After our annual audit, things slowed down at work, which meant I was at home more … which meant more fights. In spite of our problems, I threw

Darrell a surprise birthday party, hoping it would ease some of the tension.

Let's just say it didn't.

After the party, I found myself sitting at the breakfast nook, reflecting, when Reagan's friend Trish knocked at the door. I hesitated. She continued knocking and pleading: "It's Trish. I left my jacket!"

I decided not to continue hiding. When I opened the door, looking like a light-skinned Anna Mae, she got scared. "Oh my goodness, Laina! What happened?"
"Trish, now is not a good time …"

She grabbed my face, turning it from left to right, and yelled, "Did Darrell do this to you?" I pulled away and walked over to the sofa as she said, "I'm taking you to the hospital."

"I'll be fine. Trish, just get your coat and go!"

Looking down the hallway, she asked, "Are you alone? Is he still here?"

I didn't want to talk … I just wanted her to leave. She disappeared for a while and came back with a zip-lock bag full of ice. "Here, Laina. Put this on your eye. I can't believe that he put his hands on you. Oh, it's about to be on!"

I sat up on the couch. "Okay, look. Trish, this is my issue, so let me handle this my way. I would appreciate it if you wouldn't tell anyone."

There was banging at the door.

"Open the door!" It was Reagan.

I turned to Trish as she said, "Too late … I called Reagan. It's about to be ON!"

I opened the door and Reagan went off … breathing hard and yelling, "Oh … look at you!"

I pulled away. "It looks worst than it is."

As I walked back to the couch, I heard two clicks. With a revolver in her hand, Reagan began roaming through the house, cursing and yelling. "Where is he? Hit me, nigga, hit me!"

I tried to calm her. "I don't know where he is, Rea. Put the gun away!"

Scratching her forehead with the barrel of the gun, cursing, Rea paused long enough to ask, "What happened?"

"I'm not telling you anything until you give me the gun."

She got up and walked to the other side of the room. "Oh, you not getting the gun! If you don't tell me, I'll find him and make him tell me. Betta yet, I'll let Michael ask him."

Rea knew me too well. She knew that if I hadn't told her, I definitely hadn't told my cousin Michael. "Fine," I said. "Put the safety back on and put it away."

Reluctantly, she put the safety on.

"You remember Monique?" I asked. "You know,

the big-breasted chick he had in my house when I was in Chicago?" She nodded her head. "Well, I opened the door and there she was with a halter top and booty shorts. When I asked her what she was doing here, she looked me in my face and said 'I came to drop off my baby daddy's birthday present.' I said, 'Your WHAT?' When she started laughing, it took everything in me not to bust her in her face."

"Why didn't you?" Reagan asked. "I've seen you knock chicks out for less."

"I don't know … I been asking myself the same thing, I mean…" I began pacing the floor

" Anyway, then Monique said, 'You look … what's the word I'm looking for … bewildered. I guess that means he didn't tell you about our baby.'"

"Wait, wait," Trish interrupted. "She said bewildered? The hoe got a vocabulary?"

I continued, "I looked down at her stomach. She didn't appear to be pregnant so I figured she was trying to play me."

Reagan held up her hand and interrupted. "Okay, okay. Where was I when all this was going on?"

I sat back down "I don't know."

Eager to hear what happened next, Trish asked, "Did you let her in, DeLaina?"

"No, I slammed the door in her face and went

in the bedroom to get his cell phone to see if he's been talking to her. When I picked up the phone, there was a little message envelope on the screen. I bypassed that to see the call log. I saw incoming and outgoing calls to her, but that wasn't proof he's been sleeping with her."

Rea and Trish looked at each other from the corner of their eyes.

Reliving the event proved to be too much for me. I was feeling a bit erratic. I thought back to when I used to hustle on the corner. If someone tried to invade your territory you'd put one in him. Problem solved. This situation was a little more complex than that. Monique couldn't come on my block unless he gave her permission. I began to cry.

Reagan put the gun down and put her arm around me. "It's okay, sweetie."

I dried my eyes and finished the story. "I checked the messages on his phone. They were from her, telling him she didn't know what she would have done if he hadn't been there for her during the miscarriage and how sorry she was that she didn't give him a son."

Trish said, "Whoa."

From that point on, the story went through my mind as it came out of my mouth, like I was reliving it all in my memory …

I had gone back to the party, found Darrell, and dragged him into the bedroom. It became too much, and I started crying and yelling. He slammed his beer bottle on the night stand, and threw his hands in the air. Pacing the floor and cursing, he said, "What are you going off about now? We can't have a moment of peace!"

I said, "You still screwing her?" I picked up his Heineken bottle and hurled it, smashing it against the wall, missing his head by an inch. "Answer me!" I yelled.

"Naw, what is you talking about?'"

I grew angrier watching him appear as truthful as he usually did.

But then something happened. I thought about everything he'd put me through, all the truth that must have been lies. I curled my fingers seemingly one at a time, locking in all the loveless days … all the nights he came in late, all the fights he picked … clenched them in my fist, leaned back, and connected with his jaw like Roy Jones taking it to Bernard Hopkins. He fell against the dresser, knocking over the lamp. That's when I told him, "Monique said hi!"

Rubbing his face and ignoring my comment, Darrell told me, "If you eva put yo hands on me again, I'll kill you."

I felt love turn to hate like the flip of a switch. I was so embarrassed at the fool he had made of me. I went back to the party, attempting to act unfazed. After everyone left, he came into the bedroom where I was. I was sitting on the side of the bed, trying to make sense of my life.

He said, "The house is a mess, but we can clean up tomorrow."

I couldn't look at him. I just got up and left the room. He followed me and kept talking, but I wouldn't respond. Trying to plead his case, he sat down beside me on the couch, insisting that he didn't call her, that she called him.

I lashed out. "You still lying! I saw your phone."

"You went through my phone?" He went to the room and grabbed it. He came back scrolling through the phone as though he were trying to see what I saw. "Why you going through my stuff?"

Surprised that he took that angle, I said, "You sneaking around, but if that's your angle … fine. Why am I going through your stuff? I pay the bill on that phone, I pay the rent on the roof you sleep under. As long as we're going there, everything you have on, I bought." I laughed. "Your stuff! Hmm, maybe if you had some stuff, we wouldn't be having this conversation."

I could almost see the hair raise on his back. Like a cornered wild animal, Darrell attacked, grabbing my arms and throwing me against the wall as hard as he could. I lost my balance. In a struggle to stay on my feet, I grabbed and reached for anything to keep from falling. He grabbed my throat with one hand and punched me in the jaw with the other. I fell to the floor. I was stunned. I always thought that if this ever happened, I'd be like Wonder Woman, blocking blows left and right, but I was so caught off guard that I couldn't think.

He sat on top of me, punching and yelling, "You make it so hard to love you!"

In the struggle, a vase fell. I grabbed it, hit him in the head, ran into the bedroom, and grabbed the Beretta resting in the hollowed Bible in my nightstand. He charged in behind me and froze as I turned around with the pistol pointing at his chest.

Obviously startled, he asked, "Where did you get a gun?"

I didn't answer him.

He reached for it and said, "Put it away before someone gets hurt."

I planted my feet firmly on the ground and securely locked my finger around the trigger as I said, "You mad at me? YOU got her pregnant!"

Darrell humbled himself—a little—by putting his hands in the air.

As I said "You made me have an abortion," tears flooded my eyes, blurring my vision.

Though he didn't say a word, he backed away as I walked toward him. "I wanted my baby!" I yelled. "You have no idea what it's like to lay on a table in a cold room and consent to a doctor sucking the life out of you." As he stared at me with that dumb look, I contemplated pulling the trigger. I finally lowered the gun. "You're not worth the bullet."

***

Now, sitting with Reagan and Trish, I felt as beaten down and exhausted as I had with Darrell earlier.

Trish shook her head and looked at Reagan. "Rea, I told her to go to the police station and file a report."

Reagan shifted her eyes from me to Trish and shook her head. "No! No way. We're not going to the police. Trish, go get your camera!"

"Why?" Trish asked.

"Just do it!" Rea yelled.

When she got back with the camera, Reagan took pictures of me from every possible angle. Once she was done, the three of us sat at the dining room table. Reagan placed the gun on the table, put her right hand over it, and told Trish, "This stays in this room."

"What part?"

Reagan sat up in her seat, grabbed the gun securely, and said, "All of it!"

Trish leaned back in the chair.

With her hand out, Reagan ordered Trish, "Give me the camera."

With a certain degree of unwillingness, Trish handed the camera over.

"What are you up to?" I asked Rea.

She put her hand on top of mine and said, "Nothing, baby. You go get some rest. I'll be back in the morning."

After Rea let herself out, I fell asleep in the clothes I had on. Later that morning, I woke up to the sound of the front door closing, not sure if it was Reagan or Darrell. I sat up on the side of the bed. I looked up to see Darrell leaning in the doorway of the bedroom, bloody, black and blue.

"What happened?"

He limped to the bed and sat with his back to me. As I walked over to the side of the bed where he was sitting, I noticed his clothes were tattered and dirty. I stood in front of him and lifted his head to get a better look. He had a big cut just below his left eye, and the right one was almost swollen shut. I wanted to ask, "Did you at least pinch the nigga?"

Instead, I asked again, "What happened?"

He didn't answer me. He laid his head on my stomach, wrapped his arms tight around my waist, and said, "Baby, I'm sorry. I should've walked away. I shouldn't have hit you."

At that moment, I knew this was either Reagan or Mike's doing. I pried him off of me and sat on the bed beside him.

"Rell, I'm tired. I don't want to do this."
He leaned on me and said, "I'm-a take a shower. Go back to bed and we'll talk about it later."

I pushed him away. "No! Do you realize I could have killed you last night?"

"Laina, you can't kill nobody. But I would like to know when you brought a gun into this house."

I shook my head. "You have no idea who I am. I spent so much time trying to be the woman you wanted that I don't even know who I am anymore."

"What? Baby, I said I was sorry."

I laughed. "If you ain't never been right about anything else ..."

He leaned forward, resting his elbows on his knees.

"Darrell, I enabled you. I don't know whether to be mad at you or myself."

"I love you."

"No, you love the woman I tried to be for you. You don't love me! You walk around here acting superior to me in my house, on my dime, and I let you ... I let you! You out here sleeping around—unprotected, no less—gambling with my life."

His face went blank. Then he finally said, "You really think I'd be here if I didn't want to be? Come on, Laina. I got money."

I shrugged, knowing that he had won a lawsuit when he lost a finger at the meat-packing plant several months ago. As of a few months ago, he started getting a monthly settlement check.

He stood in front of me. "I don't need you." He attempted to run his fingers through my hair. As I pulled away, he said, "I want you."

I pulled away. "For what? To wipe your feet on? I would have done anything for you ... anything!"

"Laina—"

"WHAT! LAINA WHAT?" I grabbed his cell phone. "You talk to that trick on the phone, befriending her, and you won't even call me to tell me you're gonna be late." I grabbed the car keys and threw them at him as I yelled, "You ride shotgun with me, but I take a backseat to ALL of your mess! You just take, take, take." Pointing at my chest, I continued, "What about ME! Yeah, you get your little two G's a month ... NOW! But who's been taking care of everything for the past eleven months? You haven't paid one bill in here."

With a straight face, he said, "You don't ask me for money or tell me when bills are due."

"Are you ... you're kidding, right? You don't

ask to eat, but the food is always on the table in this mugg. What? You think there's a food fairy around this piece?"

"Oh, you got jokes."

"No, what I am is tired. I thought … maybe if I showed you what love looked like, you'd reciprocate."

He stood up. "Dar you go wit da big words. Just cuz I don't love the way you do doesn't mean that I don't love you. And what about you, DeLaina? Who's Trey?"

I hadn't heard that name in years. "What?"

"You heard me!"

I never mentioned the name "Trey" or that past life to Darrell. Curious where he heard Trey's name, I asked, "Why?"

He said that I called his name in my sleep … which made sense, seeing as whenever I was unhappy, I always thought of a happier time.

"Who is he?" he asked again.

I responded reluctantly. "An old friend."

"You sleeping with him?"

Irritated by his line of questioning, I quickly said, "You can question me when someone shows up at the door."

"Oh, because you ain't get caught, your dirt don't count? When was the last time you saw him?"

I let out a loud breath and shook my head. I was not going to stand there and be interrogated about Trey.

As I slipped on my sweat suit, he said, "See, you got skeletons in your closet, but you want me to be some Superman."

"NO, A MAN! I never asked you to be perfect. I knew you weren't perfect from the first time we broke up, but I learned to acquiesce. I tried to give you everything you needed, and it still wasn't enough." I could feel the bitter taste in my mouth. "This ain't love, whatever it is … I'm done with it."

He shook his head. "Don't be so dramatic. Look, baby, I need you."

"You had ME. All of ME, and all I wanted was your selfish, good-for-nothing, cheating behind …" He'd always called me weak if I showed emotion, so I always tried real hard not cry in front of him. This time, though, the pain in my chest overflowed, and I cried for all the times he'd stifled my emotions.

I dropped to the floor and sat there. "I can't do this anymore!" I yelled.

He held his head with his hands.

"I'm going to Reagan's," I said. "Don't be here when I get back."

I grabbed my keys and purse as he yelled my name.

"LAINA! LAINA?"

There's a Process

When I got back, he was gone but his presence was still there. Three days had passed and I hadn't slept a full night since he'd been gone. When he dropped by to get the rest of his things, I was lying on the couch. When he walked past me, I pretended to watch TV, seemingly engrossed in a commercial … *'cause Oscar Mayer has a way with B-O-L-O-G-N-A*. I tried to remain disconnected, but I found myself listening to his footsteps, listening to the echoes of his sighs as he roamed from room to room. He puttered around as if he was trying to buy time but didn't have exact change.

I watched him pack CDs that we listened to together: Nina Simon … Aretha Franklin … Earth,

Wind & Fire—CDs that we made love to. We played *The Best of the Isley Brothers* so much that, every time Ronald hit a high note, I moaned like it was the remix. Darrell snatched my memories and threw them in that raggedy old backpack. I was dealing, holding it together, until I saw the red t-shirt sticking out of the bag. I had been sleeping in it since he'd been gone; it still smelled like him. Guess it gave me a false sense of security ... like this didn't really happen, like he didn't really cheat on me AGAIN and he wasn't really gone.

It was just as well. I was never going to let him go, holding on to bits and pieces of him. He roamed through the house, making sure he didn't forget anything ... through the hallway, in the bathroom, in the kitchen ... like he ever went in the kitchen for anything other than a beer. I watched him take a final lap around the place before walking to the door. As he threw the backpack over his shoulder, my heart began beating faster like it was trying to jump out of my chest and go with him. I know I told him to leave, but my heart wanted him to stay.

"I think I have everything," he said.

Fighting back the tears, I said, "A'ight."

I got up and walked to the door, trying to remember that HE did this to us ... HE brought other people into our circle ... HE hit me.

We stood in the foyer, staring at each other. He

stared like he was trying to memorize each freckle I tried to mask with makeup. Then, like a criminal being sentenced, he made his final plea for mercy.

"Laina, baby, I'm sorry."

He dropped the backpack and filled his arms with me. He never felt more warm or soft or smelled more wonderful than he did at that moment. I wanted to believe with all my heart that he was sorry. I wanted to believe that he'd take back the night he dotted my "I" and crossed my "T" if he could. That he'd undo all the hurt if he could, but I was scared to take that chance.

The tighter he held me, the more I could feel him release the bull. I could feel the wall between us tremble. He pulled back just enough to look in my eyes, and for the first time he looked vulnerable … sincere. He looked at me like he was dangling from the bottom of a rope, begging me to save him. I wanted to … I wanted to do what I always did: whip out a cape and run to his rescue, but I always end up diving in and doing the breaststroke through his mess. Because I loved him.

My love for him ran deeper than any cavity he could explore. He didn't want to leave and I didn't want him to go. I flashed back to the first time he said "I love you," the day I realized I was pregnant, the day I had the abortion … to now. As I began crying, he held me tighter in his arms and kissed away my tears.

Just as my heart softened, his cell phone rang. He didn't answer it. It rang again. He fumbled around in his pocket to stop the ringer but hit the speaker button instead. The person on the other end said, "Hello? Hello? Baby, it's Mo. Can you hear me?"

It was Monique. He struggled to get the phone before she said anything else. In that instance, my irrational thoughts gained strength.

I held him tight and whispered in his ear. "I will always love you."

With tears in my eyes, I pulled away, reached around him, and opened up the door. He grabbed his backpack, threw it over his shoulder, kissed me on the forehead, and left.

I closed the door, slid down onto the floor, and burst into tears. I missed him already.

After that, I wouldn't leave the house. Called in sick the whole week and told my boss I had a virus. I laid in the same place … on the couch, wallowing in my relationship's demise. I turned the ringers off on the house and cell phones. I didn't want to talk to anyone, not even Rea. Lonely was my new best friend, and I laid there with her listening to my heart ache. The sleepless nights made the days seem so long. I struggled just to make it from moment to moment. Reliving the abortion that I let him talk me into … the way he held me … the lies … the way he smelled after the gym … that broad showing up at my door. Sometimes it seemed as though I couldn't make it to the next minute much less the next day. I laid there licking my wounds, not realizing I was infecting them by trying to place blame everywhere except where it belonged.

Get It Together

By Friday, Reagan had called in reinforcements. Constance—Reagan's older cousin—and I were close but we hadn't talked in a while. I figured she must have heard what happened with Rell and I. She called several times this one afternoon, but I wouldn't answer. She left a message that said, "You have to pray. The Word says weeping may endure for a night … but joy will come in the morning."

I wasn't trying to hear nothing about no joy coming in the morning … I needed joy right then and there.

Ain't no sunshine when he's gone … I laid there moaning the same verse over and over like a scratched 45. My Grammy Award-winning performance was interrupted by a knock at the door. I didn't get up to see who it was figuring, whoever it was would think I wasn't home and go away. The knocking went on for ten minutes before it finally stopped. Then I heard a fumbling of keys in the door knob. My heart started racing. I popped my head up from the couch, ran my hand over my uncombed hair, thinking maybe it was Darrell.

"Laina?" It was Rea and her mother.

I laid back down.

"Why aren't you answering the phone?" Rea asked. "We sittin here thinking something happened to you!"

"Obviously, I didn't want to talk!"

Ma Mitchell walked over to the love seat, took off her jacket, and said, "Baby, are you okay?"

"I'm fine, but I don't much feel like company."

She sat down and said, "Well, you're going to talk to me. Sit up!"

I laid there, thinking, *I am not in the mood for this.*

Then she took her motherly tone. "DELAINA RENEE RICHARDS! I SAID … SIT … UP!"

I sucked my teeth and sat up, leaning against the arm of the sofa.

"What's going on with you?" she asked.

I sighed. *Thinking, Like you don't know.* I looked

at Reagan.

She lashed out. "WHAT?! All diss right here … could've been avoided if you had just answered da phone."

I wanted to be alone, but the hurt on the inside began seeping out. One tear after another began rolling down my face, racing for the ground, as I mumbled, "Darrell and I broke up."

Rea reached over and handed me a tissue.

Ma took off her glasses. "Now we're getting somewhere. Why?"

Sniffling, I said, "Because of da chick Monique." I might as well have said we broke up because it was partly cloudy, or because the birds chirped too loud … none of it was true. I wanted to place the blame somewhere, on anyone for me being alone, for me waking up crying every morning because Rell wasn't beside me.

Ma shook her head. "Are you done?"

I nodded yes.

She uncrossed her legs and proceeded to read me the riot act. "DeLaina, you know I adore you."

She took a tissue and dabbed my face left to right.

"I want to be empathetic," she said, "but, baby, this was inevitable. I remember when you were Monique. You started dating this boy when he had a girlfriend, but you had to have him." She adjusted her hips in the love seat and re-crossed her legs. "You won. Now look at your prize. He cheated on her to be with you. What made you think you were the exception to the rule. Sweetheart, orgasms aren't promises. And at the risk of sounding like a pessimist, isn't it ironic that you lost him the same way you got him?"

"Ma, despite what you may have heard, I loved him!" I said.

She scooted to the edge of the chair and put her hand on top of mine. "The woman you stole him from probably loved him too. Baby, I'm not saying he wasn't wrong … I just want you to recognize your role in this situation."

Rea smacked her lips. "Screw him!"

"REAGAN!" Ma shouted.

"Sorry, Ma, but DeLaina wasn't even herself wit dat negro. She was blocking out the world, hidin' her emotions to please him. She turned into some fake Susie Homemaker and he ain't even appreciate her."

Trying to defend his actions, I said, "Things aren't always what they seem."

I wished I was madder at him, but the truth of the matter was that a part of me felt sorry for him. Part of me identified with him having a jacked-up childhood. Darrell grew up in a house watching his mother turn tricks for drugs. Like me, he'd been on his own since he was young.

I tried to explain. "I didn't do anything I didn't want to do. I was trying to build a life for us. I was trying to show him he wasn't a reflection of his family." Ma shook her head. "NO! You weren't trying to save him from his demons. You were trying to save you from yours. You're afraid of being abandoned, but God said, 'I will never leave you or forsake you.' Baby, you thought if you made yourself indispensable—if you did enough, bought him enough—he'd need you and wouldn't leave you."

I was speechless. She was right.

Ma asked forthrightly, "While you were going into debt for him, what was he doing for you?"

I know that was a rhetorical question but I gave it some real thought.

She kept going. "But something kept you going back. There was something in you that innately drew you to him—despite knowing about Monique and the girls in the bike club. Maybe in your mind, somehow being with the one that everyone wanted somehow validated your worth. I tried to teach both you and Reagan how to get with your mind what your body can't keep." She reiterated it again for both of us: "Let a man fall in love with your mind before you expose him to your body."

She sat beside me, pulled me into her bosom,

and rocked me like she could feel my pain. She said, "Sometimes you have to endure burns before you remember that fire is HOT." She stopped rocking long enough to kiss me on my forehead. I looked up at her and saw her eyes watering. I don't know where she went, but for a few minutes she was reliving her own inferno.

She said, "We'll get through this. It's a learning experience." As she looked over at Reagan, she continued, "This goes to the both of you. Write it down or get a tattoo, but remember: love is just a word until someone gives it meaning. You understand?"

Lying in her arms, I began reflecting, and the tighter she hugged me, the wider the flood gate opened. I began crying like a newborn baby smacked on the behind for the first time.

I cleared my throat and told Rea, "Thank you." Without hesitation, she said, "You're my sister …"

"I just feel so stupid for not seeing the signs."

That wasn't an accurate statement. I did see the signs; I just ignored them. My frustration with Rell had been building. I had a feeling that he was messing around again. He was picking fights and hanging out more, but I didn't have any tangible evidence. He didn't even want to be intimate anymore. I didn't cheat but I was growing more and more frustrated by the day, to the point that I hated going home knowing he was there. Knowing he was going to reject me.

You don't have to grow up in the church to know that God answers even a sinner's prayer. Two days before the surprise party, I did what I always do when I don't know what to do: I prayed …

God, I know we ain't talked in a minute, but you know my heart. I love Darrell more than I've ever loved any man, but I don't feel it being reciprocated. I'm tired of crying and trying to figure him out. I can't do anything to please him anymore. He's always angry with me. God, if we're s'pose to be together, please fix this thing. Help us to work it out. If not, please show me a sign and remove him from my life. Amen.

Even as I potentially made my bed in hell … God was still there.

Ma comforted me. "Honey, it was a learning experience. You were so afraid of being alone that you settled for a little bit of anything for the sake of having something." She wiped my face with the balled-up tissue in her hand. "Now, please, please go take a shower." I lifted my arm to take a sniff as she continued. "And Rea and I will pick up around here a little."

I stood in the shower, reflecting as the water ran down my face. Realizing he didn't love me on his own. I didn't give him a chance to. I leased his affections one dollar at a time.

Trying to Find Me

Looking back, I finally realize the unsaid: I was desperate. That relationship caused me to walk love's tightrope, doing flips and juggling while balancing on my toes like some circus freak. I didn't want to be alone so I tried to bribe love, tried to buy it in the eyes of any man that would look back. I had been abandoned by so many people that, when someone came along, I tried to be a protector, which transformed into me being a giver. Giving them everything so they wouldn't have a reason to leave … trying to guarantee their stay.

Ma Mitchell told me it was okay to feel what I was feeling. That it was only a mistake if I didn't learn from it. She told me to get out of the house, find an outlet. She told me to write down what I was feeling everyday throughout the day for the next week but not to reflect on it until the following week.

Saturday morning, I laid in bed cuddled up with my memories. As the room became brighter, I covered my head, trying to hide from another day, but the birds were taunting me. It wasn't like I could sleep anyway. I remembered Ma Mitchell saying, "Take yourself out. Put on your prettiest dress and go somewhere, anywhere." So I took a shower, swept my hair into a ponytail, and slipped into my strapless sundress. After I packed a snack, and grabbed a notebook I went to Gill Park just outside of the city.

Once I got to the park, I immediately walked down by the lake to feed the ducks. After all the bread was gone, I laid out the blanket I found in my trunk and watched the clouds, trying to see the shape in each one as they passed. Hours later, I laid there thinking, *I don't feel any daggone betta.* I rolled over onto my stomach and watched the families come and go until a young couple happened by. He appeared irritated by her very presence. No conversation between the two. They were just there. He had a caged look on his face, like he was being held against his will—and the harder I stared, the clearer I saw Darrell and me. I still didn't understand why I wasn't enough for him. I began to cry as I remembered the constant fights.

Lonely held me down, whispering, I'd rather cry in the arms of a man every night than to have dry eyes alone. I just didn't want it to hurt anymore. I grabbed the notebook and began writing as my tears soaked the page, making it barely legible …

I've scrubbed my house and cleaned my sheets but I can't get his scent off of my soul. Love is like a priceless antique … so when a man says I love u … it makes a woman weak … makes it hard to breath and even harder to speak…

When a woman loves a man …

She becomes his muse, allowing all of her energy to be used … until he's the little engine that could … "I think I can, I think I can."

We lived together but never lived … together … I was more like a prisoner … trapped by the word LOVE… I think the only reason he kept me around is because I gave him enough rope to keep me tied down … bound by the words that flowed from his lips, lost in the grip he had on my hips.

I knew … I knew he played, betrayed, strayed, and swayed women, but he told me … You can trust me …

He said he never knew love before he knew me … And I believed him … cuz every word he spoke evoked feeling … I thought it was the real thing; it just never manifested into the real thing …

Now I'm healing …

I use to say if lovin him is wrong, I don't wanna be right … Well, if that was right … I'd rather be wrong …

than to go on pretending up is down, bad is good, and that he eva loved me…

Trying to get him out of my mind … trying to find a way to redefine … me. Closer to insane than stability …

I just wanna let go.

I pushed my way through the next two days trying to find me. I had sacrificed me for him for so long that it was hard to remember where he stopped and I began.

Seeking comfort, this was about the time I started smoking. Trading one addiction for another.

Paige

I sat at my desk going through the pile that had been sitting there for the past week, trying to focus on something other than Darrell. Fortunately, I had a new client who demanded a lot of my attention. It couldn't have happened at a better time.

I was sitting at my desk when the phone rang. I answered, "DeLaina Richards."

"Hey, Laina. It's Paige."

I hadn't seen or talked to Paige in some time. She and I were very close, but I think she and Rea were a little closer. I was the "Whatever!" one of the group. Paige was the calm and rational one; whereas Rea was the "shoot first, ask questions later" type—that is, if anyone was left.

Our lives had changed significantly since the last time Paige hung out with Rea and me, hers more than ours.

About three years prior, Paige met Arlen, some freelance photographer supposedly from New York—I had my doubts. After dating for about five months, he called her one day and said, "This ain't working for me." Then Paige didn't hear from him for two months—and out of the clear blue, he showed up on her job and asked her to marry him. Shortly thereafter, she found out that she was pregnant so, they upped the wedding date, trying to beat the baby's arrival. She told me that she came home one day and Arlen had left her a "Dear Jane" letter. I guess that story was less embarrassing for her than what really happened.

A week before the nuptials, she received a page from him, asking her to meet him at the house for a nooner. When she got there, she heard noises coming from the bedroom. Paige walked in on Arlen having sex with the best man.

Rea insisted that deep down Paige had to have known, that there had to have been signs, even though Paige maintained that she had no idea that Arlen was bisexual. I never questioned her story—I figured if she wanted me to know, she'd tell me.

Paige shut down from the world for a little over a year, but when she resurfaced, she was at peace—

she said that she had given her life to Christ and that was the only way she'd been able to raise my godson, Keith.

So, sitting there in my office with Paige on the phone, all I could really say was, "Hey, Paige. What's up?"

"I just wanted to call and see how you were doing." She hadn't called just to say hi in a while, which told me that she must have talked to Rea.

I laughed. "I'm fine."

"Good! DeLaina, your blessings are coming."

"What?"

"Sometimes God has to move people out of the way to make room for your blessings. My pastor said sometimes we hold on tight to the very thing that God is trying to pull out of our grasp."

Her words brought tears to my eyes. I got up and closed my office door. "Paige, it feels like a part of me is missing."

"I know."

"But I felt things going downhill. They started getting worse, and I prayed and asked God to remove him if he wasn't supposed to be here. Both times."

"Both times? God's shutting doors and you around here opening windows? Darling, God doesn't take anything you're supposed to have. You should be shouting with joy to know that he hears your cry."

"I know."

"I don't think you do. You don't need a man to be happy."

"No offense, Paige, but that's the single woman's slogan."

"It may be, DeLaina. But I can tell you … I'd rather be by myself than to be with a man I can't be myself with. By the grace of God, I can look in the mirror and see laughter in the eyes where tears used to be."

"Ain't that Marvin Gaye … 'Precious Love'?"

She sighed. "You're missing my point."

I laughed. "No, I get it, I get it. Thank you!"

"You should come to church with me one Sunday."

"I will."

"I love you, Laina."

It felt good talking to her. However, when I left the office and went home to a quiet house and an empty bed, I quickly remembered my reality. Then it was off to bed as quick as possible, ushering the day to an end. I'd lie there with the covers pulled over my head like a child hiding from the boogie man … each night hoping the next day would ease my pain just a little.

Baggage

Reagan and Rico—the ghetto Ricky and Lucy Ricardo—were always fighting about something. Rico was Rea's on-again, off-again boyfriend.

I had special ringtones for all my girlfriends, so when my cell phone rang, I knew it was Rea: *Count on me through thick and thin, a friendship that will never end* (Whitney Houston and CeCe Winans, of course!). I answered, "Hello?"

Instead of hearing greetings, I heard Rico yelling in the background. *"Cuelgue el teléfono. Ain't que nadie yendo no donde esta noche."*

Then I heard Rea yelling. "English, Livin' la Vida Broka! In this house, we speak-a da English!"

Rico yelled back at her, "Hang up the phone.

Ain't nobody going nowhere tonight!"

I could hear Rea as she stomped around with the phone in one hand, muttering something about finding her purse and keys.

She yelled at Rico again. "Look, Enrique Iglesias, if I stay here, I'm going to jail!"

I was more afraid for him than I was for her. He acts stupid, but he's not crazy. Rea on the other hand …

"Rea? Rea-Rea! Hello!"

"YEAH! Laina, diss nigga trippin. Meet me at Frisco's in a half an hour."

It was funny how I could see the issues in someone else's relationship that blinders kept me from seeing in my own. Rea's ex-boyfriend Frankie had preyed on her naiveté. He was a salesman eight years her senior—a polished manipulator. The guy was good, he could con a crack-head out of a rock. Frankie moved into Rea's apartment and completely took over. She came home one day to find he had rearranged all the furniture and had gotten rid of most of her stuff. He criticized everything about her, even down to the way she dressed. Suddenly, what she'd wear was inappropriate—even though they were the same clothes she worn for the several months he was chasing her. But it didn't end there with Frankie—she spent too much time on the phone, in the club, at the bar, with me … anywhere he wasn't able to watch her. I called her cell phone one day to find that the number had been disconnected … at least that's what the recording said. It turned out he had her number changed. She never wanted to be groomed, shaped, or molded by a man until she found herself stuck in clay.

Reagan had always been a free spirit. Always maintaining the attitude that "There are far too many men to get caught up with one"—but I knew better. That's the role she played because she thought she'd never get married, never thought anyone would ever want to be with her for an extended period of time.

Although Rea's a beautiful girl (five-nine, about 162 pounds, with naturally sandy brown hair that complements the hazel in her eyes), it was obvious that the insecurities of that little fat kid still existed.

They say that some of the most beautiful women are the most insecure. Reagan was no exception to the rule. Although you would have never known by the way her hips swayed when she walked or by the way she occasionally tossed her hair—but if you looked deep beneath the Maybelline …

Once Frankie found her weakness, he exploited it and played on her desires, saying things like: "My wife wouldn't eat that … I wouldn't let my wife wear that … A married woman wouldn't go to those places." She was so busy playing "wifey" that she forgot she wasn't one.

I watched the most headstrong woman I knew relinquish her self-worth to a man who wasn't worthy to be in her presence. It was his insecurities that made him jealous of her. He was afraid she'd realize that she was too good for him.

One night, he eavesdropped on a conversation Rea and I were having. I told her how handsome the new guy at work was. From that one little comment, he deducted that I was trying to set her up with someone else—calling me a home wrecker. When Rea defended me, he called me a whore and said I'd made a pass at him. That's when the light came on for Rea—she knew he was lying. He thought she'd take his word and cast me aside. He underestimated the bond between Reagan and me. It was hard for her—she walked away, but not without scars ... at least not the scars I had. But it's because of Frankie that other men get the short end of the stick when dealing with Rea.

So—back to Rea and Rico, and meeting Rea at Frisco's ...

Frisco's is a bar in midtown ... I guess it's more like a lounge. We used to meet there every Friday after work before we all got tied down. They renovated it to be more upscale—big-screen TVs, sofas around the bar, sexy uniforms for the bartenders (low-cut vest with a bowtie), and a huge dance floor upstairs.

I found a seat at the bar while I was waiting for

Rea. Looking around, I noticed all the booths were occupied by couples. I missed that "we" feeling. I was still trying to move on, trying to see past my past. I just wanted to feel like someone loved me. For one night, I just wanted to lie in the arms of a man and pretend that he loved me, that he was mine and I was his.

As I looked around, I noticed a man staring at me from the other end of the bar. He was handsome, tall, dark chocolate with a medium build. Sizing him up, if I had to guess, I'd say he looked like your average barber: well groomed with a perfectly shaped goatee, like it was drawn by Rembrandt.

Rea finally arrived, late as usual. She snatched out a chair next to me, sat down, and said, "A'ight, for real doh. Let me tell you why yo boy is gonna make me shank his ... Oh, I'm sorry." She stopped to hug me and continued, "He is bent on controlling me."

"What happened, Rea?"

"A'ight ... when me, you, and the girls went out the other night, what did I drive?"

"His Jag."

"Right! Ain't nobody drove it since. So he takes it out today, and when he got back, he asked me where did I go. Man, I cussed him out." While listening to Reagan vent, I couldn't help but notice the guy across the bar still staring at me.

I asked her, "Why did he question you? Didn't

he say you could take it out whenever you wanted?"

"Exactly! He claim he filled up the tank the other day and that he had to put more gas in it today. I was like … SO!" I sat there, puzzled, as she went on to say, "Hum! He ain't just gonna be questioning me like I'm his child. I said I went out. I went out! I don't know who he think he is."

After I asked Carlos, the bartender, for two more shots of tequila, I told Rea, "You flipped out for nothing. He asked you a legitimate question… what happened to all the gas. Baby, you can't treat every man like he's Frankie. You're afraid if you let down your guard, Rico will treat you like Frankie did. Rico loves you, but you're going to run him off acting like that."

"Whateva! I bet he won't be questioning me no more."

She took her shot. Before I could take mine, I noticed that the guy who had been staring was getting up to leave. As he walked in my direction, our eyes met.

He said, "I saw a couple of guys try to get your attention, but you weren't having it."

We smiled at each other. Rea turned to check him out, starting with his shoes. Rea's not a gold digger, but she prides herself on being able to size up a man. She looked him over from head to toe, taking careful note of the fresh hair cut, Gaultier blazer, Marc Jacobs jeans, manicured hands, and size 12 Italian loafers.

He continued, "I spent the last thirty minutes contemplating the right words to say to ensure I saw that smile again."

Flirting back, I asked, "So what did you come up with?"

He reached out to shake my hand. "My name's Reggie."

Rea snickered. "It took you thirty minutes to come up wit yo own name?"

With a sly, sexy grin, he said, "Her beauty left me lost for words."

Fine and smart! He seemed nice enough, so I started to protect him from Rea—but then, if he couldn't handle her ...

He held out his hand toward Reagan. "And you are?"

She looked down at his hand and responded, "Not impressed."

"Whoa! I'm going to get out of your hair." He smiled and turned back to me. "Will you at least tell me your name?"

"DeLaina."

He reached into his pocket and pulled out a business card. "Give me a call sometime, DeLaina."

Ten minutes later, Carlos came over with another round of drinks for Reagan and me. We usually paced ourselves, so I asked Rea, "You ordered another round already?"

"No! I thought you did."

Carlos leaned across the bar and said, "The guy you were just talking to ordered the round. He paid your tab, too."

Rea and I looked at each other.

Rea said, "Dude got game; see if he gotta brother."

After two more tequila shots and three Coronas between us, I was drunk enough to feel like calling Darrell.

I've always been able to hold my liquor. I drink the most, but Rea's always the first one drunk—and cursing. I told her it was time to go. Spitting all over the place, she slurred, "I'm good … I can make it home … I'm not ready to go yet… you go ahead."

I paid the rest of our tab, waved to my favorite bartender, and said to Rea, "No, lets go."

I reached into her pink and white Coach bag and took her keys. Rea was far too drunk to drive fifteen miles to an angry boyfriend, but I knew her well enough to know she would attempt it.

I told her, "You're coming home with me."

Slumped over and reeking of every inch of the bar, she said, "No, I'm good! I wanna go home and give Rico a piece of my mind." She leaned back in the chair, nearly falling.

I told her, "Okay, I'll take you home," figuring if I got her to the car, she'd pass out.

We managed to make it to my car with Rea stumbling every step of the way. With one arm wrapped around her, I reached into my purse, disabled the car alarm, and got her in the backseat.

"Just lie down, we'll be home soon."

By the time I got back to the driver's side, Rea had passed out and was drooling on my leather seats. It was just as well; I didn't want her to know I was calling Darrell. Still sitting in Frisco's parking lot, I pulled out my phone and dialed his number from memory.

"Hey, Rell, it's DeLaina."

"Hey, girl! What's up?"

I drew a complete blank and an awkward silence took over. Once we got past the silence, we played catch up for about an hour, updating each other on friends and what's been going on. Then he said, "You know I still miss you."

I held the phone tighter, looking out the sunroof, and said, "I know the feeling." I loved Darrell. He was the one man who would always have a place in my heart, even after the music stopped.

He cleared his throat and said, "I'm not trying to go down memory lane, but I have so many regrets when I think about you and our relationship."

My loneliness made it easy for him to pluck my

emotional strings. I sighed. "Well—"

He interrupted, "I'll call you back," in a whisper—the way you did when you were fifteen and you heard your mama coming up the hall. He didn't call back.

The next day, I called Reggie. Rea insisted that I had been out of the dating game for a while and tried to give me the rules of engagement. She told me to wait at least a week before calling. I thought that would be rude considering he bought us drinks and paid a $60 tab. I only called to say thank you, but about an hour into the conversation, he asked me to meet him Wednesday for dinner. I hesitated for a moment but agreed. I had an itch that was dying to be scratched. We did dinner and a movie. We saw each other every day for the next week. By week three, we kicked it up a notch. I really enjoyed talking to him, and I could tell by his touch that he wanted to love me. He was good for me ... just what I needed. He was a wealthy, sweet, considerate man who appreciated me. Everything Darrell wasn't. So why couldn't I stop thinking about Darrell, then?

I wanted to call Rell just to say hi and see how he was doing—or at least that's what I kept telling myself. I called Rea in an effort to keep myself from calling him.

"Hey," I said.

"Hey, gurl. What's wrong?"

"Nothing. I was just calling."

"Okay, 'I was just …' Whateva! Did you forget who you talking to?"

Sometimes I hated that she knew me so well. I paused, holding the phone tighter, waiting for my heart to admit that I missed him, every trifling thing about him. I wanted to let go, but I found myself aching just to hear his voice.

I finally confessed, "I miss Darrell."

"Laina, maybe you're thinking about him cause you're scared—Reggie's the unknown. And I guess at least with dumb-dumb you know what you're getting."

"That was a good try, Dr. Phil, but I'm serious."

It was scary how I could always feel Darrell. I could think about him and he'd appear somewhere like he came from my thoughts. I could feel when he was unhappy or scared. One night when Darrell and I were still together, I was at Reagan's playing spades with her and the girls when my stomach twisted into knots and all I could think about was Darrell. I called him to find that he had been in a motorcycle accident.

I tried to explain to Rea. "I need to know he's okay."

"Girl, please, ain't nuffin wrong wit dat negro. Okay, let's say you call him and he say they chopped his foot off …"

"What?"

"Girl, dey done, dey done Kunta Kinted him. Dar ain't nuffin you can do for that crippled nigga. He ain't gonna do nuffin but walk all ova you wit dat one good foot."

"What da ...? Are you high?"

She exhaled, blowing the smoke into the receiver. "You know what I'm saying."

Rea was useless.

I really enjoyed talking to Reggie, but the more time I spent with him, the more I missed Darrell—his kiss, his touch. Over the course of the next few months, Reggie spoiled me to a fault. One evening, he called and said, "I'm taking you out, so wear something nice." He called an hour later to tell me to come outside. When I came down the steps of the condo and cleared the awning, I stopped as I saw a chauffeur opening the door of a white stretch limo. I eagerly waited to see who was getting out. It was Reggie in a black Armani suit, holding a single red rose. He looked handsome, like some *Ebony* man of the year. I didn't have a want in the world with him around. The bad part about that ... well, he was ready for a full-blown relationship.

I liked him a lot. Really. I loved going out with him; he always made me feel like he felt lucky—pulling out chairs, opening up doors, helping me with my coat. And they said chivalry was dead. I even enjoyed talking to him; he listened so attentively. But the bottom line was that I knew I was still in love with someone else. I wanted to continue to be friends, but I thought that would just send mixed signals. I didn't want to hurt him, so I decided to back away. I made myself unavailable; even began ducking his calls. After several weeks of that, I finally said, "I think we need some space," but, for him, it must have translated into, "Try harder; call me more."

A couple weeks later, I got home from work to find him sitting on the steps of the condo.

In an embarrassed yet concerned tone, I asked, "What are you doing here?"

"You won't return my calls. I figured this was the only way I'd get you to talk to me."

I felt bad. It wasn't his fault that my heart and my mind weren't on the same page.

With every right, he asked, "What happened? I thought everything was going well."

"I'm sorry! I know I've been acting like a jerk …" I was hesitant to complete that statement, but it was now or never. "I told you I had just come out of a relationship not long before you and I met—and to be honest … I'm not over him yet."

"For real! The one that cheated on you?"

Embarrassed, I said, "Yes." It wasn't like I wanted to miss him.

"Were you thinking about him when we made love?"

"Reggie, please, it's not about the sex."

"He treated you like crap," Reggie ranted. "I put you on a pedestal, but you still want to be treated like crap. Ain't that about a ..."

I accept part of the blame; I jumped in too fast. Maybe I hoped being with someone else would help me forget and move on. I should have given myself more time, but Reggie knew I was fresh out of a relationship; I made it known. He must have thought he could make me forget my past.

Timing was bad, that's all. Had it been another day in time, maybe it would have worked.

***

At that point in my life, I was looking for love without so much as a composite sketch.

In an effort to keep my sanity, I thought a change of atmosphere would do me some good. Rea insisted on taking me to a bar on the east side that she'd heard had an open mic night on Fridays. This was around that whole *Love Jones* era.

I remember sitting in a smoky candlelit bar with Reagan, listening to people recite my pain under a dim spotlight—it was anything but a movie. Listening to poetry was more than just something to do. It was more like a religion and every venue was a church.

Somehow, watching those people go to the "altar" and testify on the microphone made me feel less alone. Sitting in those venues was therapeutic—therapy in its purest form. Listening to others' issues forced me to deal with issues of my own that I hadn't realized even existed.

One night, a young girl came in with a long platinum wig and a full-length leather trench coat. It was so long that you couldn't tell if she had on clothes under it or not. When her name was called to take the mic, a hush came over the room. All eyes were on her as she walked slowly and seductively to the stage. As she approached the mic, she untied the belt on her coat to reveal her clothes. Rea nudged me. The girl wore a choker, a wife beater, a miniskirt that stopped in the middle of her upper thigh, and thigh-high boots. She couldn't have been more than nineteen or twenty. As she started her piece, her words strangled the judgment in my mind—pinned me down and forced me to reflect on my own life and realize … I wasn't that different from the streetwalker. She was looking for money and I was looking for love.

The girl looked around the room, making eye contact as she recited her poem …

If they had just told me to taste the fallen fruit from the family tree … if they had just said love isn't tangible, it's something only the third eye can see …

or that men would try to obtain me like "Boardwalk" in Monopoly …
if they had just told me.
From da womb, big mama was determined to teach me to cook and clean; how to make a mean pot of neck bones and collard greens …
but neglected to teach me what love means.
So by age eighteen … everything I knew about love, I'd seen depicted on the big screen.
And that script had me in and out of relationships based on the rotation of my hips …
looking for love in romantic places but finding it in cramped cars and small spaces without love or traces thereof.
Can't blame big mama; CAN'T TEACH WHAT YOU DON'T KNOW …
See, her great-great-grandmother's past is eva-lasting; it's been tattooed on her soul since she was bought and sold in 1823, living only to birth mastah's babies into slavery …
Neva the opportunity to teach her children or to know what love means … just a machine.
Though the women evolved, they've neglected to involve communication, leaving the same equation unsolved.
Too afraid to talk to a woman child so they just send them into the world like a declawed cat in the wild … powerless, left in distress … just prey in a dress … I pray this is addressed.
You're … too young, or I'll tell you when you get older…

turned into a twenty-year-old carrying ancestral burdens on her shoulders.
And all I can do is mimic what I see.
If they had just told me ...
maybe life and love wouldn't be ... trial and error.

Some of the onlookers looked confused by the young girl as she confessed feeling stuck in a world that wasn't defined—held down by what she thought but never really knew. It was a faint cry for help and it seemed I was the only one that heard her.

After she finished her piece, she walked off the stage and headed for the door. I didn't want to leave, but something wouldn't let me stay. I followed her out. She was about twenty feet ahead of me when I yelled, "Excuse me!"

She turned around.

Not sure what I was going to say, I walked toward her. As I got closer, I said, "That was a real nice poem."

"Really? It didn't seem like anyone got it."

I laughed. "Sometimes when you go through something, it's easy to recognize when someone else is going through it."

She nodded. "Yeah, I guess so."

I stuck out my hand and introduced myself.

Surprised, she said, "Oh," then shook my hand. "My name's Caramel."

"I'm going to get a cup of coffee. You wanna go?"

"Look, Ms. … DeLaina. I don't swing that way."

"What!" I laughed. I thought to myself that I guess it did look like I was coming onto her. "Listen, sweetie, the things you said in your piece reminded me of me, and I remember needing someone to talk to and having no one."

"I don't even know you."

"Sometimes those are the best people to talk to. They can't throw your past in your face." I wrote down my number and handed it to her. "If you ever need someone to talk to …" Then I walked away.

Reagan was standing outside the venue with our jackets and purses. She said, "You always trying to save somebody. I'm-a get you a puppy."

Final Try

Several days later, on my way home, my cell phone rang. No special ring tone, so I knew it wasn't one of the girls. Driving with one hand, I fumbled around in my over stuffed purse, resting in the passenger seat. I quickly grabbed the phone. "Hello!"

"Hey, Laina!"

Chills ran through my body. It was Darrell. I don't know how he did it … every time I thought about him, he'd contact me soon after like he could hear me longing for him.

"How you been?" he asked.

I wanted to tell him I was miserable … that I still woke up reaching for him, that I couldn't have a relationship with anyone else because he still had my heart and I wanted it back. At that moment, it felt like my heart was going to jump out of my shirt just from the mere sound of his voice. Instead, I said, "I'm fine." His voice dropped to a whisper. "I miss you, baby."

I lied and said I had another call I had to take, then hung up.

Darrell was a disease that I had yet to find a cure for. He began calling again, leaving messages, apologizing for all the wrong he'd done. One evening, I came home from work and pressed play on the answering machine. As I stood there flipping through the mail, I stopped when I heard his voice. "DeLaina, if you're there, pick up ... pick up." There was a pause, then, "My cousin Beverly said she saw you today. She said you look just as beautiful as ever. I miss you girl. Call though, I knew being with him was bad, but bad always felt so good.

He called every day for the next four days ... but I wouldn't answer. On the fifth day, I answered "Darrell, please stop picking at the scab. Just let it go," and hung up. A few hours later, his number showed up on the phone again.

"Hello?" I answered.

"This is Angela! I don't know what you tryin' to pull, but Darrell and I are back together, and there ain't nuffin you can do to come between us."

I laughed. "If you really believed that, you wouldn't be

calling me trying to convince yourself."

She yelled, "Trick! I—"

I hung up, realizing she and I had switched places yet again.

The following day, I woke up and realized I was bigger than my weakest moment. Six more months passed and I declared I was over him—as much as you can be over a man you gave your heart to.

Weeks later, I got off work a little early to go get my hair done. Something just for me. My car was on "E," so I stopped at the gas station two blocks from the office. I realized I had left my bank card in my other purse, so I had to go inside to pay cash.

"Fifteen dollars on number two, please."

As I walked out of the quickie mart, I noticed a man nearing my car. At first sight, he resembled Darrell. I convinced myself it couldn't be him because the man didn't have dreads. As I got closer, I saw that it was him, still as sexy as ever. As he stood there—pumping my gas—I could smell his scent over the octane fumes. I folded my arms and took my Whatever stance …

I said, "I can do it myself."

He leaned against my car. "You look beautiful."

I glimpsed over at the pump … $8.43. "Thanks, Darrell, but I can take it from here."

$12.87 …

He said, "I need you."

$14.97 …

I wanted to stand there and listen to him tell me how much he wanted me, tell me how sorry he was or even that he loved me, but I knew where that road ended. I hopped in the car and told him I had to go as he screwed the gas cap on. Just as he walked around to the driver's side, I pulled off. I was in tears before I merged onto the street. Missing him, hating him, loving him—all at the same time. Suddenly, I remembered everything about him … from cream and no sugar in his coffee to the birthmark behind his left ear. I coached myself sitting at the light—*You're doing fine without him … love doesn't have to be hard*. I couldn't believe he cut off his dreads. I began to think, *Maybe …*

I tried to calm myself down. I phoned to cancel my hair appointment then called Reagan. In a frazzled voice, I said, "Hey, it's me, where are you?"

"I'm at Pa-Pa's. What's up?"

"I'll be there in twenty minutes."

Mr. Johnson, Rea's Pa-Pa has always been more like a father to her. See, two years earlier, he had a stroke and never fully recovered, and since then, they'd diagnosed him with alzheimer's. Although her brother Isaiah moved in to help take care of him, Rea went by every other day to check on him.

I knocked on the door and announced myself,

yelling, "It's me," as I let myself in. As I crossed the threshold, Mr. Johnson looked at me and said, "John three-sixteen."

I hugged him. "It's good to see you."

He smiled and nodded.

Rea came down the steps, hugged me, and said, "What's wrong?"

As she led me into the dining room, I explained that I ran into Darrell earlier and how all of these emotions reemerged.

Reagan sat down at the table. "You gotta let go."

"What do you think I've been trying to do?"

"I know you still love him, but you gotta remember ain't nuffin changed but the chick he's screwing."

"I was doing fine until I saw him, Rea! Now I'm having all these flashbacks ... like the way he use to hold me ..."

"For real, for real ... Like you told me when I was going through it over Alex—it's okay to visit the past, just don't buy property there. For real, it was only a matter of time before someone really got hurt."

"I wasn't gonna let him hurt me."

"I wasn't talking about you."

"Rea, sometimes, I just want to hear someone say I love you."

She put her hand on top of mine. "Girl, I love you!"

I sucked my teeth. "You know what I mean!"

"Laina, you don't need him. Besides, I want you to meet Alonzo's cousin."

"Who is Alonzo?"

"Oh, I met him a couple days ago."

"Um, I'm going home ..."

I walked through the living room to say good-bye to Mr. Johnson. As I leaned down to give him a hug, he said, "Philippians four-nineteen."

"Okay. You take care of yourself."

As I walked away, he grabbed my hand and said, "God will supply all your needs; have faith."

On my way home, I couldn't help but wonder if Mr. Johnson was speaking randomly or if he was really speaking to me.

I went home, changed clothes, and tried to relax, but I couldn't stop thinking about Darrell. I ordered some Chinese food, poured a glass of wine, stretched out on the couch, and popped in my favorite movie—*The Color Purple* ... "You sho' is ugly!" As I grabbed the bottle to pour a fourth glass of wine, I heard a tapping. I thought I was hearing things, then I heard it again. With bottle in tow, I went to the door and looked through the peephole. It was Darrell.

I was far too sober to deal with him. I took a step back from the door—he still took my breath away. He knocked again. I stood there contemplating what to do while I finished off the bottle of white zinfandel. As I reached for the door knob, I could feel my heart pounding like African drums during a mating ritual. When I opened the door, I was lost in him—he looked like he'd stepped out of my dreams. He had on a button-up, baggy jeans, and Timbs, but he stood there with the confidence and sex appeal of someone wearing a white Armani suit.

He smiled. "Hey!"

"Hi. What are you doing here?"

"I haven't stopped thinking about you since I saw you." He sighed and handed me a single red rose he had hidden behind his back.

I sniffed it and smiled. "You've never given me flowers."

He stepped inside and closed the door. "I'm not the man I use to be."

He took my head in his hands, planted hope on my lips, and kissed away the lonely. All of the nightmares and drama seemed nonexistent. I dropped the flower and held him like my most precious secret. Everything moved so fast … between kisses, he took my shirt off; I took off his shirt. He scooped me up in his arms and said, "I missed you." He carried me into the bedroom, laid me down on the bed, and made love to me like his life depended on it. He never felt stronger to me than he did that night. Three hours later, we laid there, embracing, confused.

With his arm wrapped around my waist, he whispered, "I never stopped loving you."

I was coming down from my high; my mind was racing a mile a minute. I couldn't believe we were here again. He was like a cancer that kept coming back.

He kissed me on my neck and asked, "You still love me?"

Hesitantly, I said, "Yes."

He cuddled up behind me. "Where do we go from here?"

"Chemo."

"What?"

"Rell, we've been down this road before. You're good for about three months or until you get bored, and start picking fights."

"I promise it'll be different this time."

"How do I know that? How do I know that in six months we're not going to be where we were nine months ago? It was suppose to be different the last time. Remember?"

"Because I need you."

I was lost for words. I wanted to be rational and say, "No, we've tried before," but rationality didn't exist. It was just me and my heart—and I wanted him.

The next morning, we woke up to the phone ringing. It was Rea calling to say she was around the corner. She and I had began meeting every other morning to go running. I jumped up and threw some clothes on, determined to be ready. I didn't want to give her a reason to come into the house. I kissed him on the cheek and said, "I'll be back." Rea pulled up as I walked out the door. As soon as I hopped in her car, she began talking about the fight she and Clarence had the night before. I tried to listen, but my mind was on my situation. *Do I really want to get back with Darrell—and if I do, after everything that's happened, how do I tell the world that he and I are back together?*

As Reagan pulled into Stony Ridge Park, she asked, "Are you listening?"

"Yes, you were saying ... how you pick fights so you can have makeup sex. And who is Clarence? Neva mind ... I don't wanna know."

We laughed.

After the 2.3-mile run, we stretched and headed back to the car.

"Girl," Reagan said. "I can't wait to get to your house! I have to pee."

I didn't want to try to explain to her what I wasn't even sure about. Although there was a powder room by the front door, she noticed when anything was out of place. I had to divert her from coming to the house. I urged her, "There's a McDonald's right there. Pull over."

"No, I can make it to your house."

"I don't think I can ... you know, uh, my bladder is weak. Come on, pull over!"

Rea fussed. "Dang! You need a pull-up?"

She pulled in and proceeded to sit in the car. "Come with me."

"What da ... DeLaina, what is wrong with you?"

"Dag, Rea, you can't pee with me?"

She stared, trying to read me. She knew something was going on but couldn't put her finger on it. She snatched the keys out of the ignition. "Fine, let's go."

Standing at the double sink washing our hands, she stared at me in the mirror. Rea's like a bloodhound. I had to give her something to throw her off my scent. I began ranting about my workload and how the new director was on my tail with new processes and procedures. She began to relate. Afterwards she dropped me off at the house and kept going.

Once back at the house I called in sick. Rell and I made love all day ... everywhere that I could hold my balance. Although we rekindled our relationship over the next few weeks, I decided to hold off on telling anyone until I was absolutely sure about Darrell and me.

I felt myself falling more in love with him every

day, then the music stopped. Half asleep one night, I turned over to reach for him. When I didn't feel him, I woke up. The bedroom door was closed, but he wasn't in the room. I walked down the hall to the kitchen, to the den, then the living room. I could hear his voice but no Darrell. He was out front on his cell phone. His voice was soft and gentle—the way he talked to me, which led me to believe he was talking to a woman. He was telling someone he hadn't called because he'd been out of town. I heard him say, "Of course I've been thinking about you." I realized he hadn't changed. He was the same old Darrell. Trying to play both sides from the middle.

When he finally came back to bed, I asked in a groggy, gentle tone, "Baby, where were you?"

He quickly said, "I left something in the car."

"What did you need from your car at 2:00 a.m.?"

"I left my phone. I'm expecting this dude to call about a second interview."

I sat straight up in the bed. "And you think he's going to do it in the middle of the night?" Insulted that he didn't come up with something better, I said, "So that's where we are, Rell? We lying … and it's only been a few weeks. Who were you talking to on the phone?" He sat there silent. As he sat on the side of the bed, I couldn't help but remember the last time I saw that desolate look on his face. I just sat there, shaking my head.

He finally responded. "Angela."

Darrell went on and on trying to explain. He said that he was pacifying her because he left some things at her house and he thought she'd destroy them if she knew about us. There were so many holes in that story, but the heart wants what the heart wants, so I convinced myself I could almost understand. What I couldn't get around was him sneaking out of the bed to call her. Which made me wonder how many times he'd done that before. I couldn't help but to put myself in Angela's place; and why not … it's not like I hadn't been there before; all she had was his words. Her life, like mine, was on hold based on his lies.

I convinced myself I could feel him trying. He knew I loved him and all he had to do was tell me a good enough lie to get me through the night.

A week or so passed and I hadn't heard anything else about Angela. I don't know why I didn't force him to go get his things—to tell her about us—but I didn't. One night, he fell asleep in the living room watching TV while his cell phone sat on the nightstand. When it rung, the name "Angela" displayed. Something was provoking me … *Answer it … ask dat heffa why she's calling yo man.* I fought with myself not to answer it. Moments later, a text message came through and I couldn't resist. It read: My water broke. Momma's taking me to the hospital.

I shook him like an Etch A Sketch, held the phone in front of his face, and demanded an answer. "What is this?"

It doesn't take a rocket scientist to figure it out. As he was getting dressed to go to the hospital, he told me he wasn't ready to be a father. He said he asked her to have an abortion.

At that point, I notified him, "It's too late for that now. In fact, it's a bit late for a lot of things."

If Darrell had told me everything seven weeks ago when he came back, it would have been easier to deal with. Hiding a secret of that magnitude made me wonder what else he was keeping from me. I knew I needed to get rid of him but, I had fallen in love with him again and just wasn't ready to let go again so soon.

I wanted to be with him, but the situation made for an unhappy ending. I didn't know if I could ever really trust Darrell, but I knew I didn't at that moment.

As he blossomed into fatherhood, my feelings stopped mattering as much. The man he tried to be began to conflict with the man he really was. And since I didn't trust him, I spent my days much like my nights, waiting for him to screw up. I wasn't able to live, so afraid the relationship would die.

After about six months, we did the only thing

we could do at that point. We broke up for sanity's sake.

As I think back on that relationship, I know now that I longed for him after we broke up to try and ease the pain of it all. I reached out to him because holding on was a lot easier than letting go. It reminds me of peeling off a Band-Aid slowly—still enduring some pain but only a little at a time versus ripping it off and dealing with all the pain at once.

Reflecting back, I've concluded I was the reason for much of my own stress. Growing up as a tomboy, I was constantly told, "You're ugly," and I believed it. My bronze-colored skin and boy clothes set the scene. Being shipped from home to home, I often overheard people say, "She ain't gonna be good for nothing just like her momma." I wanted to believe otherwise, but the voices of those comments echoed throughout my life and my relationships. So it was hard for me to believe that Darrell—the one that everyone wanted—that he wanted me, the ugly girl. My insecurities prevented me from believing that he could possibly want me on my own merit, that I was good enough.

The Beginning of the End

Marcus

It's only a mistake if you don't learn from it. When you fail a class in school, you're doomed to repeat it. In life, oftentimes the same rule applies.

One evening, Rea and I met up at Melissa's house. Now, she's that girl you had to know to love—that friend that's always so willing to tell you the unsolicited truth whether it hurts your feelings or not. Melissa insisted I needed to get out and meet some people.

After four months of the same song and dance, there I was, back in the same situation trying to screw my pain away. I found myself barhopping and back in the clubs hoping to meet Mr. Right while two-stepping to "Y'all gon' make me lose my mind ... up in here, up in here." After several months of the club scene, I met a leech, a clepto, and let's not forget the dude that followed me home and sat outside my condo.

My frustration quickly began to build. I thought about learning a second language, taking ice skating lessons, or even Tae Kwan Do—anything to absorb the extra time on my hands.

While discussing this with the girls one day as we sat on Melissa's balcony, she insisted she had the perfect man for me.

"Don't do it!" Rea said. "I would pay to see the man she says is perfect and she ain't throwin' draws at him. Eww, unless she already has."

Melissa pushed her. "Shut up, Rea! No, I haven't slept with him. He's a friend of a friend."

After weeks of coaxing, I agreed to go on a blind date.

"Girl, he's a cutie-pie," Melissa said. "His name is Marcus. He's single, no kids, and he's the lead singer of a band."

I was extremely concerned. "He sounds good, but apparently he's got some issues if he's being set up."

Melissa laughed. "He said the same thing about you."

I don't date friends of the family or my friend's families. My personality is such that I'd feel some sense of obligation versus if it was just some random dude and I didn't like him, then I could just bail. Which I'm sure is why she neglected to tell me he was her cousin.

Marcus and I talked on the phone a few times before we decided to meet in person. I remember that night. We were due to meet at the China Hut, a little spot about fifteen minutes from my house. I spent about an hour trying to pick out the right outfit, considering he already had the presumption something was wrong with me, so I wanted to make sure I wore an outfit that was just right … one that said, "Whoa. Why is she single?" I washed my hair and pulled it back into a curly ponytail. I wore my white tube top with the black rose draped across the front, black stretch jeans, and my black and white, three-inch open-toed sandals. I walked in and stood at the counter like I was waiting for my food, carefully scanning the room.

I told Marcus I'd be wearing a red shirt. I wanted the opportunity to see him first and run if need be.

A tall, chocolate, bald man walked toward me. "Oh, the old 'change shirts' routine?"

I laughed. "Are you Marcus?"

He reached out to shake my hand. "Yes, Marcus Day."

Slightly embarrassed, I asked, "How did you

know it was me?"

As he told me how Melissa showed him a picture, I noticed how his dimples made a special appearance when he talked.

We sat down, ordered some food, and talked for hours. Because he was so passionate about everything, it came across a bit animated—kinda cute. As we argued who'd win between Wonder Woman and Zena, he stood up to take his jacket off and moved to the seat beside me, at which point, I closed my eyes and looked away to keep from laughing. His shirt was so tight that I couldn't tell if it was a shirt or a onesie. What is that … smedium, sm-large?

After three hours of uninterrupted talk, he said, "So tell me … how did the last man let you get away?"

Reluctant to respond, I thought back for a moment and admitted, "We grew apart."

Seizing the moment, he leaned over and pressed his lips against mine. Taken off guard, I quickly pulled back. He apologized. Moving past the awkward silence, I told him about the book I just finished reading by Adonica. He said he heard it was good and asked if he could borrow it. He followed me back to my house to get the book. While standing in the foyer, I offered him a cup of coffee. I knew I should have let that man go home, but I was enjoying the attention. We sat down and continued to talk for another two hours before we noticed the time. When he got up to leave, we stood in the middle of the floor, engaged in a ten-minute embrace without one word being passed. As he leaned down and ran the tip of his nose from my collarbone to the ridge of my ear, I felt him grow between us; it felt nice being wanted. He backed me against the wall … and as I pushed him away, he pinned down my wrists and kissed my bottom lip. I felt helpless yet hopeful. I knew I should make him stop but I couldn't make myself tell him. He released my wrists and placed his hands in mine, locking fingers against the wall. There was something about him that just wasn't right. I couldn't put my finger on it.

The next day, Melissa called to see how the date went.

I told her, "There was something about him that scared me, something that made me feel vulnerable and weak."

"What does that mean?" She said she talked to him and he said, "There's something about that girl." She insisted we fell in love.

"It was one date, Melissa. Dang!"

I think she was right. We began spending every possible moment together: movies, dinners, and long weekends. We did all the things that couples do.

Three months later, I was chosen to head up a

new office is Mississippi. The project was already two months behind schedule, which meant two months behind revenue, fueling the fierce push to get this office up and running. I wasn't their first choice; the person they'd originally chosen resigned without notice. It was such a wonderful opportunity that I didn't even care that I was plan B.

I got the news on Tuesday that I needed to be on a plane Friday morning. I didn't sweat it. I thought I'd be back in a couple of weeks or at least be home on the weekends to see Marcus, but I was working around the clock. By the time we called it quits in the evening, all I wanted to do was get in the bed. I called him every night the first week to say, "I miss you," then it was off to bed to start all over again. By week three, I was too tired to even reach for the phone. Although most nights I fell asleep at the computer, he was constantly on my mind. Absence makes the heart grow fonder. I wanted to take full advantage of this opportunity, so the job took precedence. What started out as a three-month project turned into eight months. After the three months were up, I agreed to stay—contingent upon three-day weekends. But between going through mail, paying bills, and washing clothes, it was virtually impossible to fit in a man. As hard as I tried, I only saw Marcus three times in the eight months but we did what we could. We sent cards; he sent flowers and candy. He even sent me a little, white, stuffed bunny rabbit that was holding a mix tape he'd made for me.

After eight mind-numbing months, I was finally on my way back home.

Once I got back to town, the first place I went was Groove Thang, a top-floor lounge in the city where Marcus' band played every Wednesday. I walked in just as the band finished their set. Peering through the crowd, trying to get closer to the stage, I saw him. There he was, more handsome than I remembered. My heart started beating faster as I moved closer to the stage. I tossed my hair and cupped my hand in front of my face to smell my breath. I could feel myself taking deeper breaths, thinking how I couldn't wait to—

Then I hit a BRICK WALL.

Stopped dead in my tracks. My feet wouldn't move. I could hear my heart pounding over the noisy crowd. I was still holding out hope, but I now knew the reason it seemed in the past few months, I was the only one putting in effort. The reason was five-six, about 130 pounds, with her lips pressed firmly against his. I felt like a voyeur watching, remembering what he smelled like the last time he held me in those arms.

Busy with work, schedules off, maybe even that he had broken his dialing finger. I wanted to believe anything besides another woman. Suddenly, my shirt got tighter and the room got smaller. I couldn't handle it.

As I turned to walk away, he called out my name. "DeLaina?"

I took a deep breath, put on my best smile, and turned around. "Marcus Day? Is that you?"

He wrapped his arms around me as though he were trying to make up for lost time, like we were the only two people in the room. With my nose pressed against his neck, I inhaled him, remembering every inside joke and every night we spent together. He smelled like dinner and a movie, like breakfast in bed, like marriage and kids. Then reality walked up and cleared her throat like a needle sliding across a record.

"Marcee, aren't you going to introduce me to your friend?"

Who da … Marcee? I thought.

He looked embarrassed. "Oh! Honey, I'm sorry. This is Michael's cousin, DeLaina. DeLaina, this is … my … girlfriend, Verneece."

Did he say GIRLFRIEND? And why am I suddenly Michael's cousin?

He wasn't referring to me as Michael's cousin when he was sending me flowers and saying "I love you." I wasn't Michael's cousin when we were playing doctor. Why didn't he just introduce me as an old friend?

Michael always told me, "Never let them see you sweat." So I reached out to shake her hand. "Nice to meet you Vanessa."

She smiled. "It's Verneece, and it's nice to meet you as well."

"Have you guys been dating long?" I poked.

Pulling him closer, she said, "Oh, about five or six months. Right, baby?"

He looked down and nodded his head yes.

With my best impression of a Kool-Aid smile, I said, "That's great!"

"DeLaina, you catch the last set?" she asked. "My man was great."

"Oh, I'm sure he was, but I'm just meeting my date here." I couldn't believe I let that lie roll off my tongue.

Marcus snapped his head up to look at me. "Date! You seeing someone? I thought you just got back in town."

Verneece seemed a bit concerned about his reaction.

Still smiling and batting my eyes like Miss America, I said, "Yes, Marcus, what did you think? No one would want me … that I'd just be sitting at home waiting for Mr. Right to realize distance only means you need to build a bridge."

Stuttering like a Muslim caught with a pork chop sandwich, he said, "No … I mean … uhh … not at all. I … I was … I was just saying—"

I interrupted, "I better go. It was nice meeting you, Versace."

"That's Verneece." She rolled her eyes.

"Um-hm. Take care, Marcus."

I was stuck … I couldn't leave right away since I lied about meeting a date, so I had to play it out. I walked over to the bar and flagged down the bartender. "Peach martini … light on the peach." I stood there with my drink in hand, looking around as if I were looking for someone, all the while trying to devise a plan to get out of there. I turned to the bar and looked up in the mirror to see if they were looking in my direction, and of course they were.

The one benefit of having male cousins is GAME. From the corner of my eye, I caught someone staring at me … *Prey*. Once I turned and got a full view, he looked like Tyson Beckford … wide body, full lips, and all. I found my date. I made eye contact from across the bar. As he stared back at me, I looked away, biting my bottom lip. Finally, I walked up behind him, leaned over the barstool, pressed my body against his, and put both hands over his eyes.

I whispered in his ear, "Let's play the name game. I'll give you one try to guess my name … and if you're wrong, you have to buy me a drink."

In a Barry White octave, he said, "I like games. And if I guess right?"

"If you guess right, I'll give you a kiss."

"Sounds good to me," he said. "Let's see ... ummm ... you sound like a Patricia." I removed my hands as he slowly swirled the bar stool around, stopping directly in front of me. He smiled and spread his legs so that I was standing between them. With a sly, sexy grin, he asked, "So are we drinking or kissing?"

From the corner of my eye, I could see Marcus walking past the bar toward the restroom. I leaned in, put my arms around his neck, lightly kissed him on the cheek, and said, "Call me Pat."

By the third drink, Marcus and his little girlfriend were finally gone. I just wanted to leave. I paid the tab. That's the least I could do. Although I wasn't interested in seeing this guy again, he gave me his business card. Given the night I had, I figured he just might come in useful again.

I drove around for a while to clear my head. As I pulled into my parking lot, my cell phone rang; it was a "private" number. I don't answer blocked numbers, but, since it was one o'clock in the morning, I was curious.

"Hello?" I said.

There was a faint whisper: "DeLaina?"

"Yes, who is this?"

"It's me ... Marcus."

I'm sure all thirty-two of my teeth were visible at that moment. "Why are you whispering?" I asked.

"Because I don't want to wake Verneece."

"No, you don't want Vertigo to know you're talking to me."

"It's Verneece! Okay, fine … that, too." There was an awkward pause. I sat in the parked car with the engine still running. Finally, he said, "Laina, I'm sorry you had to find out about her that way."

"Yeah, I bet, Marcee. I'm sure you wish I had gotten the hint from the 'I miss you' messages you left."

"I did … I mean, I do miss you, but I was lonely."

"Are you serious? That's what you're going with? Your punk behind could have gotten a dog! Is this your jacked-up attempt at an apology?" He was quiet, so I said "You know what … I don't have time for this."

"Wait! Laina, you're seeing someone, too. So what's with the 'tude? Look, I just wanted to tell you that it was nice seeing you. I didn't realize how much I missed you until you were in my arms."

I could feel my heartbeat in my throat. I reciprocated: "Yeah, it was nice seeing you, too."

"That's it? 'It was nice seeing you, too'? Where are you?"

"I just got home."

"Oh, okay."

"Marcus, when I first left, you were calling regularly, sending notes, flowers, then you just stopped. I got a message once a week, then every two weeks. I called, wrote … shoot, I even sent a carrier pigeon, but you still didn't respond. At least now I know why."

"No, DeLaina, that's not fair. When you first mentioned taking that project, I told you that I was no good at long-distance relationships. I told you I needed someone right here."

"Yeah, you did, but I must have gotten confused because I thought that 'I love you' meant 'Let's try to make it work.' I guess we weren't as close as I thought we were."

His voice dropped to a whisper as he said, "Baby, I'm sorry! Laina, seeing you tonight makes me want back what we had."

"No! You pretty much screwed that one up."

"Baby girl, I don't know what to say. I just have all these feeling right now. Do you miss me?"

"I did! But you moved on, so I have to move on too."

"Yeah, I saw that thick-neck bamma you were with at the bar."

"Don't hate! You know he was sexy."

"I don't know about him, but you are. You look

so beautiful tonight." His tone changed again. "Do you remember Omar's wedding? I think that was the night I knew I loved you. We danced all night, and everyone kept saying 'Y'all gonna be next.'"

I could feel a tear form in my heart and run down my face. I fumbled around looking for tissue. "Marcus, don't do this." I closed my eyes and got lost in the memories.

He said "I remember every moment with you … every kiss, every touch, and every I love you."

There was a tap on the window. I jumped. It was Marcus, standing outside my car. A little uncomfortable, I unlocked the door and stepped out. Looking down and barely making eye contact, I stood with my arms folded and my back against the car. "What are you doing here?"

"Baby girl, I wanted to say it face-to-face." With the pointer finger of his right hand, he lifted my head to make eye contact. "I'm sorry." He leaned in and kissed my forehead. As he pulled back, I unfolded my arms and wrapped them around him.

When I looked up at him, our eyes locked and the heat drew us closer. As our heads slowly tilted our lips touched. His lips were just as soft as I remembered. He grabbed my face with both hands and pulled me in deeper.

He stopped kissing me long enough to whisper,

"I missed you." He unbuttoned his shirt and placed my hand over his heart. "That's what love feels like." I blushed. His heart was beating a mile a minute. I wanted him more at that moment than ever before.

I took his hand and said, "Let's go inside." Once inside, though, reality hit me. "Marcus, I want you, but this isn't fair … not to me or Venus."

He laughed. "Her name is Verneece. And what about what I want?"

"You'd still want your girlfriend had I not wrapped up that project."

"Maybe. Until I realized I was settling. I've never felt like this before. Laina, I can't pretend I don't care about her, but it doesn't feel like this."

His words touched me deep inside. In seconds, I had to determine if I was willing to deal with the consequences as they came. Between my heart pounding and my body aching, I couldn't hear the voice of reason.

You would think that I knew better from the relationship with Darrell, but this was different. I felt like Marcus was mine; he was suppose to be with ME.

As time went on we began emailing and instant messaging. What can I say? We were drawn to each other like light in the crack of a window. We started sneaking around, and the excitement of it was overwhelming.

Marcus continued dating the both of us for about a month, with constant excuses as to why he hadn't ended it yet. I was trying to be patient, but my patience was wearing thin. One night, he lied and got out of the house to come see me. We laid there basking in the afterglow, cuddling. He must have felt himself getting tired, because he asked me to set the clock in case he fell asleep. Since they lived together, him staying out all night was a no-no. I took matters into my own hands. When the alarm went off, I quickly turned it off so as not to disturb him. Next thing I knew, it was morning and the sun was kissing our faces. He looked scared. He jumped up, and slipped one leg in his pants while hopping around trying to find his shoes. He gave me a quick peck on the cheek and darted out the door. His leaving abruptly left me feeling cheap, but I was curious how this was going to play out.

He conjured up a lie about being detained by the police, which bought him more time with her. As for me, patience had an expiration date: November fifteenth.

Marcus and I were supposed to meet for a late romantic dinner after his set, but I didn't feel much like being romantic. The fact of the matter was that I was feeling used and manipulated. I knew it was going to continue to go on for as long as I allowed. As I got dressed, I made myself a drink or two. Dark liquor has the uncanny ability to talk me into doing and saying things I wouldn't ordinarily.

Once I arrived at the club, I went straight to the bar and ordered a shot of tequila. I sashayed into the lounge with liquor in my system and no food on my stomach. I was like a heat-seeker looking for trouble. The band was accompanying a poet I had seen there before; they called her Love's Poet. When I arrived, she was almost in tears reciting her pain. She had her eyes closed and both hands resting on the shaft of the mic as she relived that moment …

I've mixed my tears with this ink to form these words, hoping you'll understand my pain through these nouns and verbs.

I honestly don't know what happened to us … what went wrong.

But now I'm left reliving my emotions through every love song

Cause … I can't remember to forget you.

I found myself caught up in her issue. I had to remind myself to focus. I went to the lounge, sure that Veronica would be there—and sure enough, she and two of her girls had a table in the corner near the stage.

I walked toward the stage, stopped, and folded my arms as if I was waiting for an explanation. Marcus looked like a deer caught in headlights. Quickly glimpsing over at Victoria, he struck the wrong chord twice. My presence obviously distracted him. Detecting something was wrong, she turned to see what had him disturbed. As I motioned for her, she glimpsed back at him then joined me at the bar.

I told the bartender, "Shot of tequila, no salt," before facing her. "Would you like a drink?"

She looked confused. "No, thank you. DeLaina, what's this about?"

I threw my head back and took two swallows, then asked, "Did you know that Marcus and I dated before he met you?"

"I figured that ... And?"

When I didn't respond, she laughed and said, "Look, sweetie, I'm missing the show, so let me put you in your place real quick—"

I interrupted to order another drink. "Can I get another shot of tequila and a Heineken?"

"DeLaina," she continued. "I see you desperately sniffing around my man, but notice the last two words ... MY ... MAN."

I smiled. "That was cute. Are you trying to convince me ... or YOU?"

She put her finger in my face and said "Heffa, let me tell you something ..." I could feel myself turning into a donkey—like a tail and ears had appeared. As I reached for my Heineken, she pushed my head with her finger and said, "Stay the hell away from me and Marcus. You hear me?"

I firmly gripped the neck of the bottle with my right hand, and reached back for strength—when Marcus ran up and grabbed my wrist. I snatched my arm away and said, "You betta handle your business before I choke this …"

When Velveeta finally put Marcus out, he moved from one girlfriend's house to another. So, at the flip of a coin, we found ourselves under one roof sharing a world.

I popped my collar and stuck a feather in my hat: I won. Everything was great for a few months, then it seemed things began to change. It was subtle at first, then the mood swings began to come more frequently. As his attitude changed, so did his pattern. Suddenly, he was coming home later and later. One evening, we went to the corner store for some junk food and a blunt. I went down the back aisle to the cold section to get us some drinks. Reaching for the freezer door, I looked up in the mirror to see Marcus walking up to some girl. Admittedly, he knew lots of people—we couldn't go anywhere without seeing someone he knew or that knew him—but this looked odd, even for him. As I watched his body language, I was sure he was coming on to her. I got the drinks and headed to the front near the register hoping for the opportunity to introduce myself but, she was walking out the door by the time I got there.

"Who was that?" I asked him.

"We went to school together."

"Did you two date?"

He yelled, "No, DeLaina!" and left the store.

I was mad that he was mad. To me it was just a question. I was trying to get an understanding of what I had seen.

It was in these times that his actions began to chip away at my trust. I guess it's funny that I thought the man I cheated with would be faithful to me … again.

Hard to Keep

Marcus was quite a catch ... just hard to keep. He promised me that nothing was going on. He wanted me to believe him, and I wanted to. Seeing him at the club, falling all over those women, really made me uncomfortable. He tried to convince me that it was just business ... that he had to appeal to the woman in the crowd to keep them coming back. Behind the microphone, he was selling a fantasy. He tried to make me think it was for them when in actuality it was a two-way street. He made them feel wanted, and their lust in turn fed his insecurities.

I didn't want to feel insecure. I didn't want to be the woman I had been with Darrell, but I couldn't help feeling slighted by him. Undervalued even.

I had to question if it was really him or if it was me. Before I knew it, I was in love with a man that at times I didn't know. He was happy one moment … angry and depressed the next. How was it that I could have a man and still feel lonely?

One evening, I stopped by rehearsal to pick up Marcus since his car was in the shop. When I arrived he and Kee-Kee—the lead female vocalist—were working on "Nothing Has Ever Felt Like This." Seemingly, anytime I came around, sista-girl would catch major attitude. As a woman, you know when something ain't right … when another woman has a thing for your man. So I asked Marcus if anything was going on with them … or previously had been. He swore up and down that there was nothing going on.

Once she saw me she picked a fight with Marcus and stormed off—and he went running after her as usual. I can't began to express how it felt to watch my man chase another woman in an effort to "console" her.

Meanwhile, the band continued rehearsing while they waited for the two of them to return. I hadn't been to one of their rehearsals in a while but as per the standard … they sounded great. The guitarist sang Marc's part. As they played, I hummed Kee-Kee's part, but as I got caught up in the moment, I began singing … "Nothing has every felt … quite like this … nothing has ever meant ..."

Satchel stood up from playing the piano and said, "I had no idea you could sing like that."

I blushed as my ego inflated.

"Look," he said. "How would you feel about doing a duet?"

"Really?"

I never considered myself a singer, but when he said it to me, it certainly sounded good.

"Do you know 'Let's Stay Together'?" he asked.

As I broke into "I ... I'm so in love with you," he said, "Yeah, that's it."

Marcus walked in slowly with a disturbed look on his face—and from that day on, his whole demeanor change toward me. Marcus walked toward the stage with both hands in his pockets. Satch stopped playing and said, "Man, why you ain't tell us Laina had a voice like this, we could have gotten rid of that Kee-Kee a long time ago."

Marcus took one hand out of his pocket and twirled his finger in the air. "Wrap it up, guys," he said. "We'll reconvene Wednesday at six." He looked at me and said, "Laina, let's go."

"Okay, I'll be right there."

As he left, Satch explained that they weren't looking for a quote-unquote new "member" but a featured artist from time to time. He ended the conversation with, "Talk it over with Marcus and get back to us."

When I got to the truck, Marcus was sitting behind the wheel, revving the engine. I got in and attempted to talk to Marcus about Satchel's idea, but he wouldn't say a word. I couldn't make heads or tails of his attitude, which frustrated me. When we got home, I jumped out and stormed into the house ahead of him. As I crossed the threshold of the condo, I heard him running up the steps. He burst through the door, grabbed me by the throat, slammed me against the wall, and yelled, "Don't you EVER disrespect me like that again."

Sadly, I was used to him trying to manhandle me. I squeezed out the words. "What did I do?"

"I step outside for a second and you all up in Satchel's face."

I pushed him off me, yelling, "You trippin'! There were at least ten other people in the room. We were singing."

He grabbed my arm. "It ain't look like just singing!"

I snatched my arm away. "What about you chasing behind Ms. Thing?"

"I told you! We work together!"

When Satchel asked me about singing, my first thought had been, *I'll get to spend more time with Marcus—*

but obviously he saw it as him losing his identity and space. I knew him better than he thought I did. If he thought for a millisecond that one of the band members or anyone else for that matter was trying to hit on me, he would have shut that club down, as opposed to holding it in until we got home.

A few days later, Marcus forgot his wallet. When I dropped it off at rehearsal, I ran into Satchel and he asked me, "So did you guys talk it over?"
Embarrassed, I looked down. "Yeah, I don't think it's such a good idea."

"Okay. I got the impression it wasn't gonna work out, so I called a friend of mine who's looking for a female vocalist, and I told him about you. Marcus knows him; his name is McElroy." He handed me a piece of paper. "He's expecting your call."

Several weeks passed and things seemed to be back to normal on the home front. I had been rehearsing four nights a week with McElroy and the band. Then it was time—my first gig. I sat at my vanity, nervous and excited, putting on my makeup when Marcus came in sweaty and funky from playing basketball.

I told him, "Hurry, go take a shower. I need to leave in about twenty minutes."

He grabbed the remote, sat on the chaise, and began flipping through the stations aimlessly.

"Marcus?"

"What?"

"I'm singing at the Love's Nest tonight."

Without taking his eyes off the television, he said, "I'm at the club five nights a week. That's the last place I want to be on my night off."

"But … I'm singing."

"AND? I've heard you sing before."

Everything Marcus did or desired to do, I was always his biggest supporter. But, on the night that I needed a little of that back, he chose the remote over me. I wanted to believe he was just kidding, that he'd still show up at the club. There I was, a grown woman, watching the door the same way I watched the window when I was little, waiting for my mother to come … and just like her … he never showed up.

When I got home from the club we of course got into a huge fight. I'm talking three hours filled with cursing and door slamming, after which he grabbed a few things and left. Days later, as I was in the kitchen packing my lunch, I heard a light tapping at the door. When I looked through the peephole and realized it was Marcus, I wondered why he didn't use his key. Instead of questioning him, I opened the door and mumbled, "Good morning," as I walked back into the kitchen.

Walking slowly behind me, he sat down at the breakfast bar and said, "We need to talk."

I continued packing my lunch. "I don't have time for this, this morning."

"I won't take long."

As I threw everything into my lunch bag, he slid my house key across the marble countertop and said, "You know I love you." I stared at the key as he tried to explicate how tired HE was. "This emotional tug-of-war has got to stop."

I was stunned that HE was breaking up with ME. If anyone should still be mad... During the past few days I came to realize that he resented me for trying to do what he was doing. He took it personally whereas I just wanted to share in his world.

I pushed the key back. With an air of insouciance, I said, "Baby, just take the key back. We'll talk about this tonight."

He confidently shook his head and walked away. As he neared the front door, he said, "I'll get my things later."

We had broken up before, so it was hard for me to believe it was real. I mean, really, where was he going to go? He had come into this relationship with virtually nothing. He told me when he got divorced, his ex-wife took everything but a living room set, a couple of paintings and the clothes on his back. He said he never recovered from it so I footed pretty much all the bills; he bought food and paid the cable bill. The question was: where was he going to go where he'd only have to pay two hundred dollars a month?

Looking back, I guess I thought, "Where are you going to find a bigger fool than me?"

I thought I'd give him a couple days to calm down and rethink this thing. Day three, I called and left a message. Day four, I called again, and on day five, his phone went straight to voice mail. Apparently, he was serious, and I couldn't understand why he'd abandon our relationship now. Although we had broken up many times, I always thought we'd spend the rest of our lives together. Maybe that was just me. I went over to Reagan's in an effort to get my mind off of Marcus, but no sooner than I had crossed her threshold, my cell phone rang—it was him.

"Hello," I said.

"You called?"

"Yes, I called. Why haven't you been returning my calls?"

In a curt tone, he responded, "I'm calling now. What's up?"

"You know what … forget it!" I hung up.

I plopped down on the couch beside Rea, laid my head on her lap, and asked rhetorically, "Why is he such a jerk?"

While she rubbed my back, her cell phone rang, but she quickly hit "end," sending it to voice mail.

"Who was that?" I asked.

"Oh, that's just Paige."

"Why you never answer the phone when she calls?"

"Cuz it's like talking to my mother. She always says the same stuff: Why you ain't been to church? Ain't God good? Won't he do it ..."

I laughed. "She's just excited about God."

"Whateva. She thinks she's holier than thou."

"No, she doesn't."

"Laina, I asked her to come with us to Frisco's and she was on some ... 'No, you know I don't drink anymore.' Ain't nobody ask her all that. She could have come and just spent some time with us. She act like she too good."

"Why you being so mean? Okay, first, you don't invite a recovering alcoholic to hang out in a bar. Second, she's saved. What would she look like hanging out in a smoke-filled meat market? She's a deaconess for goodness' sake."

"Well, she claims she's been delivered, so it should be all good."

"Maybe she didn't want to put herself in a vulnerable situation."

"I can't stand you ... you always defending her. Well, you can't get around the Bible, and the Bible says somewhere, 'Test and see that the Lord is good,' so if she's been delivered, she'll know the minute someone offers to buy her a drink."

I sat up on the couch. "Okay, seriously, Rea … YOU NEED TO STOP SMOKING! It says TASTE … TASTE and see that the Lord is good. Taste, crack-head."

My Baby Daddy

The breakup went on for six and a half months until he saw that I, too, was moving on. As time lapsed, we got back together. Broke up again and got back together. We didn't really want to be together; it was just easier than waking up alone.

This time when he moved back in, he came with more baggage than the last time.

One night, we were watching TV when the phone rang. I reached over him to answer it. "Hello?"

In a high-pitched tone, the caller said, "Yeah, can I speak to Marc?"

Thinking in the back of my mind, *He ain't been here but a few weeks. I know this fool ain't acting up already.*

"Um, sure, who's calling?" I asked.

"Rho."

I repeated the name and hand him the phone. He answered the phone, "Hey, hey, girl. What's … what's going on? Oh yeah. Well, how the kids doing? Good, good. Look, how you get this number?" His voice got louder as he said, "Oh. Tyron … Tyron gave it to you. I see. Well, this is my girlfriend's house, so please don't call here. Yeah, yeah, I heard you. I'll call you tomorrow and we'll talk about it."

I sat in the corner of the couch with my arms folded, waiting for him to tell me what just happened. He grabbed the remote and pressed play on the VCR. I snatched the remote, turned the movie off, and said,

"Don't play wit me!"

"Baby, I didn't give her the number. Tyron did."

"Okay, you need to check your boy. In the meantime, WHO is she? And what do you have to call her tomorrow to talk about?"

He sat back on the couch and shook his head. "When we broke up, I dated her for a minute."

"Why in da world would Tyron give some girl you used to date … this number?"

He shook his head. "I don't know."

His "I don't know" was ticking me off. Somebody was going to tell me something. I went to the closet where his coat was hanging and grabbed his cell phone. As I started scrolling through for Tyron's number, he called out in an innocent voice, "Baby?" The phone began ringing. Marc came around the corner and saw the phone in my hand and asked, "Who you calling?"

"Tyron!"

He snatched the phone. "I'll deal with Ty—"

"YOU gonna deal with him? Oh, nigga, you betta tell me something. I ain't playing wit you."

"A'ight, Laina, look …" There was a long pause before he continued. "She's pregnant."

"You got some girl …" I immediately had flashes of Darrell and his baby momma drama. "How far along is she?"

"I don't know. She can't be more than a month or two."

I sat there angry, trying desperately to remind myself that it happened when we weren't together.

"Do you know for certain it's yours?" I asked.

"Naw, I don't know. I mean, she said it is."

I took a deep breath and tried to put "me" aside for a minute. That kid didn't ask to be here. Marcus needed to talk to her, and since he looked uncomfortable, I grabbed my coat and said, "I'm going to get out the house for a little while. Call her back."

He grabbed my hand. "Stay. This affects both of us."

The fact that he insisted on having the conversation in front of me was reassuring. He dialed the number on the cordless and handed me the kitchen phone as it connected. When she answered, he said, "Rho, it's Marcus."

"Hey," she said. "Look, I ain't know you had a girlfriend or nuffin like dat. I just thought you should know. Hold on." She yelled, "Kivon, get-cho sista off da banister! DANG! Y'all gonna have Social Services up in here again!"

He shook his head.

"I'm back," she said.

"Okay, Rho, for real do you know for sure it's mine?"

"Wha-chu tryin ta say, Marcus?"

"Naw, my bad, I'm not trying to say anything. I'm just asking, Rhonda, that's all."

"Um-hum. A'ight den, let's not have this conversation again." She sucked her teeth and said, "Hold on." She yelled, "Joquan, go see wha-cho brother doin'!"

After she came back to the phone, Marcus said, "Okay, well, for my own peace of mind, I want a DNA test."

"Whateva, Marcus! Ya lil' GIRLFRIEND must've put you up ta dat … cuz I KNOW YOU KNOW how we was gettin' down."

"No, I'm doing this so I know what to tell her." He looked at me and said, "She's a part of my future." Unconcerned, she said, "Yeah, whateva. Look, can I call you on diss numba or do you got another numba for me?"

He looked to me for confirmation. Once I nodded my head yes, he told her, "Yeah, you can call me at this number."

"A'ight, I'll call you if I need anything."

I was proud of him. We didn't hear anything from her for months, then all of a sudden, she started calling every day … several times a day. One day, I overheard him say, "I gave you three hundred dollars last week. I don't have it."

I snatched the phone from him and said to her, "He'll call you back." I turned to Marcus and asked, "What did you give her three hundred dollars for?"

"She needed stuff for the baby."

"That's why you borrowed money from me? The baby's not even here yet. Don't let this girl make a fool of you. Just wait until after the DNA test and we'll get whatever the baby needs."

The phone rang … it was Rhonda. We didn't answer. I told him, "Look, if I tell her NO, you have to stand up and say no too."

He agreed.

She called again, so I answered. "Hello."

"Put my baby daddy on da phone."

"Excuse me? Look, Rhonda, let's not start being disrespectful."

She sucked her teeth. "Well, jus' put him on da phone den … shoot."

"No, tell me what you need."

"I need you ta… put… him… on… da phone!" She paused. "I need Marcus to come finish what he started last week."

"What?"

She laughed. "He knows what I'm talking bout."

I turned to him and enunciated, "What happened last week?"

Marcus ran and grabbed the kitchen phone. "Rhonda, don't play with her like that. Now you tell her nothing happened or so help me …"

She sucked her teeth. "I was jus' playin'. Dang … y'all ain't got no sense of humor. Look, I need some money for Pampers."

"The baby ain't even here yet," I snapped.

"You think I don't know dat? I'm nesting."

I snapped again, "Tell you what … since you have all the jokey jokes, holler at us when your water breaks. Betta yet, holler with some DNA results. Until then, don't call my house."

"DeLaina, diss ain't 'bout you. Marcus is this

baby's daddy. You can't stop me from calling him."

Her lack of respect caused me to act ignorant. "Trick, you don't know me. I can stop you from seeing tomorrow. You betta train a pigeon, holler out the window ... do whateva you gotta do ... but don't call my house." I was hot.

Twenty minutes later, Marcus asked, "Really, baby ... a pigeon?"

This whole baby thing wasn't an easy pill to swallow, considering all I had endured with Darrell. In spite of the situation, Marcus and I were in a good place, and seeing him happy made me happy.

The following month, Rhonda gave birth to a beautiful baby girl: TraNia—who happened to look a lot like Rhonda's youngest boy. Marcus's excitement caused him to see what he wanted to see. He'd say stuff like, "She looks just like me, doesn't she?" I didn't want to appear unsupportive. But after three weeks of "My daughter this" and "My daughter that," I called to schedule an appointment for the DNA test. He had become so attached that he was hesitant. Rhonda was defiantly against it. She used everything she had to fight it. The appointment was rescheduled three times, one of which she just didn't show up, so we finally stopped asking.

A couple months later, after the dust settled, I called her and asked if I could take the baby shopping.

She agreed. I picked up the baby, called Marcus home for an emergency, and the three of us headed downtown to have the test done. Two weeks later, the results arrived in the mail. Marcus got home before me, but he was afraid to open it. When I got home, he said, "Baby, what if she's not mine?"

I didn't believe she was, but I couldn't stand by and watch him becoming attached to a child that chances were not his.

So I said, "Honey, TraNia didn't ask to be here. I know you love her. If you're not the father, that doesn't mean that you still can't get her sometimes or do things for her."

He didn't say a word. He handed me the letter addressed to him. As I ran my finger underneath the lip of the envelope, I could see him bracing himself. I read the letter to myself. I skipped down to the line that stated, *Marcus Day has been excluded in the paternity of TraNia Michelle Day*. I didn't want to be right. As I looked at him, he was looking at me, trying to read my expression; waiting for me to say something. All I could put together was, "I'm sorry."

After he grabbed the letter to read it for himself, he flung it across the room, went into the den, and slammed the door.

The situation with TraNia didn't bring us together; it tore us apart. Marcus didn't know how to deal with what he was feeling, so he lashed out and pushed me away.

With his emotions going through peaks of highs and lows we did what we always did when one of us got frustrated: we broke up. He just needed space to deal with what he was feeling. This time, the break up only lasted about a month.

Father Knows Best

I understood Marcus ... parts of him at least. As weird as it was, our lives were parallel. The only difference was that I learned the hard way how to not let the past control the future, or so I felt.

His father died when he was eight. At least that's the story he told. The truth was ... his father still lived here in Annapolis, but they hadn't spoken in two decades.

As he got older, Marcus stopped trying and just numbed himself. Although his father had abandoned him, it seemed that side of the family loved him just that much more. It was as though they were trying to compensate for the pain his father inflicted.

One Sunday morning, we went grocery shopping. We were rushing to pick up food before the football game started. Every five minutes, he'd say, "I don't wanna miss the kickoff. Baby, hurry up."

With one hand in the air and frustration in my voice, I snapped, "Look, we'll just grab enough for today and tomorrow, and I'll finish shopping later this week."

As I walked away, he grabbed one of my belt loops, pulling me backwards, and hugged me from behind. He kissed me on the neck and said, "See, that's why I love you."

I was always putty in his hands when he kissed me on the neck. As I turned around to kiss him, it was as if time froze. Marcus stood six-two, with 243 pounds of pure muscle, but he looked like a little boy staring over my left shoulder with a faint smirk on his face. I turned to see what had him stunned. There was a tall, handsome man walking up the grocery aisle, wearing the same Philadelphia Eagles jersey that Marcus was wearing. The harder I stared, the more I saw Marcus in twenty years. I grabbed his hand and began to squeeze. Turning slowly, looking into Marcus' eyes to confirm what I saw, the joy on the little boy's face turned to fear and ended with anger in a matter of seconds. I had never seen him like this. The gentleman hadn't noticed us staring yet.

In my mind, *I was thinking, Today is the day. He's going to come back to the condo with us and watch the Redskins get their butts whooped. I'll cook dinner … no, maybe he'll take us out to dinner. Shoot, that's the least he could do.*

Just then, Marcus grabbed the cart and proceeded toward the man at a slow pace, only looking forward. I walked behind him. As Marcus got closer, he turned his head to the left as the man looked up from the shelf. They made eye contact, then both looked away. I shook my head in disbelief. Once I caught up with Marcus, he had his hat pulled down farther on his face than usual. Walking past me toward the exit, he mumbled, "I'll meet you at the truck."

I went back down the grocery aisles where I saw the man last. He wasn't there. I walked the entire store until I found him in the bread aisle, as though nothing happened. I walked up to him and just stood there face-to-face. He stood up straighter, as if he were bracing himself for what would come next.

"How could you walk past him and not even speak?" I asked.

He put his shopping basket down. "He's a grown man. He didn't speak to me, either."

"WOW! You're certainly no Cliff Huxtable. Yea, he's a grown man, but there's a little boy trapped inside who doesn't understand why your step-children had a father and he didn't."

In a defensive tone, he said, "Look, what do you want from me?"

My anger went far past Marcus' abandonment to my very own. I was angry that my father didn't speak, either. Angry that he'd walked away as though I should have been left on the sheets. With one tear rolling down my face, I said, "You're some piece of work. In spite of you, he's incredible. He plays the piano with his eyes closed and his heart open." Blushing, I said, "In spite of you, he's wonderful. But you wouldn't know anything about that."

He looked me up and down. "What are you, some groupie?"

My mouth dropped open. In as long as it took him to make that statement, everything Mommy taught me about respecting my elders went out the window. I took a deep breath, pushed the cart away from me and let him have it. "You selfish, inconsiderate, good-for-nothing, sorry son of a—"

He interrupted "I don't have to listen to this." As he attempted to walk away, I pushed him with one hand and said, "Oh, yes you do."

Although I could see Marcus coming down the aisle out of the corner of my eye, I continued. "You are the sorriest excuse for a man I've ever seen. You're proof that fathering a child doesn't make you a father to a child." By that point, nothing was standing between us but the grounds for a restraining order and the need for a Tic-Tac.

Marcus wrapped his arms around my forearms and pulled me back, but I continued. "When he hurts … I feel his pain."

Marcus called out my name for me to stop but I couldn't. That man needed to hear the pain of an abandoned child.

"I don't know … I guess I was just hoping that you'd acknowledge being trifling, but it would take a man to do that."

He didn't say one more word. Marcus turned me around, grabbing the upper part of my arms, squeezing with both hands and shaking me.

"I'm a grown man," Marcus said. "I don't need you trying to fight my battles. You understand? DO YOU?"

As I nodded in agreement, his grip loosened. He then grabbed my hand and led me out of the store. Later that night, once he calmed down, he said, "Thank you."

Movie Night

Everything was going well. We were really trying to make our relationship work this time. Sometimes in relationships, we become complacent and negligent, or flat out take our partner for granted. We noticed that happening, so we instituted "movie night." Every Tuesday night, we spent the whole evening together watching a movie—no ifs, ands, or buts. The number one rule was, "All phones in the house are turned off on movie night."

So when my cell phone rang, Marcus said, "Who's calling you on movie night?" He said it jokingly, but Marcus was always accusing me of messing around. I guess that should've been a sign.

Provoking me, he said, "Answer the phone, Laina!"

His antagonistic demeanor irritated me. His tone was as though he knew he was going to catch me in something. I looked down at the screen on my cell phone to see who was calling. I answered the phone, got up, and began walking toward the kitchen, stuttering in an uncomfortable tone. "Oh, hi. How are you? Um … nothing … just watching a movie."

In his deepest That's my woman voice, Marcus yelled, "Who is it?"

Not responding, I walked into the kitchen and began whispering. Marcus walked so hard that I could hear him get up from the couch, pass the stereo, and head toward the kitchen. As his footsteps got closer, I said in a sexy tone, "When am I gonna see you again?"

As he crossed the threshold of the kitchen, my eyes got bigger. I began backing away.

"Who's on da phone, DeLaina?" I just stood there. He snatched the phone from my hand and yelled, "Yo, who is diss? Hello! Hello!"

The voice said, "I'm sorry. I'm back. That was my mother on the other line."

With a smirk on his face, he said, "Ava?"

I yelled, "Gotcha! You remember this the next time you fix your lips to call me jealous."

Marcus and Ava are first cousins on his mother's side. She was organizing a huge surprise party in Memphis to celebrate their grandmother's seventy-fifth birthday, and wanted Marcus and his band to be a part of the festivities.

I couldn't get away from work. My company hired a new CEO who I reported to directly, so, there I was having to prove myself all over again. With all the backstabbing, crabs-in-a-barrel syndrome, not to mention the layoffs, taking time off to go to a party was not in my schedule.

Marcus wanted to leave a day early to help his little cousin with the party. So, being the good girlfriend that I was, I shopped for a gift, packed his bags, and dropped him off at the airport on my way to work. A hug, a kiss, and an "I love you" later, I was on my way to the office.

When I got home that night, I made dinner for one, laid on his side of the bed, and just flipped through the channels. This wasn't the first time he was away—he traveled for shows from time to time, but I still missed him. I tried to go to sleep but I couldn't.

That was my biggest issue ... I hated sleeping alone.

He Was Different

When Marcus got back, something about him was different. It was no secret that Marcus and I had an on-again, off-again relationship. It's hard to explain, but the bottom line was, I loved him. There were days we didn't want to be together, but we couldn't stand being apart. As a musician, he had women who would come to the club hoping to get a chance to speak with him. That didn't bothered me much until one night when the band was doing accompaniments, for an open mic night.

The host announced, "Coming to the stage is Consuela. Where are you, Consuela?"

The spotlight hit her as she stood, wearing a

low-cut, short black dress that stopped at her upper thigh.

She walked to the stage, turned, and looked at Marcus. "I don't need an accompaniment. Tonight, I want you to move to my rhythm."

Sitting at the table closest to the stage, I thought, Oh, that's cute. She's got a crush.

She took the mic from the stand, walked toward Marcus, ran her hand across his bald head, and began reciting her piece. The explicit content of her poem left me perplexed. I couldn't believe she was saying these things on the microphone. Astonished, I looked around the room to see if anyone else was as shocked as I was. No one seemed bothered.

A part of me took it as a compliment that she wanted what I had. The other part of me was offended that she was coming on to my man … basically offering him her services. At the end of the set, I went on stage and kissed him like a dog peeing on a tree, trying to mark my territory. I guess my actions were obvious. Later that night, he assured me I had nothing to be jealous of, that I was the only woman for him. Like he'd tell me, "Umm, I wouldn't mind tapping that."

Several weeks later, I noticed a lot of little changes. He became more accusatory. (It's amazing how a cheater can see every angle and opportunity for someone else to cheat, but can't see well enough to cover his own behind.) He began picking fights about nothing, everything. I didn't understand why he didn't just leave if he was so unhappy. He was like a trapped coyote, howling, trying to gnaw his own leg off.

Marc and I had identical flip phones. If ever they were both lying on the table, we'd have to open one up to see the wallpaper to know the difference. One morning, I was leaving for work and both phones were on the table. I went through the usual routine—only, when I opened his phone, *LOCKED* was displayed across the screen. I didn't even know the phones had a lock feature. That was suspicious but not grounds for disturbance. However, added to that was the fact that he started calling more to say he'd be late. "I'm going to get a drink with the fellas," or "I'm going to drop Trevor off," or "Joe-Joe needs a ride." Funny how in the past year nobody had ever needed a ride and suddenly ain't nobody got a car.

Common sense told me, as it did when I was with Darrell, that if you have to check up on him, you don't need him. I needed to see with my own eyes 'cause, unfortunately, intuition doesn't trump love.

I found myself trying to break the code on his phone while he was asleep. Which went to show how little I truly knew about him.

After two nights of trying unsuccessfully, it was time. I called Keisha, a friend from work. She's better than that little white lady on *Murder, She Wrote*. By noon of the next day, she not only had his cell phone bill but all the names and addresses of repetitious numbers. Although the bill showed that he'd been talking to someone late at night consistently over the past month, the one thing I'd learned was to pick my battles—or should I say my heart was in such denial, it demanded even more proof ... I needed something more concrete.

So I decided to surprise him at the club. When I arrived, the line was wrapped around the corner like they were giving away free cheese. I will say, knowing him did have its advantages. I walked to the front of the line, winked at the bouncer, and walked right in. As I walked through the glass doors, I could hear his voice titillating the microphone with my favorite song. I stood in the entrance way, captivated by the passion in his voice ... "And if I ever hurt you, you know I'll hurt myself as well..."

I tucked my clutch under my arm and sashayed toward the bar speaking and winking at people like I owned the joint. There was something about that song that always made me come alive inside. I grabbed a stool and watched the big screen over the bar as the camera man zoomed in on his fingers gently caressing the keys of the piano—"... said I love you, more than you'll ever know ... more than you'll ever know."

As they neared the end of the song, I went to the

ladies room to check my makeup. As you would imagine, it was crowded as well. Unfortunately, I didn't have the privilege of going to the head of the line, so I waited along with the other nine women. Once it was my turn, I touched up my makeup and ran my fingers through my loose curls. I headed out to the floor to look for him, but I didn't have to look far. There he was, boldly standing at the bar in an embrace with his hands resting on the lower part of her back, just above the curve of her behind. My heart stopped. As he leaned in to kiss her on the lips, my initial reaction was to go and snatch her bald. But, as I stood there listening to my heart break, I curtailed my anger. She wasn't committed to me … he was.

I didn't say a word. I walked past them with less confidence than I walked in with. Not that he noticed. I guess I just needed to see for myself.

The feeling of betrayal had become too familiar. I sat in the car for an hour, wanting to cry but unable to shed a tear. I was afraid I was becoming accustomed to being treated this way.

I finally went home and cleaned house. By the time he arrived, his things were in four lawn-size Hefty bags by the dumpster—but not before I poured bleach into each one.

When he got home about 4:00 a.m., I was still fully dressed, sitting on the couch. I wasn't up for some big fight. I'd been down that road before, and I just didn't have the energy for the ride. He came in, kissed me on the forehead, and instead of asking what I was still doing up, he said, "I'm going to take a shower, and I'm going to bed. I'm beat."

I could hear him in the bedroom, pulling out the dresser drawer. When he stuck his hand in and realized the drawer was empty, he flipped on the light and said, "WHAT DA …?"

From the couch, I said, "Oh, yeah, you don't live here anymore."

"Again, Laina? Again with this bull! You putting me out again! What did I do now?"

He kept asking the same question over and over. I was calm and nonchalant. He wanted me to jump up and down and show emotion, but it wasn't in me this time.

I guess I had prepared myself for that moment. He kept asking if I loved him. I think he figured if I knew about the chick, I would have said so. Figuring I must be mad about something else, he said, "Let's just talk, baby. You're overreacting."

Overreacting would have consisted of me shoving that cell phone so far …

Let's just say I wasn't overreacting.

Marcus had done so much dirt that he couldn't begin to guess what I found out, what had pushed me to that point. He chanted, "Whateva it is, we can fix it … I love you … Whateva it is, I'm sorry, baby … Just talk to me."

He almost looked scared, like a black man pulled over in a white neighborhood with an I Hate Rednecks T-shirt on. He was in an unfamiliar place, a place where his words meant nothing.

Finally, he said, "You know what! Forget it!"

He headed toward the door, almost running. As he reached for the knob, I yelled his name … exhaling after the last syllable in a sensual tone.

"Baby, wait …" I said.

He stood there with a smirk on his face as though he knew I wouldn't let him leave. Silence took over the room as I walked toward him, slow and seductive. Looking into his eyes, I took a deep breath and licked my top lip like I'd been practicing for that moment. Then I leaned in so close that I could feel his breath on my face and whispered, "Baby … where are my keys?"

He was stunned. Never taking his eyes off me, he reached into his jacket pocket, grabbing the Philadelphia Eagles key chain with the keys to the house, the Navigator, and the uncut key I had inscribed last Valentine's Day with "Laina's Heart." He threw it clear across the room and left.

A few days later, Marc called after he found out

I was at the club and tried to explain, but there was no excuse, no justification, nothing he could say that would make it okay for me.

So there I was yet again, driving down a familiar path. After all the pain I went through with Darrell, one would think I'd learned from my mistakes. I didn't.

There I was, hurting again from the pain I'd allowed some man to inflict. Everywhere I turned, there was his car, or so it seemed. It was as if they had just rolled out a new shipment of black, chromed-out Acura's. Every radio station I turned to was playing yet another sad love song. I put in my DMX CD. That's the kind of mood I was in. I was angry with everyone, including myself. I went through the regular routine, trying to cleanse my memory. Throwing out pictures, gifts, anything that reminded me of another failed relationship.

A couple days later, I received a call from Satchel's friend asking me to sing at the club. I declined. I didn't want any parts of it; singing wasn't my thing. I was only doing it to share a connection with Marcus.

***

I was so hurt and angry. I didn't take a break from the dating scene. I just jumped right back in, hoping to forget my woes. I tried to cover up my pain by replacing him, but when you love someone …

As I reflected, I questioned myself, *Why is this happening to me*? Every time I opened up to care about a man, it would be fine in the beginning. Then, all of a sudden, things would change.

I did what I had always done when I didn't know what to do: I prayed. I hadn't stepped foot inside a church in about two years … but now was as good a time as any. I confessed, I was afraid to be alone. Although I'm sure it had something to do with some deep-rooted abandonment issues from my childhood. Nevertheless, I was afraid. I was equally tired—tired of the insane relationships. I just wanted to be with someone who loved like I did.

I did my very best to stay away from Marcus and anyone who knew him. I loved him, but how much can you love someone that doesn't love you back? It just made it that much harder for me to pull it together. The harder I tried to forget him, the clearer the memories became.

Seven months later, Michael threw Tracey—his doctor girlfriend, as we referred to her—a surprise party at her parents' house. I went alone. Due to Rea and Mike's illicit relationship, she wasn't invited, and of course this wasn't Paige's thing. I sat by the bar downstairs, watching everyone mingling and dancing, waiting for the right time to sneak out when the DJ played

"Before I Let Go." When the party got kicked into high gear, I put my drink down and went to the dance floor. About an hour or so later, the DJ slowed it down with "Stairway to Heaven." As I walked off the dance floor, Marcus appeared.

"Dance with me," he said.

My first thought was, *Where you come from*?

Hesitantly, I agreed.

With his hand on the small of my back, he tried to make idle chitchat. "How you been?"

I thought to myself, *You'd know if* ... but, I didn't want to seem bitter. I just said, "Fine."

"I was hoping you'd be here."

I stopped two-stepping to the O'Jays long enough to look him in his eyes and ask, "Why?"

He saw the potential for a cussing-out, so he grabbed my hand and dragged me out by the pool. "Baby, sit down for a second."

I folded my arms, taking my sista-girl stance. "Naw, I'm good. Say what you have to say so I can get back to the party."

"Relax. I just want to talk to you."

"Marcus, there's nothing to talk about."

"Just let me finish. Baby, I never meant to hurt you."

Laughing sarcastically, I said, "That's because you never meant for me to find out?"

He sighed, confirming my comment.

"Fine, you wanna talk about it …" I said. "Why do you keep doing this? Why am I not enough for you?"

As he looked down, seemingly to gather his thoughts, I felt the anger build, and I wondered if I had ever been enough for anyone, including myself. I wanted him to say something, but he just stood there quietly. Frustrated, I walked away. As I got closer to the sliding glass doors, he began singing. I loved and hated that about him. When he couldn't articulate his feelings, he'd always depend on a song to say it for him.

"I'm nothing without you," he sang.

I stopped in my tracks.

"I know better now … And I've had a change of heart."

I still stood with my back turned to him.

"I'd rather have bad times with you than good times with someone else."

I walked away from his failed attempted at an apology. I went around the side of the house to my truck, with him trailing behind me, calling out my name.

When he caught up to me, he said, "Baby, I'm trying to apologize."

"No, Luther Vandross is apologizing …" Shaking my head, I said, "He's not the one who cheated on me—AGAIN!"

I opened the truck door as he said, "It's not you!" Looking down, he continued, "Sometimes it's the ones you love that you hurt the most." He lifted his head to make eye contact and said "I've never loved anyone besides you …"

"I never doubted that. You just don't respect me!"

He quickly responded, "Baby, I do. I …"

"I can't trust you. You humiliated me. It will never be the same again. Look, I accept your apology, but I'm done."

Reflecting, I admit we tried to change each other. He didn't want me to wear form-fitting clothes, and I didn't want him to sleep with other women. He wanted me to give him more space, and I wanted him to stop trying to give change to every woman that paid him a compliment.

Our relationship was infuriating, nothing but a constant tug of war. It was the epitome of trying to fit a square in a round hole.

Looking back, I can see how my insecurities caused me to smother him. I kept telling myself that I just wanted to be near him—to share in his life—but it was far deeper than that. Unknowingly, I tried to insert myself into his life at the club, the bar, and even rehearsals. My love expounded like he was the last man that would ever say "I love you."

***

I had insecurities about everything but one. The one thing I was confident about was my sexuality. I thought I had outgrown it, but I was still confusing sex with love. It took years for me to learn to separate the two.

I treated sex like an investment. Risking my savings with the hope of gain. I figured that if I could make him love the sex, I could get him to stick around long enough to notice the rest of me.

When Marcus made love to me, he'd hold me real tight and moan "I love you." Which geared us toward a more sexual relationship. I needed to hear him say "I love you," and the more I pleased him, the more he'd say it. So I pulled out all the stops trying to find new ways to arouse him—until we became addicted to one another.

After four months of begging, pleading, and chasing, I took him back … again.

This Is It

I remember that Marcus once told me, "Ain't no relationship perfect. You just find a person you can tolerate and work on it together."

I can't count how many times Marcus and I broke up before we finally got it right—or so it seemed. The things that had gone on for years became clear once he was diagnosed with bipolar disorder. One of the doctors said that sexual addiction could be a symptom of the erratic behavior. But once Marcus started taking the medication, he was different—calmer, sensible even.

I knew that this time was it, and from that point every time I went to the grocery store, I'd walk down the magazine aisle and glimpse over at the wedding magazines ... never picking them up, but just looking from the corner of my eye as to acknowledge their existence.

Several months into the newfound and medicated Marcus, we were better than ever. One night, Marcus invited the gang—my girlfriends and the fellas—to the club for The Blue Room's tenth anniversary party. I remember it like it was yesterday. The girls and I were tired and sore; we had been out all night just the night before to celebrate Reagan's twenty-eighth birthday. If I'd had it my way, I would have stayed home and slept, but Marcus made me feel guilty by saying, "You knew the anniversary party was tonight. No one told your hot tail to stay out all night."

So there I was, popping ibuprofen like Tic-Tacs. When the girls and I got together, we were like school girls. Laughing at the guys trying to be cool and the old hoochies wearing their daughter's clothes. The guys were no better, ogling and commenting on every piece of tail that came within eyesight.

The band was finishing its last set when Marcus took the mic and said, "I'd like to dedicate this new song to the woman in my life."

Everyone let out an "AWWWW" as I sat there with my face red. He was never big on public displays of affection with me, so the dedication caught me off guard. He began playing the piano, soft and slow, while staring at me. I thought at that moment that I couldn't love him any more than I did. As the song picked up pace, the saxophone came in, the guitar, and finally the drums. He stood up from the piano and slowly walked to the center of the stage and began singing.

"I've loved a woman a time or two but never knew love until I loved you..."

He always reminded me of Marvin Gaye when he swayed back and forth. By the end of the song, he was on the floor walking toward me. He grabbed my hand, pulled me up from my seat, and two-stepped through the last hook of the song. There was something in his eyes; he had never looked at me that way before that night. He kissed me on the cheek and walked back to the stage. As usual, the band received a standing ovation.

After the last set, we always met Marcus and the band in the VIP lounge. But that night, they wouldn't let us in until Marcus got there … not even me. Once "Mr. VIP" arrived, we walked in to see Chanté Moore sitting on a stool behind the mic, more beautiful in person than any magazine.

"Wow," I said. "She's performing in a VIP lounge. Has it gotten that bad?"

Marcus laughed. "No, baby, she's in town for a few days. I invited her to come and join us for a couple of drinks." He grabbed a drink and held it up. "A'ight,

I'd like to propose a toast."

Everyone grabbed a glass of pre-poured Moët. Marcus put his champagne down, which meant he had something to say. He's one of those people who talks with their hands.

"DeLaina," he said. "You've helped me to grow into a man, facing fears I didn't know I had."

Just then, I could see Melissa from the corner of my eye, jumping up and down. As I glimpsed around the room wondering what was going on, everyone had silly grins on their faces.

"We've had more ups and downs than the law allows," Marcus continued, "but we always end up back together. Baby, you're my soul mate."

Chanté begin singing: "At last, my love has come along ... my lonely days are over..."

Eddie poked Malcolm in the side and asked, "Is he really about to do what I think he's about to do?"

Malcolm nodded.

"Aw, naw, man, don't do it!" Eddie said.

Melissa smacked him in the back of the head. "Boy, don't make me ..."

As Chanté's voice faded, Marcus said, "I need you. You've seen me ... I'm nothing without you."

As I placed my palm on his cheek, his eyes watered.

"Baby," he said. "I want my daughter to have

your smile."

In spite of Reagan's obvious distaste for Marcus, even she became emotional. I could see her wiping her face from the corner of my eye.

Now sniffling, Marcus took a deep breath and said, "I want to tell our grandchildren about this day ..."

While Eddie paced the floor, shaking his head and mumbling, Marcus reached inside his jacket pocket and pulled out a marquise-cut diamond ring. He took my left hand and knelt down on one knee. My eyes began watering as he said the four words every woman's heart longs to hear: "Will you marry me?"

I could barley catch my breath; I couldn't say a word. All I could do was nod my head yes. As a single tear rolled down his face, he stood up and hugged me like a five-year-old who had been lost in the department store and just found his mommy.

Damon

I never saw Damon coming. Once he arrived, I wondered how I'd ever loved a man before him. He gave birth to a woman I never knew existed. He was everything I ever wanted, and things I never knew, I did. Somehow, the air was clearer, the stars were brighter, and I was happier than I had ever been in my life.

The morning I met Damon, I'd gotten into an argument with Marcus about his cell phone. It was sitting in the charger on his side of the bed. I was standing in front of the dresser, pulling my hair into a ponytail, when his cell phone rang. He ran down the hallway, darted past me, dove on the bed like Derek Jeter sliding into home, and slid clear across the satin sheets onto the floor, cursing. I wanted to laugh so bad, it was killing me.

Trying to hold it in; giggling between words, I said, "Baby … you … okay?"

"Yeah."

After all that, he didn't even answer the phone; he just picked it up and looked at it.

When I agreed to marry him, I told myself I was renewing my faith in him in spite of our past. I didn't want to live a life looking over my shoulder, so I promised myself I wouldn't assume anything. He would always be innocent until proven guilty.

The only thing about that … we can forgive, but we can't forget. And because there was so much I couldn't forget, it made that promise unrealistic.

As he got up from the floor with cell phone in hand, I asked, "Who was it, sweetie?"

He sucked his teeth and lashed out. "I don't have to tell you everything! What? I can't have a life outside of you?"

He could have easily said it was one of the guys from the band or someone wanting him to play a gig that he didn't want to play. Instead, he blew it out of proportion, which showed signs of guilt, which in turn Map-Quested directions to a place I didn't want to go. A place where there was no peace. A place where I questioned his every move, and checking his phone became a way of life.

In an effort to stay rational, I said, "You're right! You don't have to tell me everything ... but if I ask you, why wouldn't you tell me?"

He didn't respond.

"I just want to be happy." I pleaded with him, "How can I do that when I can't even trust you?"

"We can't be happy because you're too insecure!" Then, in a manipulative tone, he said, "And I'm telling you, no man wants to be with a woman like that."

It irritated me to no end how he always tried to manipulate me and make me feel bad for something he did. This was just one of the many signs of the old Marcus that left me angry and confused.

"You have a lot of nerve!" I said. "You cheated on your ex-girlfriend with me, then on me with her. You get caught at the club with some big-booty hoochie. But me? I'm just insecure. How did you fix your lips to say that?"

Yes ... I did have my own insecurities that I carried at times like a new Prada. The fears of the little girl that was abandoned by her mother twenty-some odd years ago still lived inside me, and sometimes she still heard the echoes of people telling her she wasn't pretty enough or good enough. Maybe it was my insecurities that made me hold on to a man that wasn't worth holding on to. I guess it made me feel like at least somebody wanted me—even if he ain't worth a … (well, you know).

I left, slamming the door behind me. So upset that I began to question the man I was marrying. At that moment, a divorce was clearer than the nuptials.

I had to do something to release my frustration, or I was going to do something irrational. I never go to the gym on the weekend. That's my "me" time, but it was now three weeks prior to the wedding, and I needed to lose seven more pounds to fit into my wedding dress without having the bridal party grease me down with Crisco.

I decided to try to catch the spin class that's usually full during the week. Upon entering the building, I swiped my card. *Beep*. I swiped it again. *Beep*. It wouldn't allow me to enter. I attempted to clean the black strip on the back of the card. As I rubbed it on my shorts, I noticed a line forming behind me. I swiped it again. *Beep*.

"Trouble?"

I looked up to respond when my eyes filled with arms the size of my thighs, attached to a smile that lit up the entire room. *And my favorite day at the gym is …*

He reached across the counter for my card, pushed the release button to open the gate, and said, "Come on through. Let's see what the problem is."

His smile was contagious. I could feel a draft on

my back teeth. I couldn't take my eyes off him. As he pulled up my account, I marveled at the definition of his olive-colored skin. I ran my eyes up and down and over every muscle. I had just made my way back up to his midsection when he said, "Your account is showing up as inactive."

"Why?"

"There appears to be an outstanding balance."

Marcus and I opened a joint account at the bank, and I'd obviously neglected to give the gym the new checking account number to debit each month. So I ran to the car, got my checkbook, and reinstated my account.

I smiled. "Thank you."

He flirted. "It was my pleasure."

I smiled and walked away like Loretta Devine in *Waiting to Exhale*. Conscious of every step, I thought to myself, *I hope he's not watching me walk away.* I refused to turn around for confirmation. Trying to shake off my impure thoughts, I continued upstairs to class. Picked out a bike and laid my towel over the seat. I was a little early, so I walked over by the mirror to stretch. I couldn't stop thinking about his smile. Facing the mirror, I spread my legs apart, bent over, and grabbed my left ankle with both hands. As I rotated to the right, I felt someone watching me. With both hands wrapped around my right ankle, I looked in the mirror. There he was. Standing in the corner watching me. Realizing that all the blessings my mother bestowed upon me were in the air, I popped up and spoke to his reflection. "Are you following me?"

In a flirtatious tone, he said, "Maybe!"

"It's because I'm black, right?"

He laughed as his reflection moved closer until he was standing directly behind me. I could feel the heat from his body. He looked over my left shoulder and spoke directly to my reflection. "I wanted to introduce myself."

Although the class began to fill, it felt as though we were all alone. We stood there, staring, as our souls recognized one another and embraced. I found myself memorizing the brownest part in his eyes, the perfect ridge of his nose, his jawline, and the shape of his lips. I watched his mouth open and his lips move as he said, "My name's Damon."

Without hesitation, I replied, "I'm DeLaina."

He smiled. "Yeah, I know. Nice to meet you." He looked around, leaned down, and whispered, "I better go. I heard the instructor is a real piece of work. Meet me for a cup of coffee after class?"

Sweat began forming in places I won't mention. I held up the back of my left hand and stuttered like an idiot, "I'm … um … Ring! Um, I'm engaged."

He smiled seductively. "I know. But you just

met the best man."

I was drawn to him like I was to those six-hundred-dollar Prada sling-backs. But, as with them, I knew I couldn't justify taking him home. I looked down and said, "No, thank you."

"I respect that," he said, then walked over to the bike in the front of the room, reached back, pushed play on the stereo, and yelled, "Let's get warmed up!" I had no idea he was the weekend instructor. Even with twenty-five people in the class, he watched and pushed me the entire time as if it was a personal session. "Come on, come on. You can do it. Come on. Three more … two more. That's it."

I tried not to blush.

I knew better than to have an emotional exchange three weeks before my wedding, but there was something about him that spoke clearly: "You need to know me."

After class, I avoided eye contact, grabbed my water bottle, and raced to the door. I got in the truck and backed out of the parking space. I looked up, simultaneously shifting into gear, and there he was—standing with his arms folded.

I put the window down. "Why you standing there looking like a black Superman?"

He laughed. "*Vine a salvarte.*"

I was taken aback by what I assumed was

Spanish. I'd noticed the beautiful shade of his skin tone, but didn't think he was Latin. "Excuse me?" I said. Smiling, he said, "I came to save you."

"What makes you think I need to be saved?"

He just smiled.

I asked, "Where are you from?"

"Chicago."

"No! Where's your family from?"

With a sly grin, he pulled his keys out of his pocket and began backing away from my truck. "I'll tell you over a cup of coffee."

Without any confirmation from me, he got in his car and pulled out. The ring on my left hand should have been reason enough for me not to follow him, but somehow it wasn't.

As I stood beside him looking up at the Starbucks menu, he said, "I'm Dominican."

We sat at a little table by the window, finishing each other's sentences, laughing, and talking for hours about everything from politics to childhood scares—from roller coasters to emotional scars.

"So, Ms. DeLaina, what's your *su razon de ser*?"

"My what?"

"Your *raison d'être* … your reason for being?"

"WOW! That's a big question. No one's ever asked me that before. I'll have to give that some thought."

"You should."

"Do you know yours?"

"Yes. I'll tell you mine when you tell me yours."

"So, do you take all the women in your class out for coffee?"

"No, you're the first."

"Whateva!"

"Serious business! I dated a trainer at another location, but never a member."

"Really? Then why me? I mean, I'm engaged, this has no potential."

"You're here," he mumbled.

"What?"

He spoke louder. "I said the sky is clear."

Laughing, I said, "That's not what you said."

"Look, I'm not trying to steal you away." He laughed. "There's just something about a woman that doesn't pay her bills that just turns me on."

Laughing, I said, "I do pay my bills."

His zeal for life and openness made me question my relationship with Marcus. I honestly believed that Marcus loved me more than he'd loved anyone else, but somehow that didn't make our relationship transcend.

Damon told me about his ex, who sounded a lot like Marcus in that she demanded a lot of the relationship but gave very little.

"We communicated well when she had a problem," he said. "But when I needed her support, I was on my own. I had to realize you need more than love to make a relationship work."

Although common sense, it made a light bulb go off. He was sincere. I could tell by the tone of his voice that he was disappointed that the relationship didn't work. I told him a little about Marcus. Like, we'd been together for four, almost five years, and we'd had more ups and downs than a roller coaster. That sometimes the way he communicated—or didn't—scared me. I told him that we broke up and when we got back together six months ago … he promised he had changed, but I was starting to see a little bit of the guy I'd broken up with every day.

Without bashing Marcus, Damon said, "Maybe you could get him to talk to the pastor that's marrying you. Or go to like a pre-marriage counseling or something."

I sat there talking to a man that for all intent and purpose was a complete stranger, but I felt as though I already knew him. There was something about him that made me smile uncontrollably. I clung to his lips, holding on to his every word. I didn't want the conversation to end. I was starting to feel bad. Through everything that had transpired between Marcus and me, I had never cheated, never opened myself up to an emotional entanglement. The guilt was on me like dollar-store perfume. I had gone to the gym to let off some steam, and now found myself having a conversation with a man that wanted to know what made me bite my lip when I smiled. I kept thinking, *How could this be happening now? Of all times, why now*?

I dug around in my purse with one hand, feeling for my cell phone to check the time … only to find that five hours had passed and I had eight missed calls from Marcus. As Damon went on about how he wanted kids someday, I interrupted. "I'm sorry. I have to go."

He walked me to my truck, handed me a business card, and said, "I wish you didn't have to leave. Why don't you stop by the gym around one tomorrow and I'll take you to lunch?"

"We'll see."

He confidently winked and said, "See ya tomorrow."

Confused

Marc had been hanging around the house a lot since things had been slow for the band. Battling his own demons had caused him to start questioning my every move.

I called Rea.

"Hello?" she said.

"Hey, it's me. Did Marc call you looking for me?"

In a curious tone, she said, "Naw, why?"

"Okay, the CliffsNotes version … I met someone. We drank coffee and talked for hours. The ringer was still off from the gym, and Marcus has been blowing up my phone."

"Oh no! Forget the CliffsNotes. I want the textbook version. You gonna get you a lil' bit before you say 'I do'? You deserve it. Shoooot!"

Nervous, I said, "Rea, FOCUS! I don't have time for this. I'm almost home. We have to get our stories straight. You know how he is. He'll try to poke holes in everything I say. Please just do this. I'll tell you everything later."

She sucked her teeth. "Fine."

"A'ight, Rea, we went to the gym—"

"Then we went to dinner. End of story. Kiss my—"

"Reagan! I still have on my workout clothes and I stink. He knows I wouldn't have gone to dinner like this. We'll stick to the basics. We worked out … went to check on the bridesmaids' dresses, then went for coffee. We both had the caramel macchiato … okay?"

"Yeah, yeah, dresses and caramel, but if you ask me … you should get you some."

"Reagan, I'm marrying this man."

In an irritated tone, she said, "Um-hum, yeah, nigga, yeah. We worked out … went to check on the bridesmaids' dresses then went for coffee. We had caramel macchiato's."

"Good! Okay, I need to clear my mind. I'll call you later."

I went over the story in my mind repeatedly so that it would translate like second nature.

His car was out front when I pulled up. I put

my game face on and walked into the house with cell phone in hand. He stopped me in the hallway.

"Where you been? I been calling you all day."

I rolled my eyes and walked around him.

"Where were you?"

Without thinking, I said, "I asked you a question this morning too. I didn't get an answer."

"Oh, you need to grow up and stop acting like a spoiled brat." He grabbed my arm as I walked down the hallway. "Where were you?"

I snatched my arm away and went into sista-girl mode. "Are you serious? We're getting married in less than three weeks … there's a grocery list of crap to do … and I'm in the gym twice a day so I can fit into this dress. Not to mention trying to find you a wedding gift. What did you do all day besides blow up my phone?"

I pushed past him into the bathroom and locked the door. I sat on the side of the tub, surprised that I opened my mouth and those words flew out. He stood outside the door, knocking. "Let me in."

Yelling from the other side of the door, I said, "I've never given you any reason to think I wasn't on the up and up, yet you constantly interrogate me. How is it that you screw up but you don't trust me?"

The tension made the night long. I slept in the guest room. The next morning, I got up with Damon on my mind. Thinking about the question he'd asked:

what was my purpose?

I showered, pinned up my hair, lined my eyes, and glossed my lips. Marcus laid in the bed with a firm grip on the remote, occasionally glimpsing up at me as he watched highlights on ESPN. Suddenly, I noticed him focused on me. He asked, "Where you going … to the gym?"

I didn't answer.

He sat up in the bed. "You showered and put on makeup to go to the gym?"

"Must you get up starting? It's Sunday! Dang, I can't put on a lil' makeup today?"

He got up. "Yeah, it's fine baby." He put on some shorts and a T-shirt, and left the house mumbling, "I ain't stupid."

I mumbled back, "I beg to differ."

I walked out to the truck to find Marcus in the front seat. "What are you doing?" I asked.

In a condescending tone, he replied, "I'm going to work out with my baby. Is that okay with you?"

It's true what they say … game recognizes game. "Okay," I said.

I saw his tactic and played along with him. I grabbed my cell and called Reagan.

"Hey, girl, I'm on my way."

"On your way where?" she asked.

Hoping she'd catch on quickly, I said, "No, we

said we'd meet at the gym at eleven."

She sucked her teeth and said, "Is dat fool wit you?"

I laughed. "Yeah, I forgot to grab a bottle of water from the house. Can you grab me one too? Oh, Marcus, do you want a bottle of water?"

He sat with his back against the passenger door, glaring at me and trying to figure me out. "No, I don't want no freakin' water."

"Okay, Rea," I said. "I'll see you in about twenty minutes—"

"Do you need me to come for real?" she asked.

"Yeah."

In an irritated tone, she said, "FINE! But you betta be coming to the gym by my house."

That worked out perfectly since Damon worked at the gym near my house.

"Yeah, maybe we can go get some food afterwards," I said.

She sucked her teeth. "Whateva!"

As I closed my flip phone and placed it in the console, Marcus said, "I know your lil' behind is up to something; I can feel it."

Without thinking, I reversed the situation. "What's going on with you? Are you having cold feet?"

He didn't respond.

Rea and I pulled up at the same time. She hopped out of her Accord coupe and handed me the bottle of water.

"S'up, Rea?" Marcus said.

She kept walking.

I nudged her.

"Yeah, nigga, whateva!" she said.

Her distaste for him was probably my fault. I always told her when things were bad. Never when things were good.

Rea and I found two stationary bikes side by side while Marcus hovered around the free weights. I explained to Rea that I was supposed to have lunch with Damon. I'd gotten so excited about seeing him that I let down my guard, and Marcus became suspicious.

After about an hour at the gym, Marc took my truck and I hung out with Rea. From the moment that he pulled out, I was on the phone with Damon. "I didn't stand you up," I said before explaining what happened.

"Um … you must have been looking some kinda' fine for him to hijack your truck," he said.

I didn't respond.

He said, "Listen, I wanna see you, but I don't want you catching flack at home because of me."

"Yeah, I know, but I haven't done anything."

"Come on, Laina. Then why do you feel so guilty?"

I did feel guilty. I guess it was because, for the past four years, I had only wanted one man. There was something about Damon, though—with him, I felt different ...

I had to see him, so I asked, "Do you know where the aviation observation is?"

"On Mills Road?"

"Yeah. Meet me there in forty-five minutes."

When we got to Rea's house, I took a quick shower, and grabbed some shorts and a T-shirt from Rea's drawer. As I was getting dressed, I noticed her sitting on the side of the bed, looking down in the face. She finally said, "Kevin and I broke up."

"I didn't know y'all were going together."

She chuckled. "Why does everyone keep saying that?" Tears ran down her face as she asked, "Why does this keep happening to me? You got two men and I can't even keep one."

"I don't have two men. I have Marcus, who is trifling, and I question every day if I really want to marry him."

"Do you know how many women would switch places with you in a heartbeat?"

That statement was ironic considering that, some days, I didn't even want to be me.

I wanted to tell her that she kept attracting the same type of men because of the bait she'd been using. I wanted to tell her that sleeping with a man on the first night didn't show good judgment, and men would question it in their minds—*If she did it with me …*

I wanted to tell her that it was that same erratic, irresponsible thinking that had her credit jacked up—living in the now and not thinking about tomorrow. Considering we were peas of the same pod, I knew she'd be less than receptive hearing it from me. But as her friend, I felt it my duty to at the very least remind her of the obvious … "Having sex with a person doesn't make him your man."

On my way out the door, I grabbed her Celtics cap and car keys. "I'll be back in about an hour," I said. "If Marc calls, tell him I went to the store."

My stomach tightened as I neared the rendezvous point. I thought to myself repeatedly, What are you doing? *How can you seriously entertain these unrealistic feelings for someone you met twenty-four hours ago*? As I backed into a parking space, Damon came over and opened my door.

He took my hand, helped me out of the car, and said, "Is this what you were wearing when ole boy hijacked you?"

"No!" I said, laughing.

He wrapped his arms around me. "I missed you."

I wanted to believe him, but aside from the fact that I was getting married in a few weeks, I had enough failed relationships to know that things take time. So I tried to maintain rationale.

I said, "You don't know me to miss me."

He smiled. "You don't have to play hard with me."

We walked along the trail, talking. When he asked if I had siblings, I told him about Mike and Rea.

"There were five of us," he said. "I had an older sister but she died when I was six, and my baby brother passed a few years back."

"Oh, wow, I'm sorry."

"Oh, naw, it's cool."

In an effort to change the mood, he snatched the cap off my head and took off running down the hill toward the lake. I took chase behind him and jumped on his back, causing him to fall. He rolled over, straddled me, pinned my wrists down, and said, "Now what?"

The next three weeks were nothing short of amazing. We stole moments whenever we could. It started with five minutes here, ten minutes there—but that wasn't enough. Before I knew it, I was neglecting work, emailing him all day, taking long lunches, leaving work early, and lying to Marcus about my whereabouts. Although Damon and I weren't having sex, we were intimate. Being with him was as intoxicating as a fifth of vodka.

Friday night, Marcus always played "poker" with the boys, which meant they'd be at the strip club at least till two. Damon wanted to get a bite to eat and maybe go dancing. I agreed to meet him at Marco Polo's, a bar on the other side of town—the kind of place you take a date you don't want anyone to see you with. I kept trying to convince myself that, since I wasn't sleeping with him, I wasn't really cheating. I guess that's why I chose a spot across town where I was sure not to run into anyone Marcus or I knew. I was excited to be able to spend more than a few minutes with Damon.

I got home from work early enough to spend some time with Marcus, stroke his ego a bit, and let him beat me at NBA Live. He asked me where I was going as I threw on my raggedy sweats. "Over to Patricia's, then probably to Rea's."

"Who is Patricia?"

I used the fact that his memory was bad to my advantage. "You never listen to me. She's the woman doing the makeup for all the bridesmaids."

I had already snuck clothes out earlier in the week and dropped them off at Rea's.

I was running a few minutes behind schedule. When I arrived at the bar, there he was, engaged in conversation with a beautiful woman who had her hands all over him. I stood at the other end of the bar for a few minutes, watching to see how far he'd let it go. She pulled him closer to her. She leaned over, ran her fingers through his hair, and whispered something in his ear. He looked up and caught me staring with little excitement on my face. Irritated, I headed for the door. As I got outside, he ran out behind me, asking, "Where you going?"

"I'm just going to go back home. I'm tired."

"Why? You came clear across town to turn around and go right back?"

I stood there not saying a word, fumbling through my purse for my keys. He stepped in closer, lifted my chin with his index finger, leaned down, and kissed me passionately. At the end of the kiss, he said, "I didn't know that girl. She just came and sat beside me."

"You were letting her do a lot of touching for someone that doesn't know you. You know … what … whateva."

He laughed. "You're jealous"

"Why would I be jealous?"

"You're cute when you're jealous."

"I'm not … jealous!"

***

When I looked up, the weeks had flown by. It was already Thursday … two days before my wedding. I had plans to meet Damon for lunch as I had every day for the past three weeks. I dreaded this day, as this would be our last lunch, since I had appointments all day on Friday.

The guilt made me promise I wouldn't carry Damon into my marriage, but I honestly wasn't ready to lose him. He had somehow become the best part of my every day. Although I realized I was being selfish, I still wasn't prepared to wake up the next day knowing I couldn't see or talk to him again. Wondering why I couldn't have met Damon seven months ago, I found myself wishing Marcus made me feel the way Damon did.

When I arrived for my dreaded lunch date, he was already there. I sat across from him, silenced by fear. Afraid I was making a mistake.

"You haven't said more than three words. What's wrong?" he asked.

"Nothing."

"Yes, it is. Tell me what's wrong, baby."

I lifted my head from my plate. "I can't see you anymore."

"What are you talking about?"

"I'm getting married Saturday."

In a surprised tone, he said, "You're still marrying him? You don't even like dat dude!"

I nodded my head yes.

He adjusted his fitted baseball cap. "I really didn't think you'd go through with it." He stood up hastily, reached for his wallet, threw two twenties on the table, and said, "My bad, I thought you wanted to be happy. Good luck with that."

Confused by my emotions, I watched him walk away. I didn't want him to leave. I wanted to grab Damon's arm, explain that he and I barely knew each other. All relationships are grand in the beginning. I wanted to explain that Marcus and I had a past, that at least I knew what to expect with him—but I couldn't move.

Wedding Day

After the girls got dressed and my makeup and hair was done, I asked everyone to leave the room. I needed time alone with my thoughts.

On my wedding day, I sat on the edge of the chair in my robe, staring at my wedding gown and wondering if I was about to make the biggest mistake of my life when Rea came back to check on me.

"Girl, why you not dressed?" she asked.

"Rea, what if he's not the one I'm supposed to be with?"

"Oh my goodness! Are you serious? Laina, you're just nervous."

The door opened. "It's me," Melissa announced herself as she entered. "Look, I know it's your day and all, but don't you think you should be getting dressed?"

I walked toward the window, rubbing my hands as if I were lotioning them, and said, "I don't know about this …"

Pointing at me, Rea said, "I told her it was just nerves!"

Grabbing a tissue from the box, I begin twirling it around both index fingers as I paced the floor trying to explain. "No! I don't think I can do this!"

Melissa took a step back. "What's going on, Laina?"

"I don't think I'm as happy as I could be."

"What?" Melissa asked. "Did you and Marcus get into a fight?"

My voice began cracking. "No! I … I just don't think that loving someone is a good enough reason to marry them."

Melissa went off. "Are you freakin' kidding me with this? My cousin is waiting for you at the altar and you decide to develop common sense today?"

Rea mumbled, "Oh snap!"

"All my family is here!" Melissa said in an irritated tone. "Laina, dat boy loves you, and right now I can't understand why!"

Rea stepped in. "A'ight, that's a-nuff! She feels bad as it is. Besides, it ain't like he ain't done enough for her to have second thoughts. Shoot, you know I can't stand dat nigga no how! If she don't wanna marry him, she don't have to."

Melissa rolled her eyes at Reagan, then turned and scolded me. "So all of a sudden you don't love him?"

I tried to explain. "No, of course I love him, but loving someone doesn't mean that you're supposed to spend the rest of your life together."

Melissa walked over to me, pressed her left shoulder against mine, leaned in, and whispered, "And you just figured this out today?"

Rea moved and stood between us. She looked at Melissa. "You need to calm your lil' behind down." Rea took my hand and said, "Laina, you need to tell her!"

Melissa rolled her neck. "Tell me what?"

With a deep breath, I said, "I met someone."

"What do you mean you met someone? You're engaged!" Melissa's eyes grew wide. "Wait! You cheated on Marcus?" Pointing at Rea, she asked, "You knew about this?"

I grabbed Melissa's hand. "Can you stop being a cousin for five minutes and be my friend?"

She snatched her hand away and folded her arms.

"Look," I said, "You have every right to be upset,

but just listen to me for a minute. He's … he's not just anyone, Melissa. I can't really explain it … WE FIT! I've never felt so complete in my LIFE." Smiling from ear to ear, I said, "Girl, he makes me happy. I've never heard my name sound more beautiful than it does when it rolls off his tongue. He—"

She cut me off. "How long Laina?"

I turned and walked toward the window. "Three weeks."

She threw her hands in the air, pacing the floor. "So you're willing to break my cousin's heart for a crush? Three weeks! Are you kidding? Oh, I get it … he put it on you!"

Defending the situation, I argued, "Melissa, I haven't slept with him. It's deeper than that."

"Whateva, Laina! Marcus has been there for you for what … the past three or four years, dealing with the baggage you brought from previous relationships." She held out her hand and began counting off. "Darrell, Tyrone, Jeff … and he neva judged you, Laina."

Her lack of understanding was ticking me off. "Okay, first, it's been four and a half years that we've known each other, but if you take into account how many times we broke up, we've been together about two years. Second, let's be real, Melissa; you were there. He never even noticed the baggage! He was too busy sleeping with Tonya, Kee-Kee, Monique, and who-eva else, trying to be a playboy."

"Girl, he's a man. That's what they do!"

Quickly checking Melissa, Reagan raised her hand like a fifth-grader sitting on the front row waiting to be called on. "Excuse me, Ms. 'That's what they do.' Is that what you was sayin' when you was bashing out Mario's windows or when you switched cars with me so you could follow Isaac when you thought he was hitti'n off da receptionist? By the way, we need to talk about that bail money."

"Whateva, Reagan!" Melissa sucked her teeth; she was visibly frustrated. Her voice got louder as she said, "You know how hard it is to get a man to claim you in public, much less commit to you in front of God."

The door swung open—it was Auntie Mona. Mona's my great aunt on my mother's side. Even though she moved to the city with her son and his wife about a year ago, I didn't see her much, but she made sure she called me every Sunday to see how I was doing.

Melissa took a deep breath and walked toward the door. Mona put her right hand on her hip and started cursing. "What's going on?"

No one made a sound. Mona was one of those irrational relatives you had to be careful what you said around. Almost seventy years old and always ready to fight.

"Y'all was loud a minute ago," Mona said. "Somebody betta get-ta speakin'."

As Melissa walked out the door, in a calm voice, she said, "Ask Laina."

Mona closed the door behind Melissa and said, "Lookin' like a Doberman! I ain't neva liked dat sassy, fass-tail gal."

Laughing, Reagan shook her head. "Dat's Laina's girl!"

Rea hugged me the way that only she could. She wrapped her arms around me tight as if she were trying to absorb my pain and said, "Sweetie, look, it's gonna be okay. You're da only one that's gotta live with your decision. Don't worry about what anybody else thinks or says."

As Reagan left the room, Auntie said, "So you havin' second thoughts 'bout marrying diss boy?"

I nodded.

She stood there for a moment, staring at me, before she said, "Lainee, let me tell ya something ..." Only my family calls me Lainee. "Da man dat he is today is da man dat he will always be. 'I do' ain't gonna change him ... ya hear?"

"Yes, ma'am."

"One more thang: if you marry him ... get ya-self

a good insurance policy cuz if he eva … EVA puts his hands on you again …"

I don't know how she knew. I hadn't told anyone, not even Rea. My bruises were between me and my makeup kit.

Mona hugged me, kissed me on the cheek, and walked toward the door. "I'm-a pray the Lord work diss here thang out in ya favor. Whateva ya decide, Auntie's behind ya … wit a sawed-off and a shovel." Walking out the door, she mumbled, "Cuz if he eva … EVA!"

I wasn't afraid of Marcus. Yeah, he pushed me around a little, but I pushed back.

I needed to talk to him but my phone was nowhere to be found. I dug around in Reagan's bag, feeling for her cell phone. I paced the floor as I dialed his number.

He answered, "Hey, sexy."

"How did you know it was me?"

"Of course it's you. Is everything okay? Did you forget something?"

"Marcus, why me? All the women you've dated … Why me, why now …"

In a concerned tone, he asked, "What's going on, DeLaina?"

I begged, "Please, just answer me."

"I mean, dang, we been together off and on for

years. It just makes sense, you know. I mean, everybody has crap with them. You just find someone whose crap is tolerable and try to make it work. You having second thoughts?"

"I'm scared."

"Me, too. But I do know that I love you."

"I love you too."

"A'ight, see you at the altar."

I'm not sure what I was expecting or what I wanted him to say, but I'm sure he didn't say it.

I was still a bit confused. I stood there alone, playing with the lace on the most beautiful gown I'd ever seen. It was an A-line cut, strapless, one piece with beads outlining the embroidered roses. As I ran my hand along the train, I wished Mommy were there to tell me how to fix this mess … to put my mind at ease. Pacing the floor with tears in my eyes, I did the only thing I could do.

"Okay, God, I know you haven't heard from me in a while, but you know my heart. Damon makes me feel something I've never felt before; I feel like I can do anything. Please, give my heart clarity. God, I just want to be happy …"

I wiped away my tears, walked over to my wedding gown, grabbed it, and held it against my chest just as I heard, *What are you waiting for?* I slipped into the dress, twisted my arms behind my back, and wiggled to maneuver the zipper up. I swirled around to the mirror. Suddenly, a calm came over me. It was a perfect fit; I'd never felt more beautiful. I felt the way every woman wants to feel on her wedding day: I felt like a princess. I stood there staring at the reflection. I couldn't believe it was me.

Denise, the wedding planner, poked her head in. "Five minutes till—WOW! You look beautiful! Five minutes until you become Mrs. Marcus Day. Just come out to the foyer when you're ready."

I attached the crown to the bun in my hair and slipped my feet into my shoes; I was ready. I took one last look in the mirror and walked out to the foyer of the church where my cousin, Michael, was waiting. He'd always been very protective of me, the way a father would protect his daughter, so it only made sense for him to give me away. "WOW! Lainee, you look beautiful." As he stared, he asked, "Are you okay? You been crying?"

"I'm fine, Mike. Just a lil' nervous."

"Are you sure?"

"Yes."

"Look, I wasn't going to say anything, Lainee, but I saw you last week at Marco Polo's with some guy. I don't care that you were with another guy. My concern is that you looked happy! I haven't seen you smile like that with Marcus since you've been back together."

I primped and adjusted my dress as if there was no validity in what he was saying.

He continued, "Is there anything you wanna tell me, 'cause it's not too late to shut this thing down." He took a step toward me as his voice got louder. "I'm serious! Regardless of the situation, you know I got you."

I looked him in his eyes and smiled. "It's my wedding day!"

He ran the back of his left hand down my right cheek. In a calm tone, he said, "You look beautiful. I wish Mommy and Daddy were here to see you."

I hugged him, kissed him on the cheek, and whispered, "They are!"

His joy lightened. "I wish all the family could be here today." Looking down, he went on, "I got a letter from Calvin. I still can't believe he's in jail for raping that lil' girl."

In a firm tone, I said, "I can."

Mike looked surprised at my certainty but he left it alone. He had no idea about the things Calvin had done to me when no one was looking, and it wasn't something I was willing to discuss, especially on my wedding day.

As Mike adjusted the crown on my head, I heard what sound like a harp.

"I thought you were walking down the aisle to the wedding march?" Mike asked.

"So did I."

Then I heard the most angelic voice …

"I believe in you and me …"

The church doors opened, everyone rose to their feet.

Mike smiled and gestured for me to take his arm.

"I believe that love will never end …"

I took a deep breath. As we took our first step down the aisle, returning smiles to people I didn't know and listening to comments—"What a beautiful dress!" … "She makes such a beautiful bride." … "Girl, you know she shouldn't be wearing white."—all I could think was, *You can do this. It's just nerves. I can be happy with Marcus.*

"Just to be right where you are, my love."

Maybe he really has changed. Maybe all a good relationship needs IS love. I do love him. I love him … I love him.

Marcus looked so handsome standing there waiting to make the leap of a lifetime. As I neared the altar, I noticed that the strapless dresses fit the girls perfectly; Melissa winked and nodded like the godfather giving his approval.

Mike handed me off, and kissed me on the cheek. I handed Reagan my bouquet and took Marcus's hand.

"I believe in yoooou and meeee ... ooooooo."

The pastor cleared his throat and began. "Dearly beloved, we're gathered here today to join Marcus Elliott Day and DeLaina Yasmen Richards in holy matrimony. If there's anyone who feels that these two should not be joined, let them speak now or forever hold their peace."

Silence.

"AMEN! Marriage is not to be entered into lightly. The Bible says when a man finds a wife ... he finds a good thing, and we're here today to celebrate the finding and witness the joining of two hearts. I believe DeLaina and Marcus have written their own vows."

The church doors flew open,

"Lainee, WAIT!"

Mona looked to the ceiling and said, "Lord, that was quick."

I didn't have to turn around ... I knew the voice. It was my smile ... Damon.

Melissa began cursing. "OH NO!"

You could hear the shuffling as everyone turned around in the pews. Nothing but mumblings as he walked toward the altar.

Looking at Marcus, he said, "Look, dude, I apologize! I don't know you, but I have to talk to her!" Marcus looked perplexed.

Melissa threw down her bouquet and started

toward Damon, yelling, "Get out of here! You were not invited!"

I couldn't breathe. Reagan grabbed Melissa; Marcus's brothers grabbed Damon.

Struggling to get away, Damon yelled, "I love you!"

Mona said, "Rut-ro!"

Mike stood up.

Rea mumbled, "Oh snnnap!"

I took one step toward Damon. "You do?"

He said, "I feel like I can fly when I'm with you … and now… I can't imagine just walking for the rest of my life."

Ooh's and aah's came from the pews.

Mike yelled at Marcus's brothers, "Hey, Ren and Stimpy! Let him go!"

They backed away. I just stood there, staring at Damon, trying to catch my breath.

Melissa snatched her arm away from Reagan. "Gimme a break! Marcus, say something!"

Marcus looked at me, searching for the words to undo what he knew was being done. I had to make peace with my heart.

Searching for the words myself, I said, "Marcus, I'm sorry! Something has been missing from us, and I finally figured out what it is."

Pointing at Damon, he asked, "What, this dude?"

"No. Marcus, we're not happy. We're just used to being together." Looking at Damon, I said, "This feels right!"

I grabbed my gown from the bottom to walk away when Marcus grabbed my arm. "Wait. How do you know it's right … I mean, really, how do you know it's right when all you've ever been is wrong? DeLaina, don't do this. We can fix it! What happened to me and you against the world?" He grabbed my right hand, kissed my palm, and placed it over his heart. "Do you feel that? Baby, that's love."

I saw the pain build in his eyes and run down his face. With his voice cracking, he sang in a whisper, "I'd rather have hard times with you …"

"Marcus, I didn't plan this!" Fighting back the tears, I said, "Please don't ever think for one second that I didn't love you, because I did … I do, even now. But love isn't enough to make a relationship work. I should have told you that I had doubts, but I tried to pretend they weren't there."

I took off the engagement ring, handed it to him, and kissed him on the cheek. "Forgive me." I turned and ran toward Damon.

Melissa called out, "Laina! You didn't answer him. How do you know it's right when all you've ever been is wrong?"

I took Damon's hand. "I've been wrong enough

to know what that feels like, and this feels like … answered prayers."

New Life

We finished off two bottles of Pinot Grigio. I celebrated being a free woman a little too much. The next morning, I awakened to my head pounding. Not able to clearly remember the night before, I looked down to see that I still had on the sweats I changed into after the wedding. As I squirmed and tried to hide from the sunlight, Damon kissed me and whispered, "I love you." As my mind and my heart received it, I began crying. I flashed back to every failed relationship. It seemed every man had loved me until they realized how much of me there was to really love. I pushed him away from me. I thought to myself that I'd rather have him as just my friend for the rest of my life than to chance him falling in and out of love and not having him at all.

Surprised by my tears, he asked, "What's wrong baby?"

"I'm scared."

"Of what?"

"I'm no good in relationships. I don't know how to make them work."

"I don't either, but we can figure it out together. Baby, I think you're carrying stuff from past relationships. I don't know all the situations, but I'm sure you weren't the cause of them all ending. It wasn't all you." He held my hand. "I don't have all the answers, but I think we can do this."

I was scared to cross the line into the next level of intimacy. But I was also happier than I ever thought possible. Everything was so perfect that it scared me. I got to wake up and just be me. Not the person he wanted me to be. Just be me.

A couple weeks later, I was READY, but Damon suggested we hold off on being intimate, citing that he didn't want me to be confused by sex. He wanted to make sure that I wasn't still attached in any way to Marcus. I agreed.

A month or so later, one evening after work, I stopped at Blockbuster and then headed to Damon's. I had it all planned in my mind that we'd have a quiet evening at his house. He had other plans. Plans that included him hanging out with several of the guys from the gym … plans that didn't include me. I flashed back to every failed relationship and took him going out personally. The proverbial suitcase (baggage) flew open. I thought it meant he was tired of me, that he was ready to meet someone else, that he wasn't getting his needs met, or even that he was going to leave me. I freaked out, and before I knew it, I had become that five-year-old that used to follow her mother from room to room as she got dressed on Saturday nights. I tried to think of reasons for him to stay home, but I couldn't come up with anything I thought would keep him.

I followed him into the walk-in closet, watching him pick out clothes for the evening. I was so close that he stepped on my toes, twice. When he went into the bathroom, I was right behind him. I quietly sat on the sink like a little girl watching her daddy shave for the first time. Up the hallway to the kitchen for a drink, then back to the room.

He stopped. "Okay, baby, what's wrong?"

I looked away. "Nothing." I was embarrassed by my actions, but I couldn't make myself stop.

"What is it?"

He looked at me in a concerned way that I'd never seen him display before. I feared he thought I was crazy, but I couldn't undo the way I had acted or how I felt. Wrapped in an amazing amount of fear, I said, "I don't want you to go."

"Why, baby?"

"I don't know … I …"

He knew quite a bit about my past, but not everything. Of course he knew I came with some baggage, considering how we got together. But he hadn't seen this side of me. My emotional baggage had unknowingly erupted. I knew what I was feeling, but I didn't know how to articulate it without sounding like I needed one of those little white jackets that make you hug yourself.

"Come here." Hugging me, he said, "It's okay." He stared at me like he was trying to read my thoughts, and I guessed that he did—even the unconscious ones. "Do you believe this is real?" he asked.

I nodded my head yes.

He asked, "Do you believe I love you?"

I began to tear up as I nodded yes again.

"I'm sorry for all the pain you've been through, but you can't punish me for it. I'm not them. Baby, you following me around this house like you're afraid to take your eyes off of me … I'm not going anywhere."

I held my head down, embarrassed that I had become transparent; that my abandonment issues had yet again taken over.

"I'm not going to cheat on you. I'd leave you

first. Okay?"

I nodded in agreement.

"You have to let me be a man. I'm going to hang out with the fellas, have a few drinks, talk a little trash, and then I'm coming home … TO YOU. Not because I have to …" He pulled me close and said, "… because I want to."

He put a fresh coat of love on the situation by taking the time to listen and understand me. I couldn't help but to think, if it were Marcus, he would have said something like, "Whateva. You really need to see someone 'bout that cuz you trippin." Maybe I did need to see someone, but Damon soothed my every ache like an ibuprofen.

I kept waiting for something bad to happen, but the only thing that happened was me falling more in love with that man by the second.

Still Attached

As the weeks passed by, turning into months, Marcus started calling. Initially, it was just to claim the things he'd left behind. One afternoon, I was leaving to meet Damon for lunch when Marcus showed up at my job with a single red rose, smelling like cheap booze and weed.

"Marcus, what are you doing here?"

Staggering back and forth, he said, "Look atcha, lookin' all good."

Trying to hold him up, I said, "How did you get this drunk before noon?"

He cleared his throat as though he were preparing to sing. Instead, he spoke the words to our song. "At last, my love has come along. My lonely days are over … at last."

The security guard stood up from behind the desk and asked, "Ms. Richards, is this man bothering you?"

I shook my head. "Everything is okay."

Marcus mimicked the officer, saying, "'Is this man bothering you?' Wha-cha gonna do … blind me wit-cha flashlight? Hit me wit some keys?"

"Marcus!"

"Yes, baby, look atcha, looking just as good as you wanna look."

It was nothing short of a miracle that he'd driven across town without a scratch. It would have been easier for me to take him to Melissa's house, but that would have no doubt caused an argument that I was done participating in. What he needed was to sleep it off. I felt obligated; guilty is probably a more accurate account. I called Damon and told him what was going on. He didn't agree with me taking Marcus home, but understood why I felt I had to do it. He warned that this wouldn't be the end of it. He further explained that Marcus was still in love with me, and showing him any form of attention would be misinterpreted. Damon was right. There was no way he could have anticipated the chain reaction of events that would soon come after I took Marcus home that day.

The more Marcus called and showed up, the more he was on my mind. I knew that Damon was the best thing for me, and I loved him, but I couldn't stop thinking about Marcus. Knowing me the way he did, Marcus sensed it and used it to his advantage. He knew that I was spending a lot of time at Damon's house, so he continued calling me at work, sending me flowers and balloons. After about five weeks of this, he invited me to lunch. Without giving it a second thought, I said, "Sure." I convinced myself that it was just lunch, just a meal—the same way I convinced myself that it was nothing when I was sneaking around with Damon behind Marcus's back.

But it was much more. When I arrived at the restaurant, he was already there, waiting. As the hostess showed me to my seat, Marcus was standing there, talking to a gentleman. He put his arm around me and said, "Mario, this is my ... friend, DeLaina."

Marlon reached out to shake my hand and said, "A pleasure."

"Nice meeting you as well," I said.

I stood by as they exchanged compliments.

"Marlon's the man. This is just one of his establishments ..."

"No, you da man," Marlon countered. "If I had a voice like yours, I'd be dangerous. Shoot, the women wouldn't have a chance."

They both laughed as they ended the conversation with the one-shoulder hug.

"DeLaina," Marlon said, "it was nice meeting you. Enjoy your meal."

Marcus pulled out my chair and kissed me on the cheek. I remember thinking, *I didn't know you knew how to do that*. We laughed and joked the way we did in the beginning of our relationship years ago. I excused myself to use the ladies' room. When I returned, there was a big white box with a pink bow around it sitting on my chair. I looked at him, then stared at the box for a moment.

I asked in a confused tone, "What is this?"

"Open it."

Still standing, I began addressing the issue. "Okay, look, you have to stop doing this."

In a calming tone, he said, "Just open it."

Hesitantly, I took off the bow, thinking, *I can't keep accepting gifts from him*. I slowly peeled off the tape, contemplating opening it …

It was Charlie, my teddy bear. Pulling him out of the box, my eyes welled up as I remembered all the nights I soaked his fur with my tears. He still had a faint essence of my childhood.

Charlie was just as full and beautiful as the day Daddy gave him to me. All choked up, I asked, "Where did you find him?"

"Remember when we first moved in together? I put some stuff in storage and you boxed up a few things to make room for me. A few weeks ago, I went through my storage unit and there he was in one of my boxes."

I wrapped my arms around Marcus and kissed him on the cheek. "Thank you so much."

I sat at the table of a five-star restaurant with my arms wrapped tightly around a stuffed animal with no regard as to who was watching.

After lunch, he carried the box with Charlie in it to the truck. I thanked him again and again, but he brushed it off like it was nothing. As we said our good-byes, he leaned in to give me a hug. With his arms around me, I thought, *This is the Marcus I fell in love with.* He pulled back to look at me … and as fast as everything was happening, I saw him leaning toward me. I knew it was wrong, but I couldn't stop me from leaning in too. He kissed me, soft and passionately. But when he placed his hand in the small of my back, pulling me in deeper, wanting more of me … I pulled away, suddenly remembering that there was no more to give, that I had a man at home waiting for me, trusting me. He grabbed my hand and said, "There's still something between us."

I said, "I gotta go" then climbed into the truck.

He stood between the door and the truck. "I'm

not ready to let you go. Girl, I still love you."

"I'm not doing this with you. I'm in love with Damon."

"He can't love you like I can."

I pulled off, went back to the office, and sat in the parking lot, confused. Sitting in the truck, guilt ridden, gripping the steering wheel, all I could hear was Marcus saying, "He can't love you like I can."

I called Reagan, hoping she could shine some light on the situation—do her best-friend thing—but she didn't answer. So I sat there trying to make sense of what I was thinking and feeling. As I continued questioning it in my mind, it came to me like wisdom. It wasn't that I wanted Marcus; it was that he was finally showing me the attention I'd been longing for from him. As his voice echoed, "He can't love you like I can," I realized it was true. We had a history of co-dependency. Marcus needed me whereas Damon wanted me. I never had anyone just WANT me. Damon wasn't a boy who needed to be coddled and coaxed into being a man. He was a man with or without me.

I loved Damon too much to put our relationship in jeopardy.

I went back to the office and finished out the day. I stayed late since it was a Monday night during football season. I knew I wouldn't see Damon.

The whole way home, I couldn't help but think

of the situation I'd created, knowing if Damon ever found out from anyone other than me, it would be all bad.

As I stuck the key in the door of my condo, I heard a heavy baseline. Once the door was opened, I was greeted by Maxwell's "Sumthin' Sumthin'." I walked into the kitchen to find Damon two-stepping as he stirred in a small pot. I stood outside the kitchen and admired his body movement as he sang along with the CD.

"Even though she pays me no attention ... All I wanna show is my affection ... Lose myself inside her ebony ..."

He caught a glimpse of me from the corner of his eye and tried not to act surprised. I asked, "What are you doing here?"

He put down the spoon and walked toward the door with a sly grin as he said, "I'll go someplace where I'm wanted."

I grabbed him and held him. "I want you." Laughing, I said, "It's Monday night."

He rested his hands on the small of my back. "I came by to take you to lunch, but I must have just missed you. Susan said you were at a client site."

I thought, *I gotta get that girl a raise.*

"And as for football, the 'Skins playing Tennessee," Damon said, "It ain't worth watching. I'd rather hang out with you." He kissed me. "Is that okay?"

"Always."

I excused myself to take a shower and throw on some sweats. I couldn't have been gone more than fifteen minutes. As I came up the hallway, I noticed the house was dead silent. Damon was sitting on the edge of the couch with his coat on. *If looks could kill …*

"What's wrong?" I asked.

He walked over to the answering machine and pressed the blinking red light. I thought to myself, *It wasn't blinking when I arrived earlier. Someone must have called while I was in the shower.*

The voice said, "Yo, what's up girl …" It was Marcus. I closed my eyes, hoping he didn't say anything stupid. "Marlon found your phone underneath the table … I guess you must have dropped it when your hands were full …" He laughed. "Anyway, yo, I gotta tell you … that kiss got me messed up … two more minutes and we would have been in the back of your truck. Call me when you get this message."

I couldn't believe he left that message on my phone. I was so embarrassed that I couldn't even look Damon in his face. I kept my eyes to the ground and shook my head.

Damon didn't say a word. He just looked at me with a dagger-like glare. I had never seen him so angry.

"Damon, it wasn't like that."

With both hands on the sofa table, he leaned down to eye level, broke his silence, and enunciated each word: "WHAT ... WAS ... IT ... LIKE ... DELAINA!"

He never called me DeLaina. I opened my mouth to explain but nothing would come out.

"So you sneaking around with Marcus?" He laughed. "I didn't see that coming." He paced the floor, shaking his head. "I would ask if you were sleeping with him, but I think that's obvious."

"I didn't sleep with him."

He laughed. "I wondered why we hadn't heard from him lately. Now I know."

As he grew angrier, I tried to explain, "Baby, this whole thing is out of context. I love YOU!"

In a condescending tone, he said, "Really?" He continued, "Out of context? Was there a kiss?"

Reluctantly, I nodded my head.

As he headed toward the door, he said, "So it's just as he said."

I didn't have any words of defense.

He had already taken my key off his key ring. He placed it on the table as he said, "I expected you to be a little confused, but I thought you'd tell me about it. I didn't think you'd sneak around behind my back." He laughed sarcastically. "You gotta see the humor in this. You cheated on me with the dude you cheated on to be with me ... who is coincidently the same guy that repeatedly cheated on you." The hurtful glare pierced my heart just as much as him saying, "I guess that's my fault for expecting more of you." He had never looked at me that way before.

As he attempted to walk away, I grabbed his arm in an effort to plead my case. He stopped walking, just long enough to snatch his arm away. He looked at me with such scorn and contempt. As he walked out the door, I followed him pleading, "Baby, I was gonna tell you. Damon, I was gonna tell you."

He left. For two weeks, I called, emailed, and even sent him a letter. The letter was returned unopened and marked, Return to sender.

I stopped accepting Marcus's phone calls and started sending the flowers back, return to sender. I blamed him for me getting caught. It never should have happened, but it made me check myself.

Damon wouldn't accept my calls or return my messages. After four weeks of being ignored, I stopped calling. I loved him. I knew I loved him, but I didn't realize how much until I was faced with not knowing if we had a future. After weeks without communication, I figured I had nothing to lose. I waited outside the gym for him to get off and met him at his car.

"I know you don't want to see me—"

"Look, wha-cha doing here, DeLaina?"

I began stuttering. "I … I know … you … you hate me, but we need to talk …"

"Don't flatter yourself. I don't care enough to hate you."

That hurt.

As I stood there with my mouth open, a woman walked up and said, "Okay, I'm ready."

I looked at her, looking at him then looking at me. I became emotional while he remained emotionless. Finally, I threw my hand up. "Whateva!" Then walked back to my car. I pulled off, crying, wondering how he could even entertain the idea of seeing anyone.

Two days later, he showed up and apologized for being rude. I apologized for allowing things to get to this point. I told him how much I missed him. He nodded and said he knew the feeling. When I reached out to hug him, he stepped back.

"Baby, what do I have to do to fix this?" I asked.

In a nonchalant tone, he said, "Look, we can be friends …"

I felt him pushing me away. "Friends?" Seeing as how our relationship was not based on any one aspect, it caused a flux of emotions.

"I don't wanna be friends," I said.

He called me selfish, then said, "Laina, we were

such good friends … you're willing to throw all that away?"

I checked him, "No, you're willing to throw us away."

"Oh, my bad … I was the one sneaking around with my ex."

He was hurting. I knew he still loved me, but he needed to realize it all on his own. If there was a chance for us to get back together, he needed to get his mind around what happened, and I knew I couldn't force that. The breakup was still on—and for the next two months, it took everything in me to not call him. He needed to miss me enough to want to fix it, but it didn't seem like it was going to happen.

Another one bites the dust.

Family Secrets

Damon was the love of my life. I'd never been happier than when I was with him. More and more I missed the little things, like the way he looked at me across a crowded room or the way he told me I looked beautiful in the mornings with eye crust and dry drool on my chin.

I couldn't blame anyone but myself for our relationship being over. He forgave me but said he only wanted to be friends.

I had friends. What I wanted was my boyfriend back. I couldn't bear only having a piece of him. It was easier to not have him at all than to have a little bit and to want the MORE he wasn't willing to give.

In order to maintain my sanity, I threw myself into my work. My newest client was looking to invest in some real estate but needed some financial guidance. My role was to take a look at their books and find the funds needed. I was on a serious deadline, so I asked Susan to hold all my calls. As I sat hunched over the keyboard crunching numbers, my phone rang. I didn't answer it. Five minutes later, it rang again and again and again till finally I answered it in an irritated tone. It was Mike.

"Oh! Hey, Mike." Continuing to plug numbers, I asked, "What's up?"

"Uncle John-John died."

You'd have thought that I'd be numb to death by this point, but I wasn't. I sat back in my chair as I remembered how nice he was to me when Daddy died. "What happened?"

"I don't know, Lainee. They seem to think he was driving and fell asleep behind the wheel."

"The eighteen-wheeler?"

"Yeah."

"Oh wow. How's Tilley handling it?"

"I don't know."

"Didn't you talk to her?"

"Actually, no. The attorney called me looking for you. John-John's Will is being read next week and you're mentioned."

"What? Why would I be mentioned? I haven't talked to or seen that man since I left Atlanta."

Mike paused for a moment before saying, "It would be nice to get back home." Before I could ask, he volunteered to accompany me.

Once we arrived at the law offices of Wainwright & Dunbar, I developed this uneasy feeling in the pit of my stomach. I chalked it up to jetlag, and continued to wait impatiently with Mike. A young woman escorted us to the large conference room with a view overlooking the city. After she put out several bottles of water and offered coffee, she assured us Mr. Wainwright would be in shortly. Mike sat down, but I was drawn to the beautiful sixteenth-floor skyline peeking through the blinds. The doors flew open. I quickly turned, hoping it was the attorney. It was our cousin Tilley. I hadn't seen her since she shipped me off to Minnesota after Daddy died. She walked through those doors like she owned the place.

"Hey nah, wha-ch'all doin' here?" she asked. "Look atcha. You've both grown so much!" She hugged and kissed Michael on the cheek, then walked toward me. "It's nice to see you, DeLaina."

As she leaned in to hug me, I took a step back and said, "I'm sorry for your loss." Time hadn't healed that wound just yet. I was still angry at the way she'd mistreated me all those years ago.

Acknowledging my demeanor, she took a step back and looked at her nails. In a nonchalant tone, she said, "I miss him so much." She continued, "Hey, y'all ain't answer me … wha-ch'all doing here?"

Just then, the attorney walked in with his eyes fixed on the legal-size manila folder in his hands. With his head buried in the file, he continued flipping through the pages as he introduced himself. "I'm Amos Wainwright. Please take a seat and we'll start the proceedings." He closed the file and took his glasses off, resting them on the table. "First, let me say John was a very good friend of mine. He will surely, surely be missed."

He looked at me, put his glasses back on, and said, "You must be DeLaina." I nodded yes. "I'm very sorry we had to meet under these circumstances." With a half grin, he continued. "But it's nice to finally meet you."

I thought, *How does he know who I am*? But I tried not to give it too much thought.

Mr. Wainwright reopened the folder and said, "This is the reading of the last will and testament of John Aaron Mosby II." He turned to Tilley and said, "To Tilley Mosby, I leave one less person to argue with." She rolled her eyes. Mr. Wainwright turned to me. "Now, DeLaina Richards—"

Tilley interrupted, "Hey nah, wait. Aren't you

gonna get done wit me first?"

"Oh, I'm sorry for being rude," Mr. Wainwright said. "I'm done!"

Her mouth dropped open.

Mr. Wainwright turned back to me. "To my daughter, DeLaina Richards, I leave—"

I interrupted, shaking my head, "I'm not … his daughter."

Tilley agreed. In an authoritative tone, she said, "She's not his daughter!"

The attorney handed me a signed affidavit from Delores Clinkscale—Tilley's older sister—confessing her knowledge and role in Tilley's web of deception. I looked at the paper, unsure as to what I was seeing. Flipping through the pages of the file, Mr. Wainwright then placed the paternity results alongside the letter and said, "You are his daughter."

Shaking my head, I confessed, "I don't understand."

I stared at the paper that clearly stated John Mosby could not be excluded from the paternity of DeLaina Richards.

Tilley argued, "Where did you get that? She's not his kid." She rose and leaned over the table. "Look, this is not the Will that we signed last year. Hey nah, if … if I gotta hire my own lawyer …"

Without looking up from his documents, Mr.

Wainwright asked her, "Did the church ever figure out who stole the building-fund money? I think it was about fifteen thousand dollars, wasn't it, Tilley?"

Her eyes widened as she slowly sat back down. Still shaking my head, I pushed the papers back to the attorney. I grabbed my purse and said, "I don't want anything to do with any of this. He knew I was his and he did nothing."

As I walked toward the door, Mr. Wainwright called out my name. "DeLaina, he didn't know."

Confused, I asked, "How did he not know? The paper right there says—"

He interrupted, "Tilley and her sister changed the results."

Michael sat up in his seat. "WHAT?"

I stood there, unable to say a word, as Mr. Wainwright continued. "Delores found out she was dying and wanted to put things in order. Before she passed, she contacted John and told him what she and Tilley had done." He pointed at the DNA results. "She gave him the test that was done all those years ago."

Still confused, I inquired, "Okay, so he found out five months ago. Why didn't he come to me then?"

I turned slowly toward the door again as Mr. Wainwright continued. "And say what? His life … your whole life has been a lie. He felt like he let you down. But, even more so, he blamed himself for not trusting your mother in the first place."

Mike turned to Tilley. "I can't believe you did this."

I turned to her, looking for an explanation, but she had this smug look on her face, which ignited something in me. I walked toward her with anger flickering inside. As I got closer, Mike jumped up in an effort to be the wall between us.

With tears in my eyes, I said, "You are so evil. Why would you do this?"

She didn't respond. Which only more so aroused my anger.

Pushing Mike out the way, I yelled, "ANSWER ME!"

Even as the tears streamed down her face and mine, she remained silent.

Mr. Wainwright explained that he and Uncle John-John grew up together. He told me he was there the first time my father laid eyes on my mother. He said, "Your father and I worked at the cotton candy stand when the fair came to town. One day, my sister dropped us off late, so we found ourselves running through the crowd trying to get to the stand so old man Cooper wouldn't fire us. But your father ..." He laughed out loud before continuing, "... stopped running when he saw this beautiful young girl standing in line at the dunking booth." He laughed again. "I remember yelling for him to come on, but he just stood there enamored by her beauty. I literally had to grab his arm. So for the next hour, I had to hear about how beautiful she was … how beautiful your mother was.

That was about the time Tilley walked up. I told John, 'Look at that girl over there staring at you.' I convinced him to go talk to her to try and take his mind off the other girl/your mother."

Wiping the tears from her eyes, Tilley said, "I remember that day. I was standing there in that cotton candy line. I couldn't take my eyes off him. Oh, he was so handsome." Tilley searched for a tissue to wipe her face. "He looked at ME and smiled. We smiled back and forth; it seemed like hours." She laughed. "But it couldn't a-been more than a few minutes. I was next in line. I finally got up the nerve to say something. He came to the front of the counter to introduce himself, but when Felecia walked up, he hopped over the counter and asked her name instead." She shook her head. "She always thought she was better than me."

Mike interrupted, "Felecia never thought she was better than you."

"All I ever heard was 'Felecia so pretty, Felecia so smart,'" Tilley said. "Felecia this, Felecia that."

Mr. Wainwright continued, "Your mother and father fell head over heels in love. You never saw one without the other. But Tilley was still hung up on him, so she spread a rumor that Felecia was cheating." Shaking his head, he continued, "I told John it wasn't true but, well, we were kids and he couldn't get his mind around the idea of it. Felecia was offended that he'd even doubt her; who could blame her? So when they broke up, Tilley swooped in like a vulture to pick up the pieces. I think that's about when your mother found out she was pregnant. Tilley tried desperately to taint the way John looked at Felecia. She knew he'd never love her the way he loved your mother."

"That explains it!" Staring at Tilley, I said, "You were threatened by me. That's why you were so mean."

Tilley blurted out, "John and your mother—"

I slammed my palm on the table and yelled, "I was fourteen! I was a child! You made my life a living hell." As I paced the floor, cursing and crying, the room went silent. "You stole my childhood."

Tilley interrupted, "Your mother—"

"SHUT ... UP!" I said. "I never asked you to take me in. You took me in and treated me like sh—"

"DeLaina!" Mr. Wainwright interrupted. "Let's finish the reading."

Although John-John left me everything, the business, the trucks, even the house Tilley lived in, I explained that money and things couldn't make up for growing up not knowing who my father was.

In the cab on the way back to the hotel, neither Michael nor I said a word. Once we got back to the hotel, Mike offered to take me to dinner, but I just wanted to be alone. I went back to my room, drew a hot bubble bath, and remembered every conversation I ever had with John-John and wondered if he ever saw himself in me and thought for an instance that I could be his child. I wondered what type of father he would have been if he had known. I wondered if John-John had been around, would my mother have stayed?

I opened the mini bar and drank myself to sleep.

The next morning when we got off the plane, Damon was waiting at the airport terminal. Drained and hung-over, I asked, "What are you doing here?"

He took the carry-on from my hand and said, "I thought you could use a friend."

I looked at Mike and silently mouthed, "Thank you."

This situation opened up the lines of communication between Damon and me. Sometimes a man just needs to feel needed. In spite of my financial expertise, I asked him to help me come up with an investment strategy … a keen way to let my money work for me. A few weeks into the planning, we were back together. I bought a six-floor apartment building already established with reliable tenants and a thorough building superintendent only six miles from my condo.

Neo

Since the failed wedding, Rea and I had become estranged. I wasn't really sure as to the reason why. In every attempt to spend time with her, she was always busy, or she'd cancel on me at the last minute. Granted, we were both busy with life, but it seemed she didn't want to be bothered with me. When I ask her about it she apologized and said she'd make it up to me. That day never came.

While riding around one Saturday night, Damon and I decided to have dinner at his favorite restaurant: Mr. Jack's. When we arrived, the hostess told us and another couple that if we didn't have reservations, it would be a forty- to fifty-minute wait. We decided to wait and just kill time at the bar. We walked through the east side of the dining room to the lower-level bar area, and lo and behold, who did we run into? Reagan. When I called out her name, she looked caught off guard, almost guilty.

I wrapped my arms around Rea, pulling her in close and whispering, "Why haven't you called me?"

"Oh, gurl, you know how it is. I just been busy."

I smiled, looking her over. "Are you here by yourself?'

A little hesitant to answer, she said she was meeting Randy, her flavor of the week, for a drink.

There was something going on with her. But I couldn't put my finger on it. Apparently feeling a little left out, Damon introduced himself. I apologized and introduced her. "Baby, this is my best friend Reagan." Rea stuck out her hand and said, "Nice to officially meet you."

Shaking her hand, he replied, "Yeah, it's nice to put a face with a name." Excusing himself, he said "Baby, I'm going to get a drink. What do you want?"

"Peach martini."

He asked Reagan, "Are you ready for another one?"

"No, I'm good."

As Damon walked toward the bar, I asked, "What happened to Trent?"

"Gurl, you knew that wasn't gonna last."

"Why? He was nice."

"Dat nigga looked like a gremlin. And I don't mean dat cute one … dat lil' bad one wit da mohawk."

"Rea, that's ugly."

"Shoot, he started it."

We laughed.

"No," I said, "he didn't look like Blair Underwood, but he was nice. Rea, you have to learn to look at the inside."

"Girl, the inside was all that was left cuz the outside was jacked up! Ray Charles could have seen he was ugly. Gurl, he would've touched dat nigga's wrist …"

Laughing, I said, "You know you wrong for that! There's more to a man than just the physical."

In a condescending tone, she said, "Says the woman wit da fine boyfriend. DeLaina, I know all about beauty only being skin deep. I was the fat girl, remember?"

Eagerly changing the subject, I said, "Well, Randy must be doing something right; you look good."

She laughed. "Randy ain't got nuffin to do wit diss. I always look good. Check my resume … I said look at the fine print!"

I laughed. "I know that's right"

"But you look great! You and Christopher Williams glowing like two nightlights." She broke into a chorus of "Don't wake me ... I'm dreaming."

"Why he gotta be Christopher Williams?"

"I don't know, but thank his momma for me ... umh."

"See, I can't take you no-where." I sighed. "I miss this ... I haven't seen you since the wedding."

"It ain't been that long."

I turned my head to the side with that Negro, please look.

"Okay, my bad," Rea said. "There's just been so much going on, but I think I'm getting back on track." She sipped her drink, positioned her glass just so on the table, and said, "I saw Marcus."

"Really? How is he?"

She shrugged her shoulders. "Okay, I guess."

Curious, I asked, "What did he say?"

"Uh, about what?"

"Did he tell you about the restraining order?"

"What?"

Thinking back on the incidents, I said, "Once I started sending the flowers back 'return to sender'—" She interrupted, "FLOWERS! He sent you flowers?"

"Yes, girl! He kept popping up at my job, causing so much drama that they got him for trespassing. Then he started harassing Damon at work."

Damon was leaving work one evening and found Marcus had busted out his windows. "Girl, it took three of the trainers to get Damon off him." Shaking my head, I explained to Rea, "It's funny, the most beautiful woman that a man will ever see is the ex he did wrong on the arm of another man."

"Are you serious, Laina? He ain't say nuffin about that."

"Where did you see him?"

"Oh … uhh, at the mall."

"I just feel so bad. I know I caused a lot of the confusion …"

Peering over my shoulder, she said, "OH NO!"

I quickly turned around. "What?"

"Dat trick all up in Damon's face." She stood up, reaching for her earring. "Let's get her."

I laughed. "Girl, sit down!"

"WHAT?"

I confidently said, "I trust the man I chose." With a baffled look on her face, she said, "Whateva. Look how dat trick is lookin' at him."

"Girl, please … the dude is FINE! Women are gonna try him. My job isn't to run off every woman that looks his way." I explained, "I was miserable chasing behind Marcus and Darrell trying to make them be faithful, checking their phones, trying to hold the relationship together with bubble gum and a shoe string."

My past relationships had standardized love as lies,

abuse, and infidelity. Every day was something, and somehow I held on to what I had and tried to make it work. But being with Damon was effortless, like breathing. I didn't have to dummy myself down to make him feel like a man. Or walk around on eggshells, afraid he was gonna flip out. Damon was everything I ever wanted, and things I never knew, I did.

I gushed. "Damon's different; he's the one."

"You've known him … what? Five minutes … and already you've cast him as Neo. Dang, Laina, did you take the blue pill?"

I laughed. I knew everyone probably saw our relationship as a knee-jerk reaction, but I had never been happier in my life. Damon could see me—everything I was and everything I wasn't. It was like I never existed before he laid eyes on me.

Reagan asked, "What about Marcus?" Looking down, she asked, "You still love him?"

"Of course I do; I almost married him. But I stopped being in love with him a long time ago."

"So you ready to have lil' Neo's?"

"Girl, yes!"

She crossed her legs, leaned in close, and asked, "How's the practice sessions?" Rea and I had always shared bedroom stories, but with Damon it felt different. I wanted to keep him all to myself. Although it would have put some color on the picture I was painting, I didn't disclose that Damon and I hadn't been intimate as yet. I smiled and said, "I love him."

She stared with a confused *What have you done with DeLaina*? look on her face.

For the first time, I knew what it felt like to be in love. The kind of love that's not embellished, fabricated, or tainted by lust … real love. I've loved before, but it wasn't triggered by these types of emotions.

Proposal

I was where I wanted to be: with Damon. Though the fiasco at the church happened five months ago and I stayed at his house four out of seven nights, Damon and I still hadn't been intimate. There was no rush. We were confident that the other wasn't going anywhere. Whereas in every other relationship, I felt obligated to sex. As in I had to attempt every erotic thing my mate's mind could conjure, in fear that if I didn't, he'd find someone else who would. So I read books and watched tapes to become a woman who could make a man crave a cigarette - and he doesn't even smoke. Loveless relationships where sex was the prize and everything else was the bonus. I was a woman who kept my bag of tricks beside the bed in an effort to keep him satisfied.

When multiple orgasms are the basis of a relationship, it's the equivalent to a house without a roof. It's fine if all you need is a place to lay.

***

My company was going through a tedious reorganization. The project director insisted on implementing a new structure that depleted my staff but not the workload. On any given day, I was doing the job of two people, maybe three. I was stressed to say the least. To put icing on the cake, Melissa called to cuss me out yet again and tell me that Marcus was in the mental hospital and it was my fault. I was completely drained.

When I got to Damon's house, the table was set beautifully with candles. I walked into the kitchen and slid down onto the floor beside the island and recounted the miserable day I had. He knelt down, took my shoes off, and rubbed my feet. He had the uncanny ability to make my troubles seem nonexistent. He took my hand, pulled me up from the floor, and led me to the bathroom, where the sounds of Boney James bounced off the flickering flames of the candles surrounding the rose petal filled tub. A warmth came over me as I thought of the trouble he must have gone through … just for me.

I released a quiet, "Aw, baby."

He smiled, kissed me on the cheek, and said,

"Get in and relax. Call me when you're ready for me to wash your back." I laid back in the tub and contemplated the change that was coming. I knew this was THE NIGHT. Although I had practically moved in, I always slept in shorts or sweats. I was still a little apprehensive about the possibility of change. After about twenty minutes, I called for him. He came in with a Victoria's Secret nighty ... you know, the ones that hold no secrets. I leaned forward to cover all the things he'd soon see. He leaned down and kissed my shoulders just before he began the slow circular motions with the loofah. After he left, I dried off, put on the tell-all nighty, and walked into the dimly lit room. He laid across the bed, looking like every woman's dream. He stood up, reached for my hand, and said, "Um, that's my baby."

What made our relationship amazing was that we left our egos and pride at the front door. He didn't feel he had to hide his feelings or the life he had outside of me. We were able to be ourselves, the selves that don't have to filter our thoughts. We could just say whatever we felt. I loved that he knew me, at times, better than I knew myself. He knew me ... the me without makeup ... the me without a smile ... the me that wasn't pretending to like something for his sake ... the me that was afraid ... and he loved me anyway.

He wrapped his arms around me and made love to me in a way that made me question the masculinity of every man I'd been with before him. My trust in him released all inhibitions like ganja. I imagined that moment in my mind at least a thousand times and it was never like that.

Lying face-to-face in the afterglow with our bodies glistening ... I stared aimlessly while tracing his eyebrows with my pointer finger. I asked him, "Why are you so sure about us?"

He propped himself up on his left arm. "You breathe life into me. I feel closer to you than people I've known for years."

I clapped my hands. "Good answer, good answer."

He laughed. "Serious business." Which translates into *It's the truth.*

***

Michael and I always had a very close relationship, so anyone that came into my life would have to love and respect him as I did—or at least fake it well. As I expected, Mike and Damon became boys. With Mike's birthday rapidly approaching, he said the only thing he wanted was a birthday dinner like Mommy use to make. I cooked dinner at Damon's for the four of us: Mike, Tracey, Damon, and myself. After we cut the cake, Damon turned to Mike and said, "Lainee was telling me that after your father died, you became more of a father than a cousin." My conversation with Tracey stopped midstream. I sat on the edge of my seat in anticipation of Mike going into one of his infamous stories about me as a little girl; I lived for those stories.

"Yeah, Lainee and I were always close." Mike looked at me. "We've been through a lot together."

Before he could go any further, Damon said, "Yeah, I know. That's why I'm asking you..." He reached into his pocket. "For her hand in marriage."

I covered my mouth with surprise. Mike smiled, as he and Damon slapped palms like old college buddies, and leaned in giving the one-shoulder hug.

Damon never ceased to amaze me. Although marriage was imminent, I didn't foresee a proposal so soon. As he walked toward me, removing the ring from the box, he said, "I've been looking for you." He knelt down on one knee and slid the ring on my finger as he said, "I found you ... just in time. Will you marry me?"

"Yes, baby, yes!"

Elope

Damon was the first man I was ever able to strip far past my clothes for. I was finally able to expose myself naked, bare to the bone.

One night, cuddled up next to the fireplace, he said, "I'm going to put my motorcycle in the shop tomorrow, so I'm going to take yours when I go riding with the fellas … if that's okay?"

"Um, well, baby, I don't let anyone ride my bike."

"I'm not just anyone!"

I sat up. "Mike doesn't ride his bike. I'll ask if we can borrow his."

"What? NO! I'm not asking Mike … We're getting married DeLaina. What's this about?"

I felt the door opening to a conversation that I had evaded for almost sixteen years. When asked by guys in the past, I always said it was my daddy's bike, and that was the end of the conversation. But I loved Damon too much to fathom lying to him.

"It belonged to an old friend."

"Who? Darrell?"

There was an awkward pause before I said, "Trey."

"Who?"

I sat there, buried in the flicker of the flame. I never wanted to completely expose myself to anyone. Fear held my tongue; I was afraid he'd look at me differently.

He sat up, turned me toward him, and said, "I don't want any secrets between us. Don't be elusive."

I took off a layer, exposing myself, and told him about my days on the streets. I removed another layer telling him about Trey, the first man I ever cared for. Layer after layer came off as I relived Ricky knocking at the door, telling me Trey's car had been found. I exposed it all. Confiding that Trey died an unnecessary death. The bike was the only thing that I had to remind me of that time and who I used to be and how far I'd come.

Without flinching, he said, "Everybody has a past."

I had been carrying the burden that came with that secret for many years. After I said it out loud, I felt lighter. I didn't realize I was holding on to my past. Maybe it was time I let Trey rest in peace.

Damon poured us another glass of wine and took off a layer himself, revealing that he spent his teenage years hustling and gang-bangin on the unforgiving streets of Chicago, working his way up the chain from being the man next to the man to becoming THE MAN.

He said, "I had everything a man in my position could want: power, fast cars, fast women, and money." He sat quiet for a moment like he was thinking back on that time.

I asked "Why did you leave the life?"

There was a long pause before he said "When we were kids, my mother use to always tell us you reap what you sow."

He went on to tell me he left the life, and everything behind when a junkie, some guy he noted as one of his best customers stuck up his baby brother for his tennis shoes.

A single tear rolled down his face as he said "I guess he wasn't moving fast enough." That was the only time I'd ever seen Damon moved to tears.

***

The next day at work I was feeling really tired, almost weak. Although it was only wine I considered that maybe I drank too much the night before.

Nonetheless, I just couldn't focus so I left work early to get some rest. When I got to Damon's house I went straight to the bedroom to lie down only to find Damon on the phone whispering. All I could make out was, "Are you going to keep it?"

I interrupted, "Who you talking to, baby?"

He quickly turned around, seemingly startled. He said into the phone, "Reagan, she is here. Yeah, yeah, okay, okay, a'ight, I'll tell her." He pressed the End button on the cordless and said, "She said she'd call you back."

I placed my left hand on my hip and pulled my cell phone out of the holster to review the call history. "Okay, so she didn't call my cell, but she called your house to say she'd call me back?"

He placed the phone back in the cradle. "A'ight, Nancy Drew … I think she's trying to plan a surprise or something."

"Oh." I felt foolish for the thoughts I was having.

I just needed some rest. I felt much better once I got up from my nap but then, Damon seemed irritable and a little distant. I questioned him about it, but he said it was nothing. A little while later he came into the den and said "Baby, I love you …"

I laughed. "What's wrong?"

There was an uncomfortable silence. He had this weird look on his face, then he said, "Marry me!"

I held up my left hand to show my ring "We've already had this conversation, remember."

"Look at me!" Whenever he said those three words, he wanted me to see how serious he was. "Baby, we love each other in a way that most people only dream about. We don't have to stand in front of people we don't usually see or talk to and profess our love. I just wanna make you mine legally."

He was right. We didn't need anyone to validate us. I didn't need the big wedding. All I needed was him. He placed his hands on either side of my face and said, "Let's go to Vegas this weekend!"

Smiling, I stood on my toes and wrapped my arms around his neck. "Yes, baby!"

He kissed me to seal the deal.

My mind begin racing, thinking of all the things I needed to do. *I need to get a dress … What am I going to pack? How long will we be gone? Should I ask Reagan and Mike to come*?

He went downstairs to watch TV.

I called Reagan.

"Hello?" she answered.

"Hey, girl, are you busy?"

In an irritated tone, she said, "Yeah, kinda. What's up?"

"Damon and I are eloping! We're going to Vegas this weekend … and I need my best girl at my side."

In a nonchalant tone, she asked, "Um, why you eloping?"

I laughed. "Because I love that man."

"Ahh, well, I kinda got plans ..."

In an excited tone, I said, "I said I'm getting married! Your girl is getting ready to do the I do thing! That trumps any plans you have."

I heard a voice in the background. After I asked her if she had company, she quickly ended the conversation and said she'd call me back. Something was bothering Rea, but I decided to give her some space. Standing in the closet setting aside clothes for the weekend, I got lightheaded, lost my balance, and fell against the wall.

I went and sat on the bed for a while to calm myself and called Michael.

"Hey, you!"

"Hey, Lainee. What's going on?"

"Damon and I are going to Vegas this weekend and I need you there."

"I'm there. Hey, have you talked to Rea?"

"Yeah, I called her a little while ago and she sounded weird. Why? You know something?"

"She called me the other day. I'll let her tell you. I gotta go but call me tomorrow with the details."

"Okay, love you!"

"Love you too."

I was ashamed to say that, even after Mike confirmed something was going on with Rea, I didn't give her awkwardness a second thought.

Till Death Do Us Part

I was up for three more hours planning the weekend. Once I finally laid my head on his chest, I laid there thinking how much I loved that man.

I couldn't have had my eyes closed more than a couple hours before a loud noise woke me from my sleep. I turned over to grab Damon when I noticed he wasn't there. I sat up in the bed. "Baby?"

No answer. I heard rumblings downstairs. As I got up to check out the noise, I heard two gunshots—pop, pop. I flashed back to my days on the block as I took off, down the steps two at a time. Halfway down, I remembered Damon's gun. Back up the steps, into the walk-in closet … the gun box was on the floor, empty. I heard a loud crash. Back down the steps into the den. "OH NO!"

There was just enough light from the hallway for me to see someone standing over Damon with a gun as he laid slouched against the wall. It seemed everything was moving in slow motion. I yelled at the figure. "Take whatever you want!" Startled, the figure quickly turned the gun on me and said, "It was an accident."

That voice …

I reached over and turned on the lamp.

"Oh my goodness! Marcus! What have you done?"

He waved the gun, mumbling, "This wasn't supposed to happen. I was trying to get the gun …"

I sidestepped toward Damon as I begged him, "Put the gun down."

He yelled, "Stop moving!" He toggled between Damon and me, seemingly evaluating the situation. "I didn't mean to!"

I turned to Damon and asked, "Baby, are you okay?"

Barely able to move, he nodded his head yes.

Marcus mimicked me, "'Baby, are you okay?' DeLaina, do you know what this nigga did?"

"Marcus, stop it! Just stop it!"

He paced the floor, talking and responding to

himself for several minutes, before he finally took action ...

Marcus ran the barrel of the gun from my temple to my jawline, whispering, "You're so beautiful." Although I'd played Tina to his Ike on several occasions, this was the first time he inspired fear in me. The man standing in my living room was crazy. Not the confident, ladies' man I almost married.

I glimpsed over at Damon's motionless body slumped against the wall; he needed me. As I tried to move closer, Marcus wiped the sweat from his brow and yelled, "Stop ... moving!" As he paced the floor, he tugged on the bottom of his shirt with his left hand, saying, "Just let me think." He continued pacing and talking to himself.

I asked, "Have you been taking your medicine?"

He didn't respond. Instead, he asked, "Did you ever love me?"

Although my heart was pounding, without hesitation I responded, "Of course."

"Then why you with this fake Al B. Sure-lookin' nigga? He's not who you think he is!" His tone lowered as he said, "We should be married with kids by now. We should be having kids!"

In an effort to calm him, I said, "Marcus, you're not thinking clearly." Pointing at Damon, I said, "He needs an ambulance. You don't want murder on your hands. Marc, right now it just looks like a botched robbery. If … if you just … just leave … I-I'll …"

He yelled, "No!" then went back to pacing the floor, ranting, "I love you! We're s'pose to be together." With the gun at his side, he asked, "Marry me?" When I didn't respond, he stopped pacing and his face went blank.

From across the room, he pointed the gun in my direction and this time commanded, "Marry me!"

As I shook my head proclaiming I can't, he aimed the gun at my head and said, "IF I CAN'T HAVE YOU …"

All the nights on the block, with Trey and the boys, I never stared down the barrel of a gun. I took a deep breath and prepared myself for the next moment.

With nothing to lose, I said, "So this is the answer… love me to death?" I walked toward the gun, yelling, "If you gonna do it, do it!"

He didn't flinch.

"It's still all about you, huh, Marcus!" I said. "What you want when you want it. You want somebody to feel sorry for you … 'DeLaina left me.' DeLaina should've left you a long time ago. You wanna blame somebody? YOU did this. You diminished our relationship. For four years, you tried to checker your way through a chess game using hereditary cheating habits as an excuse. You running around here screwing anything with a pulse and I let you because I didn't think I deserved better."

I grew angrier as I flashed back to the purgatory he called love, to the cheating and manipulation. I opened my arms wide and yelled, "WHA-CHU WAITING FOR?"

I was staring at a man that I no longer recognized. He backed up, sat on the love seat, and almost in a whisper said, "You're still the prettiest girl I know."

As a single tear ran down his cheek, he placed the barrel in his mouth.

I realized the reality at the eleventh hour.

As he gripped the trigger, I called his name. "Marcus!"

POP!

Screaming … I could barely hear the sirens racing up the block. I heard the officers outside the door banging, but I couldn't move. With guns drawn, they kicked the door open. I heard one of the officers dispatch an ambulance. Moments later, the paramedics rushed in. One yelled, "I can't get a pulse!" They placed an oxygen mask over Damon's face—"One, two, three"—then lifted him onto the gurney and rushed out with sirens blazing.

Still in shock … I stood there crying, staring at the wall splattered with blood. I walked toward his body, fell down at his feet, and rest my forehead on his knees. Crying and rocking, I moaned, "Marcus, I'm sorry! Baby, I'm sorry! I'm sorry!"

I heard one of the officers say, "Cover up his body and get her out of here!"

An officer grabbed my arm, pulling me up from the floor, saying, "We need to secure this scene."

I looked down at his motionless body, hoping he was finally at peace. I told the officer I needed to get to the hospital. He quickly offered to drive me. I ran upstairs, threw on some jeans, and grabbed my purse and cell phone. On my way to the hospital, I called Reagan. Once she answered, I blurted out, "Damon was shot!"

I burst into tears as she questioned me about the events. I tried to explain what happened, but I couldn't calm the crying enough to explain clearly.

With one hand on the steering wheel, the officer gently removed the phone from my trembling hand. "This is Officer DeLuca of the Anne Arundel County police department. I'm taking Ms. Richards to County General. Meet her there."

Soon enough, Rea rushed into the emergency room and ran to the nurse's station, yelling, "Damon Montgomery! Where's Damon Montgomery?"

"Calm down, sweetie," a nurse said. "Let me take a look." She quickly flipped through the pages on her clipboard. "He's in the operating room, but you can wait with his family in the waiting room." Pointing, she said, "Go through these double doors, and at the end of the hall make a left."

As I sat in the waiting room, numb, Rea did a Jackie Joyner-Kersee through the ER. She knelt down in front of me and asked, "Is Damon okay?"

"I don't know … they won't tell me anything."

"What happened?"

With tears in my eyes, I told her, "Marcus shot Damon then turned the gun on himself."

"WHAT? Marcus did what?" She plopped her body down in the seat beside me. "Is he…" I nodded my head. "Did he … did he say anything?"

I relayed Marcus's last words as Reagan rested her head in her hands and began chanting, "What have I done? What have I done!"

Confused by her comment, I asked, "What are you talking about?"

Before she could respond, a doctor pushed through the double doors toward us. Removing his mask, he asked, "Are you the family of Damon Montgomery?"

Reagan and I collectively said yes. I stood up, looking for hope in his eyes as he tried to explain the complications of the surgery.

He went on to say, "We've done all we can. Unfortunately, it may not have been enough."

He insisted Damon needed his rest but said that one of us could see him just for a minute. I didn't know what to expect walking into his room.

I was so taken aback by the tubes running in and out of his body I couldn't contain myself. I cleared my throat enough to say, "I'm here, baby." It all seemed so surreal. I stood beside his bed, holding his hand, telling him that he had to fight. I held his hand a little tighter as I sat there silently questioning my role in him lying there helplessly. I hadn't had any communication with Marcus in months, so what made him show up at the house with a gun?

Suddenly, Damon's eyes rolled to the back of his head. He began to convulse. I screamed for help as he flatlined. The nurses rushed in, warmed up the paddles, and shocked his heart. Nothing. They shocked it again. He laid there unresponsive.

I moaned, "Oh God!"

The doctor yelled, "Get her out of here!"

But I couldn't be moved. They tried several more times before the doctor said, "Call it."

I screamed, "NO! Keep trying."

The doctor took off his gloves and said, "I'm sorry," as he left the room, seemingly disappointed.

Overwhelmed with emotion, I felt Reagan standing beside me. She tried to comfort me as I stood there paralyzed, staring at Damon's motionless body.

Completely overwhelmed with grief, I had to remind myself to breathe. Trying aimlessly to gather my thoughts, I said, "I can't … I-I didn't … I-I wanted to … Oh …"

Reagan grabbed my arm as I gave into the pressure and collapsed to the floor. With tears in her eyes, she said, "DeLaina, I'm so sorry … I didn't …"

As I watched the nurses remove the tubes from his body one by one, I cried, "We were going to get married."

Once the nurse was done, she said, "I'll give you a few minutes."

Reagan excused herself from the room. Crying uncontrollably, I laid my head on his chest as the life we'd never have flashed before my eyes like a home movie. He looked so peaceful. Crying, I looked up and traced his face with my finger the way I did when he'd lay his head on my lap. His eyebrows, down his nose, and shaped his lips. I laid my head back on his chest and told him all the things I never got a chance to say, like the best part of my day was coming home to him. Like he couldn't cook but the fact that he tried for me gave it that special seasoning. I never loved anyone the way I loved him.

The nurse returned with two orderlies. "I'm sorry. It's time."

"Just give me a few more minutes! Please!"

They stood around the bed as I held his hand and said, "What am I supposed to do now?" I stared at his chiseled face, memorizing it the way I did the first time I saw him, until they pulled the white sheet over his still body.

I never knew the kind of love that I felt actually existed. I was caught between emotions … one minute planning a wedding … the next planning a funeral.

Standing there overwhelmed by grief, I remembered what it took to make a person want to give up.

As I walked into the hallway, I noticed Rea on the ground near the nurses' station. It appeared they were giving her oxygen as Paige held her hand. I hurried down the hall to take inventory of the situation, when the nurse insisted, "She'll be fine. It's just a lot for her to deal with right now."

I thought to myself, *She's dealing with a lot?*

Paige wrapped her arms around me, saying, "In spite of your situation … he's still God." Paige took my hand and the nurse's hand who was holding Rea's hand, and began to pray "Father God, I come to you not questioning your will, but asking that your will prevail on earth as it is in heaven. Father, I pray that you bless everyone under the sound of my voice … that you give everyone the strength to endure the days to come, Lord. In Jesus' name, I pray. Amen."

You could always count on Paige to go to God

on your behalf.

Paige offered to drop Rea off and bring her back later to pick up her car but Rea insisted she was fine … she just needed a few minutes.

I wanted to go back to Damon's house, but Paige insisted on my coming to her house.

I laid in her bed and moaned for the next twenty-four hours. I woke up to Mike and Paige whispering in the hallway. It sounded like he asked her if I had spoken to Reagan. I wasn't sure, but I thought I heard him ask, "Does DeLaina know?" My natural instinct was to think, Know what?—but I didn't have the energy to delve into the conversation.

Mike came and just stood in the doorway for a while, as if he were trying to figure out what to say. When I noticed him standing there, I jumped up and ran into his arms.

"Aw, baby girl. I'm sorry. I really am." He walked me over to the chaise and sat down beside me. "Can I get you anything?"

I shook my head no.

As I laid in his arms, in a soft tone he said, "I can't believe Marcus did this. How can you murder someone and take your own life?"

My eyes welled up as I relived wanting to die. I turned to Mike. "I never told you what happened at

Tilley's house. After Daddy died, I became depressed. Mike, he was my everything … my father, mother, friend, chef, chauffeur..."

He nodded his head in agreement.

With tears flowing from my eyes, I said, "Daddy was all I had."

"You had me."

"It didn't feel like it. After he died, it felt like the walls were closing in. Everyone was going on with their lives like nothing happened when it was hard for me to even smile. Sometimes when it hurts that bad … you don't feel like you have any options."

His tears washed over me as he held me tighter.

Why?

I don't know what I expected walking back into that house for the first time since the incident, but the feeling was uneasy. The crime scene cleanup crew had been there. They'd cleaned and placed everything back in its place, but everything seemed out of order. Although there wasn't a drop of blood anywhere, all I could see was Marcus sitting on the couch and splatters of his blood all over the wall and ceiling.

I went upstairs, took a shower, put on Damon's T-shirt and sweats, and laid down on his side of the bed.

Mike came in and sat on the side of the bed, staring at the wall. Not knowing what to say, he just laid beside me until I fell asleep.

I woke up to noises downstairs. Morning had arrived. I walked downstairs one step at a time, hoping I had awakened from a bad dream, even though the throb of my head and the emptiness in my heart told me otherwise.

As I neared the kitchen, I heard Reagan's voice. She was telling someone, "I guess I knew he neva really wanted to be with me. After a while, I got used to him asking about DeLaina. He used to ask every day, then it dwindled to every few days ... 'Have you talked to Laina? Did Laina call?' I knew he still loved her."

I stood outside the kitchen in the hallway, listening, unsure of what I was listening to. Unclear on the he that she was referring to.

"I didn't think he was coming over here when he left my house," Rea said.

It was quiet for a moment, then I heard a man's voice say, "So let me make sure I understand ... Marcus and DeLaina dated. They broke up, and she took up with Damon, and you took up with Marcus. Is that right?" Someone must have confirmed because the man then said, "Okay, go on."

Rea said, "Marcus ain't know I was pregnant till he came home and caught me throwing up. Without even asking if I was pregnant, he said 'Get rid of it.'" I could hear the cracking in Rea's voice as she said, "I told him no ... I wanted it. That's when we started arguing about the last time I had an abortion. I tried to smooth it ova, saying maybe we could be a family."

The man asked, "Why hadn't you told him?"

There was a pause before she admitted in a quiet tone, "I wasn't sure if it was his."

"Ahh, I see. Well, who is the other possible father?"

"Does it matter? I mean, Marcus didn't want a child anyway ... at least not with me."

I could hear her crying as I stood there trying to piece my life together. Making sense of every awkward moment between Reagan and Marcus. I always thought it was because she couldn't stand him. Apparently, it was quite the opposite.

Then I heard Mike's voice asking, "Detective Bullock, does she have to do this right now?"

"We're almost done," Bullock said. "Let me ask you ... how did Marcus and Damon get along?" After Michael recounted the wedding fiasco, the detective said, "Okay, that was about a year ago. I'm trying to figure out what happened that day ... from the time Marcus was at Reagan's house to the time that he came here and two people lost their lives. What happened after you told him you weren't having an abortion?"

Sniffling, Rea said, "Let's see ... uhh ... he grabbed me by the throat and slammed me against the wall. A little while after that, he left."

I sat on the floor, numb to what I had heard.

"You got off easy," the detective said. "He had a girlfriend about seven years ago who wasn't as lucky as you."

Mike and Reagan both said, "WHAT?"

"Marcus Day had two assault charges, and it appears he was a person of interest in a homicide case, but nothing ever stuck to him."

Silence laid over the room. Mike finally asked, "Why wasn't he locked up?"

"He had a history of mental illness, so we couldn't touch him. He had some sort of chemical imbalance. It's when you have extreme bouts with depression. Which really explains a lot."

Mike asked, "How so?"

"I got a call from forensics on my way over here … the gun Marcus used to kill himself was Damon's." Reagan said, "I don't understand what difference it makes whose gun he used."

"There wasn't another gun," Bullock said. "Marcus didn't come here with malicious intent. He drove all the way over here, thirty-seven miles without a gun, but somehow things got out of hand. Something is missing." I heard him get up to leave. "I'll be in touch."

I heard the door shut as he let himself out. Exiting through the living room, he never saw me sitting on the hallway floor. I sat there for a few more minutes, gathering my thoughts. A part of me felt as though I had no right to be upset about Reagan's relationship with Marcus. I was trying to get myself together to go into the kitchen when I heard Mike say, "Okay, what else happened?"

Rea sighed. "Mike, for months he was staying at my house. I gave and gave and gave, hoping he'd give me just a little bit of him. I think he thought the next best thing to being with DeLaina was being with me. It didn't bother me too much at first cuz … it was just sex. After a few months of him staying there, my feelings started to get involved. The other night when he said he loved DeLaina … I just got so upset—"

Mike interrupted, "You knew he still had feelings for DeLaina. Plus, you were sleeping with someone else."

"Yeah, I was only trying to make him jealous, but he didn't even notice. So when he said he loved her, I said, 'You're so stupid. Why would DeLaina want you when she's got all that man ova dar? I hope this baby ain't yours.' That's when he …"

She got quiet.

"He what?" Mike asked.

In a cracking voice, she said, "He flipped out. It was like watching David Banner turn into the Hulk. He drug me into the bathroom by my hair, mumbling. For real, I thought he was gonna kill me. He slammed my head against the mirror and yelled, 'Look at yourself. You too old to be this dumb.'" Rea started crying. "He said, 'You could never be DeLaina.'"

I got up and walked into the kitchen and silence took over the room. They both looked at me as though they were seeing a ghost. Reagan hung her head and said, "Good morning," in a solace-filled tone. Under ordinary circumstances, she'd throw her arms around me and ask if there was anything she could do. Apparently, she had done enough. Mike got up to make me a cup of tea.

"What were you saying Reagan?" I asked.

Shaking her head, she said, "It was nothing."

She sat at the kitchen table, staring hopelessly into a cup.

I leaned against the refrigerator. "Tell me about you and Marcus."

Mike placed the tea on the table, kissed me on the forehead, and said, "I'm gonna give you ladies some privacy."

Rea took a deep breath. "Laina, I'm sorry I ain't tell you about me and Marcus. It never seemed like the right time ..."

I folded my arms, thinking, It was never gonna be the right time. I tried to remain calm. I insisted it wasn't that I was angry ... I was hurt. Which wasn't true. I was hurt but I was also hot as fire. Of course a part of me still loved Marcus. A little less than a year ago, I was planning to spend the rest of my life with him.

"Why him, Rea?" I asked.

Her tone changed. "You think you're the only one that wanna be happy? I didn't plan it, Laina. After the wedding, he was a wreck."

It felt weird to hear her talk about my ex like she knew him. I guess she did—I'd told her everything.

"He needed someone and I had just broken up with D'Sean," Rea said. "I don't know ... somewhere down the line, I fell in love with him. I wanted to tell you that I did ... and the one day I decided to tell you ... you were all excited about your engagement and I couldn't get a word in."

"Oh, I see. Now, was this before or after you started screwing him?"

She sighed and looked away.

"You're so full of it!" I said. "Let me just make sure I'm clear ... Since I didn't let you tell me that day, then that made it okay for you to sleep with my ex. You know, it's just like you to try to blame someone else for what you did. Whether you had talked to me or not, you would have done whatever Reagan wanted to do. You completely disrespected me and our friendship."

Every group of girlfriends has its own code of ethics. But the number one rule that translates in any language is: you don't have dealings in any sense of the word with your girls' ex-boyfriend, ex-lover, or anyone she has/had an affinity for without prior approval.

I sat there, befuddled, recounting each time Rea told me in my relationship with Marcus that I deserved better, that Marcus wasn't man enough for me. It was never about me. True, Marcus had his share of issues, but maybe I would have tried harder, stayed home more. There's no telling what would have happened had she not been in my ear with her own agenda.

I had sat in that hospital with Reagan, disconcerted, replaying the suicide, both in my mind and aloud. I kept thinking, *Why would Marcus do this?* Not once did she cop to her relationship with him. I guess that's what she meant when she said, "What have I done?"

Nothing made sense then—and it still didn't. I had more questions than answers.

The next half hour passed without a word. Finally, Rea said, "Laina, just talk to me."

So I asked, "Were you sleeping with Marcus when he and I were together?"

She got quiet.

"You wanted to talk," I said. "So talk."

"Don't ask a question you don't really want to know the answer to."

"I wanna know."

She slowly nodded her head yes. "Once or twice, but it was strictly sex back then." She let those words breeze through her teeth and past her lips like that made it okay … like she just gave clarity to the laws of physics.

I shook my head in disbelief. I was feeling the same sense of betrayal that I'd felt the day I found out Ricky killed Trey.

I was so angry that my head began to pound and I couldn't speak. I grabbed my cup and went back upstairs. I laid there about an hour with my mind racing a mile a minute, thinking how I had trusted her, how she was like the sister I never had.

Another hour or so passed before I got up and went downstairs for more tea. When I got down there, she was still sitting at the kitchen table. As I stared at her, I couldn't help but feel as though our entire relationship had been a lie. All the while that she was smiling, hugging me, patting me on the back, she was just feeling for a soft spot to stick the knife in. I wondered how many other times she'd raped my trust. Standing at the island, pouring the tea, I asked, "How many others were there?"

She lifted her head from the table as I asked, "What about Darrell?"

"No!"

"Alonzo?"

"No!"

"Reggie?"

"No!"

From the den, Michael yelled, "Ronny, Bobby, Ricky, Mike?"

I stood at the island, gripping the corners, trying to hold on to a piece of my sanity. She got up to get water as I was trying to come to grips with my best friend playing "dress up" in my life.

She wiped her hands on the dish towel. "What about Damon?" she asked.

I glared at her. If looks could kill … "What about him?"

"You didn't ask about Damon."

My mouth dropped open. I couldn't believe that she said that … that she'd be so cold as to speak of him. "Trick, I don't have to," I said. "Damon wouldn't sleep with you!"

She sucked her teeth. "At the end of the day, he was just a man. Under the right circumstances …"

At the insinuation of her with my fiancé, she became just some random chick. The smug look on her face caused an out-of-body experience. It was like I was watching myself momentarily trying to talk me out of lodging the butcher knife sitting on the counter into the place in her chest where her heart should be.

As a consequence, I reached back to when

Marcus and I were dating, pushed forward to all the times she told me he didn't deserve me, pushed through all the betrayal, then reached across the island and planted my fist on the side of her mouth. I raced over, grabbed her by the throat, and squeezed. As her face began to turn red, she pawed at my hands, but I wouldn't let go. Hearing all the commotion, Michael ran in and pulled me off of her.

Although she stood there bleeding and gasping for air, I felt unfulfilled. I thought hitting her would ease the pain of betrayal. I thought it would somehow dim the thought of what she had done, but it didn't.

As Mike dabbed the blood on her face with the dishtowel, she said, "I guess I deserved that."

"Oh, don't worry—trust me, you gonna get what you deserve." I paced the floor. "Marcus was unstable, and you would've known that if you had gotten off of him long enough to think about someone other than yourself."

She attempted to plead her case: "Laina, for real, it wasn't like that." She paused for a moment. "He was … I mean, I tried to love him … but he …"

With a scornful look, I said, "Save it! What the both of you know about love could fit in a thimble."

I paced the floor, trying to regroup, trying to suppress the urge to stomp a mud hole in her.

The doorbell rang. Mike told me to go get the door, no doubt afraid to leave us alone.

I opened the door to see that it was Detective Bullock again. Before I could say a word, he said, "I'm sorry to disturb you, Ms. Richards. Is Ms. Mitchell still here?"

I opened the door wider and pointed toward the kitchen.

Entering the kitchen, the detective said, "Ms. Mitchell, can you come down to the station so we can further discuss this case."

"Can we just do it here?" she asked.

He looked around the room. "Okay. What did you say the name of the other possible father was?"

"I didn't."

"Why won't you tell me?"

"That's none of your business. Look, what is this about?"

"Something has been bothering me since I left here earlier. Let me tell you what I think happened. Marcus told you he still loved DeLaina and you weren't good enough to carry his baby." He shook his head. "And after everything you had done for him, you had to be mad. I think he knew who the other potential father was. That's how he ended up over here. Not to confront Damon … because let's be honest: he didn't care about you that much. He came to tell DeLaina about you and Damon. Does that sound about right?"

"You have got to be kidding!" I shouted. When he said "Damon," it felt like my insides turned inside out. I loved and trusted Damon in a way I had never loved or trusted a man before. I couldn't fathom him betraying that trust. Trying to stay calm, I said, "That's not possible!"

Michael backed away from Rea as she stood there silent.

"I checked your phone records," the detective said to Rea. "You sure did call Damon a lot." He flipped through the pages of his little notepad. "You even called him the day he was shot."

I looked at her stomach. "Who's the father?" I demanded.

She didn't respond.

I walked up to her. "Were you sleeping with Damon?"

Mike attempted to separate us, but the detective held him back. Reagan didn't respond; she just stood there with that silly look on her face.

At that moment, I felt hatred covering my toes, creeping up my legs and my thighs like a second skin. Something in me snapped. "ANSWER ME!" I yelled.

She didn't blink.

I clinched my fist and started swinging with my right, yelling, "Answer me, answer me!" until the detective pulled me off her. In a faint voice with blood dripping from her nose and her lips, she said "No."

That's what I wanted to hear, but something in me didn't believe her.

Barely able to catch my breath, I took a step back. "Get out!"

"Yes, Ms. Mitchell, I think you should leave" the detective said.

"No, you, too, Columbo … get out. Now!"

As Detective Bullock walked toward the door, he said, "Again, I'm sorry for your loss."

He stopped, though, when Rea insisted we needed to finish this conversation. She folded her arms and stood there with her feet firmly planted on the floor like her name was on the deed.

"Oh yeah," I said. "Stay right there."

I went to the hallway closet, ranting, "Oh, this trick is trippin'."

I grabbed Damon's steel baseball bat, went back to where Rea stood, and pointed the bat at the front door like Jackie Robinson pointing toward the outfield.

"One …" I said.

"Lainee," Mike said, trying to calm me, "please put the—"

"Two!"

"Put the bat down, Ms. Richards," Detective

Bullock said.

As I walked toward Rea with the bat positioned to swing, Mike stood in front of her, imploring me to stop. "Lainee, you have to calm down."

Rea tried to step around him, but he kept pulling her back. So she yelled around him, "I'm sorry, DeLaina. I didn't mean for any of this to happen."

I was so angry. With tears in my eyes, I said, "I believe you. But what do I know? I believed you were my friend."

"DeLaina, I am your friend."

Laughing, I said, "I'd hate to see what you do to your enemies."

Rea and I had been friends for fourteen years. If anyone ever said she'd betray me, I wouldn't have believed it. A true friend is as rare as a virgin on a wedding night, but not unheard of.

It was her conniving, selfish antics that played a role in Marcus showing up at the house. She might as well have pulled the trigger herself.

Damon's Funeral

I had always believed that everything that happens, happens for a reason … until I lost Damon. Nothing made sense. The morning of the funeral, I laid in the fetal position, waiting to give birth to understanding. As a rush of emotions came over me, I clutched the tear-stained pillow that still smelled like Damon. I laid there remembering every laugh, every kiss, every smile, and every touch.

Mike knocked on the room door, saying, "Someone's here to see you."

Sniffling, I yelled back. "I don't want to see anyone. I'm not going."

He came in, sat on the bed, and said, "Lainee, there are a lot of people downstairs that came to support you." He rubbed my head. "No one can make you go, but I think you should be there. You deserve the opportunity to say good-bye properly."

After giving some thought to his words, I got up and showered, preparing for the worst day of my life. Preparing to say good-bye to the only bit of real unadulterated happiness I could clearly recall.

Damon's mother asked if it would be okay if the funeral cars picked everyone up from our house ... Damon's house. How could I refuse.

Once his family began to arrive, a calm came over me. I felt some sense of peace being around people who loved him as much and I did. The first time I spoke to Mr. and Mrs. Montgomery on the phone was the day Damon asked me to marry him. Although we'd never met face-to-face, his mother and I shared conversations as if I sat at her dinner table every Sunday afternoon. When her foot touched the foundation of her son's house, for the first time her eyes bounced from ceiling to floor, wall to wall, person to person, until she laid eyes on me. She walked toward me, leaning her head slightly to the right, the way Damon did. She put her arms around me and held me like I was one of her very own, whispering, *"There's nothing God can't handle."*

Mr. Montgomery introduced himself with a warm embrace. He stepped aside and introduced their eldest son, Meyer, and his girlfriend, Candice. Meyer and I had spoken on the phone only a couple times. He only called when he needed something.

Mrs. Montgomery said, almost in a comforting tone, "Dion should be here any minute. When I spoke with him, he said that he and Shawn had just gotten into town and they were coming off of I-95. I thought they'd beat us here."

There was a light tap at the door. As it opened, there was a collective gasp for air in the room. As I turned around, there he was. My heart began pounding as I covered my mouth with a faint, "Oh my God!" I had forgotten until that very moment that Damon had a twin. We spoke at least twice a week, but had never met face-to-face.

"This is my other son, Dion, and his girlfriend, Shawn." Holding his hand, Mrs. Montgomery introduced him to everyone by name. Once she got to me, she said, "And, of course, this is DeLaina."

I stared at Dion like he was my wish come true … my *If I could just hold him once more*. Looking him over from head to toe, I could see that they were almost identical. I noticed that Dion had more freckles on his nose and a scar on the left side of his neck. I wanted to touch him, to hold him. I fought the urge to wrap my arms around him until I couldn't fight it anymore. He wrapped his forearm around my neck, pulling me in closer, the way Damon used to. My knees buckled, and I moaned a sound I'd never heard come from my body.

Dion's presence increased the hurt. Shaking his head, Mr. Montgomery tried to hold it together for the family. As he visibly became unglued, he got up and headed toward the kitchen, but as he neared Dion, he stopped alongside him. Seemingly unable to look at him, he rested his hand on his shoulder briefly as he passed through the hallway. Meyer joined in the hug with one arm around me and the other around his brother. Paige and Mrs. Montgomery began praying as Shawn sang, "Somebody needs you, Lord, come by here. Somebody needs you, Lord, come by here. Somebody needs you, Lord, come by here. Oh Lord, come by here."

Once we arrived at the church, Mike sat behind me with his hand on my shoulder the entire time. I sat in the front pew with Paige flanked to my left. Damon's brothers, Dion and Meyer, sat on the right beside their mother and father. I remember feeling that this couldn't be happening.

Damon's friend, Frank, gave the eulogy, and his eldest brother said a few words. I was so lost in my own emotions. I was asked to speak but didn't know if I'd have the strength to do so. After Meyer's final words, he looked in my direction and asked, "DeLaina, would you like to add anything?" Hesitantly, I nodded yes. The night before, I'd written a few lines trying to capture what our relationship meant.

I grabbed my little journal and walked toward the casket, eager to see him one last time. Staring at his motionless body, I fought back the tears as I thought of all the things we didn't get a chance to do, all the things I didn't get a chance to say. I adjusted his necktie, brushed the lint from his lapel, and whispered, "You look handsome," as I pressed my lips firmly against his cold face.

I stood on the altar, looking down into the casket, and said, "I guess I should consider myself lucky to have experienced a love that most can only imagine." Remembering all the things he taught me, I got choked up and mumbled, "I'm a better woman for having loved you." I took a deep breath and spoke over the podium. "I could stand here and tell you all that Damon was my best friend, but if you never saw us together, you can't understand the extent of our love." I chuckled as I remembered his smile. Making eye contact with Mike, I said, "After Damon asked me to marry him, I asked, 'Why me?' He said, 'Because you're the best thing since red Kool-Aid.'"

I heard laughs from the pews.

With my journal in hand, I peered down into

the open casket and spoke directly to him. "It's so hard to believe that the best thing that'll ever happen to me already has." My arms began trembling. "Before I met you, love was just a word ... but you ... you gave it meaning ... my life meaning. If I could have chosen my family ... I would have picked you ..." The tears blurred my vision as I continued. "I would have given up the chance to be your wife if I knew it meant I'd always have you in my life." As the rush of emotions took over, I moaned, "I can't imagine walking for the rest of my life."

After the Funeral

After the funeral, everyone returned to the house to pay their respects to the family. Within moments of our arrival, the house was jammed packed. I shuffled from room to room, trying to be alone, but found myself accepting condolences. It proved to be more than I could handle, so I went on the deck for some air. I stood at the railing, looking over the side at a group of the guys drinking and laughing like it was an annual cookout. I yelled, "What's the joke? I could use a laugh."

As Dion stepped out onto the deck, someone explained, "We meant no disrespect. We were just remembering the good times."

Dion gave the head nod to the fellas and told

me, "We all miss him. We just express it differently." I couldn't help but think, *That sounds like something Damon would say.*

He sighed. "I had never seen my brother so in love." I smiled as he said, "We're here if you need anything; you're family, DeLaina."

The next day, I didn't leave my room. I just laid there, listening to my heart beat. It wasn't the same. The following evening, Dion dropped by. As I opened the door, he said, "I didn't know where else to go." I opened the door wide and gestured for him to come on in.

He went into the den and sat on the edge of the sofa. He confided that he'd been driving around all day but spent the last two hours at the cemetery. He said it just didn't seem real. Dion told me stories about him, Damon, and Meyer getting into trouble as kids.

I got up, determined to pull myself together, and offered, "You want some tea?"

"Got anything stronger?"

Two hours and five Crown & Cokes later, my thirst still hadn't been quenched. As I turned the glass up to get the last drop, I said, "It's your turn to make the drinks." He got up without a problem and headed toward the kitchen. I staggered behind him and hopped up on the counter. After pulling out every liquor bottle under the cabinet, he stood over the sink and began mixing a concoction with lemon juice, orange juice, peach schnapps, amaretto, and sprite. After pouring a glass, he tried to coax me into tasting it. He approached me swirling the alcohol around in a rock glass, trying to get me to take it. I balled up my lips like a four-year-old and shook my head no. He stood between my legs and gently placed the ridge of the glass to my lips. In a soft, sensual voice, he said, "Taste it."

Never taking my eyes off him, I loosened my lips and tilted my head back as he poured it into my mouth. The phone rang. Never losing eye contact, I ignored it. As the answering machine picked up, he moved the glass from my lips and moved in slow like he had next. I was centimeters away from his mouth; I could feel the heat of his breath on my face when the voice on the answering machine said, "DeLaina, this is Mrs. Montgomery." I nervously pulled back like she could see us. "Shawn just called and said she hadn't seen Dion all day." Her tone changed as she said, "TELL HIM TO CALL ME." There was a pause, before she continued, "If you see him."

As she hung up, we looked at one another, uneasy, then looked away. The message was sobering; I jumped down off the counter and stood with the island between us. I wanted to apologize and tell him that he reminded me of Damon, that I just wanted to be close to him but I was too embarrassed to say a word. I

Change Is a-Coming

The Past Is Gone

Before she left town, Mrs. Montgomery stopped by to say good-bye and to see if I was interested in buying the house. Although I continued maintaining my condo, after I broke up with Marcus, I unofficially moved into Damon's house. I eagerly said yes as if to say Of course. I thought if I could hold on to the tangible memories, I still had a part of him.

Every inch of that house reminded me of him. In a mournful effort to feel him near, I stayed in the house with the blinds drawn, phones unplugged, nearly drowning myself in the memories.

Crying day in and out ... I completely shut down.

Mike stayed over to keep an eye on me. After a week of me not saying a word, he called Paige.

I heard him tell her, "She just sits in the closet crying. I'm worried about her. She won't eat, and if she does, she can't keep it down."

In his concern, Mike gave Tracey his key and asked her to stop by. She let herself in, came upstairs, and knocked on the bedroom door.

"DeLaina, it's me … Tracey."

I laid there for a moment, trying to get the energy to get up. I felt so weak. She turned the knob to find it was locked and knocked again.

I sat up on the side of the bed. "I'm coming."

I sat there trying to muster up the energy to get to the door. As I opened it, she hugged me, asking if I was okay. Walking back to the bed nodding my head yes, Tracey yelled, "Your pants!"

Eager to lie back down, I ignored her. As I leaned forward to crawl back into bed, I noticed the blood soaked sheets. I looked down at my saturated pants and began to panic, hyperventilating.

Tracy told me to sit down and take deep breaths. She grabbed the afghan resting on the chaise and wrapped it around me. After insisting we had to go, she slipped my flip-flops on my feet and got me down the steps and out to her car. She grabbed a T-shirt from her backseat and put it on the passenger seat for me to sit on. As she fastened her seat belt, she called the hospital and said, "This is Dr. Willard. I'm about fifteen minutes away with a thirty-one-year-old black female. Five-seven, about 145 pounds. She lost a lot of blood. Without an examination, it appears to be vaginally."

As she ran through red lights, cutting people off, she told me, "Everything is going to be just fine."

I must have blacked out at some point, because the next thing I knew, a nurse was hooking me up to an IV and the attending physician was walking into the room. The first question he asked was, "When was the first day of your last period?"

I thought for a moment and realized I had no clue. I shook my head. "I don't know."

Trying to jog my memory, he asked, "Did you have one this month, or was it last month?"

"I don't know."

After a vaginal exam, the doctor ordered an ultrasound, which showed two empty sacks. The doctor explained "Ms. Richards, there's some scar tissue in and around the reproductive organs. Extensive scaring like this, is commonly seen with abrasive abortions." I asked Tracey, "What is he talking about?"

She stared at me for a moment as if she was hesitant to translate. I took a deep breath and told her, "Tell me already. It can't get any worse."

She said, "You miscarried … twins."

I guess I was wrong.

I never knew you could miss so significantly what you never knew you had.

Once I was finally discharged, Mike stayed at the house to take care of me. He didn't realize I just wanted to be alone, or maybe he did and was afraid of what that may have meant.

I went back to spending time in the walk-in closet; Damon's scent was strongest there. I'd lie there and imagine what the twins would have looked like and the type of parents we would have been. I imagined it would have been twin girls. He probably would have wanted to name them something like April and May. They would have been beautiful … probably tall like him with olive-colored skin and that beautiful Montgomery smile.

I missed him so much. I kept his cell phone activated so I could call and hear his voice whenever I wanted to: *You've reached Damon Montgomery. I'm sorry I'm not available to take your call right now. Please leave a message and I'll return your call at my earliest convenience.*

After a few weeks of Mike asking "How you feeling today?" and telling me "You need to eat something," I made him go home. I should have taken his key. He stopped over every morning on his way to work to make coffee, claiming his coffee maker was broken. Mind you, there were at least two coffee shops between our houses, but whatever.

***

The lonelier I felt, the more unbearable the pain became. Several weeks into my depression, I called one of my old contacts like I'd call Domino's—to have some "pain relievers" delivered. Before I knew it, I was smoking my days away. After awhile, the days just seem to blend into one another.

One day, Ma Mitchell showed up at the house unannounced. The anger that I felt for Reagan … I had to fight with myself not to project it onto everyone associated with her. After she came in and sat down, I offered her some tea.

She declined and said, "You look well. How you holding up, baby?"

"I'm here."

She moved closer and put her hand on my knee. "Rea's having a very difficult time. She could really use a friend."

"Good luck finding one."

Inspite of the coconut rum in my tea I thought to myself, *I'm far too sober for this.* As I cut my eyes at her, my heart rate increased and I realized at that moment that she didn't come to comfort me but to seek comfort for Reagan. I was trying to understand how she could ask me to talk to Reagan, like her hurt was more severe or more significant than mine.

She sat closer to the edge of the couch, turned toward me, and said, "Rea's been hospitalized twice with the threat of miscarrying."

As I thought about the babies I'd lost, my eyes watered. "She put on a pair of shoes that were too big for her." I stood up. "Let her wear 'um."

I pulled away as she reached for me. "Laina, haven't you ever done anything you wished you could take back?"

"Yeah, befriending your daughter." I reached my level of frustration. I picked up my cup of tea and headed toward the steps. As I neared the top step, I stopped as she said, "Judge not lest ye be judged."

"Oh yeah? The Bible also says knock and the door shall be opened." I knocked on the wall twice—knock, knock. "GET OUT!"

I didn't realize how much anger I was actually harboring. In my heart, I still believed that she was the reason for Damon's death, so the very mention of Reagan's name caused a chain reaction of emotions, resulting in the change of my demeanor.

That very same anger prevented me from mourning Marcus's death.

***

A month or so later, in an effort to remind me I wasn't alone, Mike and Paige came up with the bright idea to have a small dinner party at Damon's house. Missing so intensely the one I loved left me with a lonely feeling even amongst the crowd. There could have been a thousand people there; it wouldn't have mattered. I just wanted to go upstairs and be alone with my memories.

Everyone trying to coddle me certainly didn't help, but I forced myself to stay downstairs to join the party.

As Paige started a pot of coffee, I went into the den, sat on the sofa, and remembered the last time Damon and I were in that room together. I smiled to myself and held my head with my hand as the memories took over. I overheard Tracey and Mike bickering back and forth. She insisted on checking on me even after he told her to just give me some space. She came into the den, sat beside me, and said, "It's gonna be okay."

I shook my head. "That's just something that people say."

"No, I know how you feel. It'll be okay."

"No, you don't! Sleeping with Michael doesn't mean you know what it's like to walk a mile in my shoes. Do you know what it's like living your entire life afraid of being abandoned, confused about who you are? Do you know what that's like?" She shook her head no. "Do you know what it feels like to lose the love of your life? We ain't break up … he's dead.

You talk to me when you lose a fiancé … and twins." I noticed Mike standing by the entrance way with an I told you so look on his face.

Tracey tried to fix it by saying, "DeLaina, I'm sorry … I …."

I pushed past her, grabbing my keys and mumbling, "I'm tired of everybody trying to act like they know how I feel."

Paige tried to stop me as I stormed out, slamming the door. In a calm voice, Mike said, "Let her go."

I drove around for hours with my mind racing. Still full of thoughts, I ended up at the condo. As I cleared the threshold, I was immediately drawn to the box of pictures on the shelf in my closet. I stood on the tip of my toes trying to reach the box. It was so far back that I was unable to grab it with both hands. While still on my toes, with one hand I pulled it closer and closer a little bit at a time until it reached the edge. Still on my toes, I reached up with both hands; the box was a lot heavier than I remembered. I lost my balance and the box toppled over, spilling pictures everywhere. As I kneeled down to pick them up, my eyes focused in on a picture of me and Trey at the carnival about sixteen years ago.

Then, it came to me: "It's me," I whispered.

It seemed that every man who loved me paid

the ultimate price.

There was a knock at the door. I tried to ignore it until a voice said, "I see your car. I know you're here." It was Paige.

Then another voice said, "Open this cotton-pickin' door! It's dark and cold as hell out here." Mona. Without eye contact or a word spoken, I unlocked the door and went back to my closet.

Moments later, Paige found me sitting on the floor in the closet, crying with the pictures scattered around me. She sat down Indian-style in front of me and wiped underneath my eyes with her thumb. In the most caring voice, she said, "The company was a bit much for you tonight, huh?"

"It's my fault Marcus killed Damon."

"We've been over this … it's not your fault"

Mona walked into the room, threw her bag on the chair, and said, "Naw, it ain't your fault. Dat boy was crazy!" Mona placed her hand on her hip. "How crazy you gotta be to take your own life?"

I looked at her with an If you only knew look. "When men love me, they die," I said.

"DeLaina, what are you talking about?" Paige asked.

I picked up one of pictures from over a decade ago and said, "Trey died too."

She turned her head sideways in confusion.

I explained that Trey was the first boy that ever cared about me. "He lost his life too. Am I cursed?"

Without hesitation, Paige began to plead the blood of Jesus. She got up and ran out to the car. She came back with her big, tan Coach bag, quoting the twenty-third Psalms: "Yea, though I walk through the valley of the shadow of death, I will fear no evil: for thou art with me."

As she finished the quote, she took out her Bible and opened it up. She reached back into her purse, got the holy oil, and poured it in the palm of her left hand, then began rubbing her hands together.

"Um, the blood of Jesus. Laina, let me get this straight. The enemy has been after you for over a decade, but since he can't kill you … hallelujah! He gets the ones closest to you! DeLaina, he can't kill your body, so he's trying to kill your spirit! Can you imagine the call and purpose on your life that the enemy is trying to kill you?" I got up and stood in the corner as she began walking through the house, touching the doorways and windows. "God has given you an anointing that has the enemy scared. Every time he tries to kill you, God is telling death to behave. Hallelujah!"

She took my hands, but I snatched them away. It all seemed a little spooky.

With her hands out, she said, "Let's pray."

"I'm standing here with pictures of dead men

around me ... I don't quite feel like prayin'."

"But you're standing. Pray with me."

I shook my head. "No!"

I remembered seeing Mommy lay hands and pray for people, but I didn't understand it. I went to church, but I never really had a real relationship with God. So, to be honest, I was scared.

Paige stared at me several minutes before saying a word. She paced the floor with her hands lifted, pleading the blood of Jesus and singing hallelujah.

When she stopped, she grabbed both my hands and said, "Father God, in the name of Jesus, first and foremost I want to thank you for being God and God alone. Lord, I want to thank you for another day. I wanna thank you for all the blessings seen and unseen. Lord, without you, we're nothing. Lord, I'm not coming to you for me. God, I'm standing in the gap for my sister. Lord, she's been under attack for years, and I want to thank you for making death behave. Thank you for being her rod and her shield. Thank you for your hedge fence of protection. Lord, I dare not question your will, but pray that thy will be done on earth as it is in heaven. Lord, you said if two or more come together in agreement, it shall be done. She's feeling alone and lonely. In Hebrews, you said, 'I will never leave nor forsake you.' Lord, I'm praying that she's able to feel your presence. Be a fence all around her. Be her comforter. I'm praying that you correct her vision, Lord God, so that she may see you. Give her a miracle ear so that she can hear you clearly, God. Lord, she's in so much pain. I pray that you mend her broken heart and give her peace of mind. Lord, restore her spirit so that she knows that, with you, all things are possible. We declare and decree that it's already done. In Jesus' name. Amen and amen."

As the words of her prayer resonated in my spirit, I cried out.

She rocked me. "You've let so many people into your heart, undeserving. Laina, I believe God had to break your heart so that it could be rebuilt in him."

I heard what she was saying, but it sound so unreal. Why would he want to rebuild my heart?

The next two days were the first bit of peace I'd had since the ordeal. Life was starting to feel okay again. Then, one evening, I was at the light on Main Street when I saw Dion going into The Coffee House. I thought to myself, *He didn't tell me he was coming to town.* I was pulling over to park when he came out with his arm around someone who wasn't Shawn.

I held my head out the window and yelled his name as they crossed the street. "Dion!"

He looked at me like a deer caught in headlights. He gave her the keys to his car as he walked over to me. As I got out the car, I could tell something was wrong.

He had that same look in his eyes that Damon use to have when he was hiding something.

I hugged him. "You didn't tell me you'd be in town. I would have cooked you dinner or something."

He looked back at the car. "I'm only in town for the day."

"Where's Shawn?"

"She's home."

"Okay, you're acting weird. What are you doing here?"

He looked uncomfortable. "I'm here for the DNA test."

"What are you talking about? What DNA test?"

"To see if the baby is Damon's."

"WHAT! What baby?"

In a low tone, he said, "Reagan's baby."

I backed against the car. "You joking right! This is … You joking, right?"

He stood there with his eyes closed.

With tears streaming down my face, I asked, "It was true?"

He didn't respond.

I pushed him in the chest with both hands, yelling, "Why didn't you tell me? I asked you! I asked you at the funeral and you told me no." Sniffling, I recalled the conversation, saying, "You said, 'No, Damon wouldn't sleep with that girl. She's lying.' You knew he was sleeping with her!" I began to curse.

In his attempt to nullify the situation, he said, "He told me it only happened once."

I stood there in tears, more confused than ever. Did Damon ever really love me? How did this happen? I thought our relationship was perfect. Dion tried to hug me, but I pulled away, cursing. "You're no better than he was. I guess Shawn thinks you're here alone."

He looked down as he said, "Look, I didn't want to be the one to tell you. In fact, I hoped you'd never find out."

The woman sitting in his car blew the horn. As he looked back to acknowledge her, he said, "I gotta go, Laina." As he backed away, he said, "None of this changes things; my brother loved you."

He was wrong. It did change things. In the moment I stood outside speaking with Dion, Damon tittered over and came crashing down from the pedestal I'd placed him upon. He was no longer this amazing man who could do no wrong. Our entire relationship fell to the ground and broke into a million pieces.

Out of Control

My anger with Reagan engulfed me all over again. Over the next several months, things spiraled out of control. I felt powerless, which took my level of anger to new heights. Constantly misdirecting my rage, as I wasn't able to release my frustrations on the one that inflicted the pain I was left to deal with.

I was left to question every memory, wondering if there was a lie hidden in there I had overlooked. I wondered if Reagan was the only one Damon slept with. I began to torture myself with "What if" questions that I'd probably never know the answer to.

I was on a clear path of destruction, drinking my breakfast and smoking my dinner.

Getting to work just before noon—the days

I'd show up—I'd sit in my eighth-floor office with a panoramic view of the city and wonder how long it would take me to hit the ground. Some days, I'd sit there for hours imagining all my pain and memories taking flight as my body rushed toward the ground. As long as I was high or drunk, I was numb to the pain and didn't have to deal with it. It went on and on for months. I tried to hide it at first, gargling and febrezing my clothes. After a while, I stop caring who knew. That's about the time my boss insisted I take a leave of absence, promising my job would be there when I returned.

Sitting at my desk, I reached into my past and called Darrell. I wanted to see a familiar face. I mentioned to him that I'd been through a rough time and just wanted to be held. He gave me directions to his place, which turned out to be a waterfront apartment overlooking the Baltimore Harbor. I didn't inquire about what he was doing with his life, but from the size of the loft, he was doing okay.

Before he could offer me a drink or take my jacket, I asked, "Did you sleep with Reagan?"

"Who? Your girl?"

Before he could say another word, I explained, "Look, I promise I won't be mad. It's been years. I just need to know."

"Naw, Laina, I didn't sleep with your girl."

"Seriously, I won't be mad."

"Laina, naw. Did she say we slept together?"

"No."

I didn't have the desire to regurgitate what was going on. I just wanted to pretend for one night that my life didn't exist. Although he pried, I reiterated, "I don't want to talk about it."

The next morning when I woke up, I popped up, anxiously looking around, unaware of my surroundings until I remembered I was at Darrell's. Still fully clothed, I sat on the side of the California king-size bed, inhaling the scent of freshly brewed coffee.

He came in, handed me a cup, and said, "I have to get to a meeting, but I'll be back in a couple hours if you want to stay."

"No, I'm gonna go."

That was the first time he'd actually felt like a friend.

Sobering

I sobered up the night I left Frisco's with some guy I didn't know. He and I had been talking and drinking for several hours. As the night came to a close, I realized, like many nights, I was too drunk to drive home. I usually just slept in the parking lot, in my car. The guy of course offered to take me home and I let him. When he pulled up to my house, I thanked him and said good night. I remember standing outside the front door, fumbling for the keys, when he came up behind me and said, "Let me get that for you." That's all I can recall of that night.

The next morning, I don't know if it was the sunlight or the thumping of my head that woke me up. I held my head up to see the clock; it was 9:48. When

I turned my head, away from the window, I screamed and hopped out of bed—it was the man from the bar. Realizing I was naked, I quickly snatched the blanket off the bed. Confused, I asked, "How did you get in here?"

He got up, wrapped the sheet around his waist, and said, "What are you talking about? You let me in."

"I couldn't have!"

He recounted the evening, saying after he helped me unlock the door, I invited him in and started kissing him.

I interrupted, "Did we ..."

Proudly, he said, "Yeah, we made love."

"Made love? What are you, a girl? You acting like we in a relationship. I don't even know your name."

In an effort to calm me, he said, "My name is—"

"Look!" I interrupted. "I don't care! Put your clothes on and get out!"

I folded my arms and shook my head in disbelief. I didn't know if he slipped something in my drink—if he raped me or if I was really that far gone. As I watched him put his clothes on, I grew angrier. Not with the stranger ... with me.

After he left, I went back upstairs in an effort to destroy any evidence or memory of my actions. I stripped the sheets, febrezed and flipped the mattress.

As I bent over to uncoil the vacuum cord, I noticed an empty condom wrapper. I went to the bathroom to get a piece of tissue to pick it up when I caught a glare of something shiny. I got on the floor to see what it was. There was glass on the floor, but it seemed to be contained to just that corner. I checked the dresser and the nightstand. Nothing. I stood in the middle of the room trying desperately to remember what happened the night before. I couldn't. I picked up the big pieces of glass and prepared to vacuum. When I moved the nightstand, I found the culprit. The glass came from the frame I'd taken Damon's picture out of. It must have gotten knocked over somehow. My stomach tightened as I picked up the empty frame. In spite of what Damon had done, I felt as though I had desecrated our room, the house.

Realizing that last night could have ended a million different ways, I sat on the floor rocking, thinking how I could have been raped, killed—anything could have happened. I was disappointed in myself. I didn't know what had become of me.

In my younger days, sure, I'd taken guys home from the club. I had my share of one-night stands. Back then, I went into the situation knowing what I was getting into. Even though I felt raped, I had no one to blame but myself. I knew I was drunk, but as usual I just kept drinking.

After I finished cleaning, I stood in the shower, crying, trying to figure out what happened to me. I got out the shower and laid on the bed with the towel wrapped around me, but I couldn't get comfortable. I dried off, put on a T-shirt and some panties, and laid back down. I didn't know if it was my sense of guilt or the disappointment I had in myself.

After about an hour of lying there, I began to smell the man from the bar. I got up, packed a bag, and went to the condo.

The first thing I did after walking in the door was pour a shot of Crown to calm my nerves, but as I put it up to my lips, the night before flickered through my mind. I could see him touching and kissing me as I laid there. I hurled the glass against the wall, hoping to shatter the memory.

I grabbed the scissors from the desk drawer in the den and went into the bathroom. I just wanted all of the pain to end. I got in and laid back in the empty cold tub. I was tired of being tired. As I laid there, reliving the pain, the tears rolled from the corners of my eyes. Feeling angry and helpless, I held the scissors tight with both hands, fighting through thoughts of thrusting them into my stomach.

I sat up in the tub and grabbed a fist full of the hair that hung just below my shoulders and began cutting. The hair fell all around me, as did the tears. I didn't stop until I was covered in hair. I was unknowingly trying to assert some sense of control in my life through the strands scattered about in the tub and on the floor. I just wanted my life back.

I Ain't Ready

My cell phone rang the following Sunday morning around seven. It broke my sleep, but I tried to ignore it, hoping it would stop. It did, but only for it to start again.

I grab it and answered angrily, "HELLOO!"

It was Paige. With no hello, she said, "Where are you? I've been calling the house."

I said, "At the condo," and hung up.

She called right back, and without me saying hello, she said, "I'll be there around ten."

In an Asian accent, I said, "Wrong-a-numba. No call back. She-a no live here." I refused to entertain the only reason she'd be calling me that time of the morning.

Without skipping a beat, she said, "You need

Jesus. You got an appointment at ten," and hung up. I pulled the phone back slowly from my face mumbling, "She ain't my momma."

About 8:50, there was a knock at the door.

I sat up in the bed and said out loud, "You have gotta be kidding!" I got up and looked through the peephole; it was Paige. "Seriously, not today, Paige."

"You do know I have a key, right?"

I sighed and opened the door. She walked in, placed coffee and muffins on the cocktail table, and looked around the room. When she finally turned and looked at me with my back against the door, she said, "What happened to your hair?"

I ran my hand over it. "I cut it."

"I see that! Is … there a reason why?"

"Did you really come over here to give me beauty tips?"

She laughed. "No, I came to take you to church."

"I know you mean well, but I ain't ready."

"What does that mean?"

"What does it mean?" I laughed sarcastically. "You didn't ask me why I'm at the condo—"

"It doesn't matter where you are. What matters is where you're going."

"Okay, Paige, for real with the optimism and the Chinese proverbs. I'm not up for this today!"

With a half smile, she said, "I want you to come with me to church. I'm not asking you to join … I'm not asking you to sing when the choir sings … I'm just asking you to come with me."

"I'm not ready. I gotta get myself together."

"Together? Tell me when you think you'll be good enough for God?"

"Look, Paige, I respect your relationship with God, but I not trying to hear all that." I sat down on the sofa thinking of everything that happened in the past two years, trying to remember when DeLaina officially left the building.

Paige sat beside me. "I'm sorry. I just want Laina back." I curled up like a little kid and laid my head on her lap as she said, "I miss her."

I laid there for a moment before saying, "Me, too."

She took a deep breath and confessed that Arlen, her son's father, didn't leave her a "Dear Jane" letter. She gave me the sordid details about walking in on him and his boy. I never told her that I already knew. I just let her tell the story her way.

"After Arlen," she said, "I sent my son to live with my mother and started partying hard again; drinking, snorting. There were so many men; one emotionless escapade after another."

She sat there quiet for a moment before saying,

"Then I miscarried."

"You never told me that."

"I was on the love seat, hovering around second base with some guy. I don't even remember who he was. When he started unbuttoning my shirt, I got this sharp pain." She laughed. "It felt like I had to poop. I thought I was constipated. I went to the bathroom, doubled over in pain promising I'd never eat cheese again if I could just get this out of me." Her voice lowered a little. "I kept pushing and pushing, trying to make the pain stop. One last push, and something splashed in the water. When I looked in the toilet …" She paused for a moment. "There was a little bloody ball-like thing." I sat up and looked at her as she continued, "I didn't even know I was pregnant, much less who the father was." Reflectively, she said, "I think it was in that very moment that I turned to God."

As ignorant as it may have sound, I asked, "Why?"

"Because I wanted to stop what I was doing and didn't know how."

Understanding the message, I agreed to go to service with her. I had never been to Paige's church before. I showered and got dressed in my Sunday best: my double-breasted black and white two-piece suit, natural-colored stockings, and black pumps. As for my hair, I wet it, put mousse on it, and brushed it away from my face as it maintained its natural curl.

Once we arrived at the AME church, I saw men with jeans and T-shirts, and women with miniskirts and halters. I wasn't sure if we were going to church or to a cookout. I grew up in a Baptist church—this sort of behavior just wasn't normal to me.

Paige caught me staring and said, "Man looks at the outer; God looks at the heart."

"I hear you, but let's be real ... she ain't here looking for God with a skirt that short."

Paige was a part of one of the ministries, so she sat on the front row. I personally didn't need to be that close, so I sat a few rows from the back trying to blend in, trying to conceal my pain. I didn't want to talk to anybody and I didn't want anyone to talk to me. The pastor—a beautiful brown-skinned woman with long jet-black hair—took the pulpit. She looked more like a super model than a pastor. As she opened up her book, she said, "Introduce yourself to your neighbor and tell them one thing God did for you this week."

I thought to myself, *Well, God and I ain't talked in a while, so…* I got nervous and uncomfortable because I didn't have anything to say on the matter. The woman sitting beside me introduced herself and said, "He blessed me this morning when he woke me up." She was happy she got another day, while some days I was mad I did. I just smiled and nodded my head.

I was ready to leave. I began planning my escape. I figured since I rode with Paige, I'd have to walk down to Main Street and flag down a taxi. I wanted to go home, roll a joint, do a line, and go back to bed. As I got up with my purse tucked under my arm, the pastor told everyone to get their Bibles in their hands and turn to Luke, chapter thirteen. Everyone stood up and began flipping through the pages. With my seat in the middle of the row and everyone standing, I was stuck. I had to wait till everyone was sitting to get by. After she finished reading about repentance, she told everyone to be seated. I stood and tried to make my way down the row, but the usher shook her head and told me to wait. I excused myself past one more person and insisted I had to go. She insisted I had to wait. So I made my way back past the four people I just stepped over. I sat there, impatiently shaking my leg, waiting for the usher to turn her back so I could make a move. The pastor said, "We're going to get into today's message in a moment, but I have to sidestep for a minute."

I thought to myself, Fine, hurry up.

"I feel the spirit of depression in this place." She paced back and forth. "Some days, you don't even recognize yourself."

Paige turned and looked at me.

"Even in this room full of people, you feel alone

right now."

My leg stop shaking as I listened. The people around me began to react as though the pastor were talking about them, even though it felt that this woman I never met was speaking directly to me.

"You've had setback after setback, and as hard as you try, it seems you can't recover from the thing that happened years ago. And you feel like God has forgotten all about you."

Tears streamed down my face.

"But I'm here to tell you that he said, 'I will never leave or forsake you.' I bind the spirit of suicide right now in the name of Jesus. You shall live and shall not die. If he was going to let you kill yourself, you would have succeeded at fourteen."

The floodgate opened up.

"The assignment of the enemy has been canceled. Your season of pain is over!"

After the pastor spoke that word, I thought angels would descend and everything would be perfect from that point. The reality of it was this: it was something for me to hold on to. It was a promise that things would get better, but things had been bad for so long that it was hard to keep holding on.

Grieving

The following Sunday, Paige called to see if I wanted to ride with her to church.

"No, not this time."

"Laina, you need to go!"

"Would you stop trying to force church down my throat! I'll go when I'm ready!" I hung up.

A couple weeks later, Paige called to see how I was doing. After I assured her I was fine, she said, "Go with me to get some chicken."

Of course I argued that I wasn't hungry, but she promised it was the best chicken in town.

After she picked me up, we rode around for a little while before she said, "You know, they started a new ministry at church?"

"That's nice."

"It's the YNA ... the You're Not Alone ministry."

You have to understand that Paige doesn't speak randomly. Everything she does and says has purpose.

As I turned to look at her, she said, "It's to help grievers, grieve."

I told her it had been two years and that I was done grieving.

She argued, "You never mourned Marcus, and after Dion told you about the baby, you stopped mourning Damon. Now you just sit around destructive, feeling sorry for yourself."

"SO!"

After the funeral, I just sucked it up. So for the first six months, I was on autopilot, just trying to get through the day. So for the past eighteen months, instead of mourning, I had just been ANGRY.

We pulled into the church parking lot. I turned and looked at her, demanding an answer. "WHAT ARE WE DOING HERE?"

She pulled into a parking spot and turned the car off. "Girl, Sista Brooks makes the best fried chicken in town."

I sat there with my elbow resting on the door, holding my head with that hand. "Paige, I don't feel like sitting around a bunch of judgmental church folk, talking about my feelings."

"Okay, look. For me, please just give it twenty minutes, and after that, if you want to leave, we can go." I sat there glaring at her as she reiterated, "Just twenty minutes."

We went in the side entrance and downstairs to the fellowship hall. There were about eight people sitting in the half circle, all of whom were older than Paige and me. After we made ourselves a plate and found a seat, the coordinator, Sister Brooks asked everyone to introduce themselves and say a little something about the loved one they lost.

I sat there uncomfortable, half listening, moving the collard greens from one side of the plate to the other when it came to the lady sitting two people down from me: Mrs. Ellie-Mae Bridges. As she talked about her Clydale, her smile widened and red tones stained her cheeks like the glow of a sixteen-year-old with her first crush. Sista Brooks asked, "When did he pass?"

She responded, saying, "Oh, 'bout a month ago now."

My interest was piqued. Shocked, I stared at her, wondering how she was able to be around other people and smile after only a month. It had been two years, and I still didn't want to talk about it. I wondered how she wasn't in tears after losing her mate of fifty-two years.

"Sista Bridges, I remember the pastor sharing

your story," Sista Brooks said. "Would you share with the group where your strength is coming from?"

Mrs. Ellie-Mae began flipping through her Bible to the page she had turned down. "God said, 'Cast all your cares on me.'" She closed her Bible. "God favored me wit a … a wonderful husband and father for my chil-ren. He gone nah, but God allowed me to have 'um for fifty-two glorious years. Chile, some folk don't even get to live dat long, much less spend it wit-cha best friend." She smiled. "Diss ain't da end. I'll see him in dat mansion in the sky."

I wondered how she could talk about tomorrow and still go home to that empty house every night.

Then Mrs. Ellie-Mae said, "He's da only man I eva loved."

"Well, you seem to be doing well," I said.

She laughed. "Ain't it funny da thangs you notice when ya don't hear 'um anymo'e. I use ta fuss, 'Clydale, pick up yo feet.' But, chile, I do miss hearing da shufflin' of his ole raggedy slippers on da flow. I miss him. But he got a promotion … he gone on ta glory nah."

Though she sound like Mommy talking about God like that, I still wasn't certain that God was there or even that he cared anything about me. I wanted to know how she was so sure.

She turned to me. "Oh, chile, ya know, dem kids

of ours would get some kinda embarrassed."

Curious, I asked, "Why?"

She blushed, adjusting the bun in her hair and said, "Chile, he couldn't keep his hands off me. Humph, we got seven kids, ya know." We all let out a little giggle. She said, "Shugah, Clydale had hip surgery last year, but, chile—"

Sista Brooks cut her off, saying, "Sista Bridges, THANK YOU! Thank you so much for sharing."

I sat there wondering how Mrs. Ellie-Mae was holding it together. How was she able to be so positive after losing her best friend, head of the household, her children's father?

Spontaneously, Sista Bridges proclaimed, "Oh, the God I serve is a mighty God."

I knew who God was, or at least as much as the average person, I guessed, but I wanted to know the God that Mrs. Ellie-Mae knew. She made me question everything I had ever known, what little it was.

As the next person introduced themselves, Mrs. Ellie-Mae came and sat beside me, put her hand on my leg like she could hear my thoughts, and whispered, "Stop focusing on wha-chu done lost and look at wha-cha got." She put her open palm on my cheek. "It sho-nuff coulda been you, but-chu still here. Chile, he kept you." There was something so warm and benevolent about her smile. She shook her head. "There must be an awesome purpose on yo life dat ya still here."

Since everything happened, I believed there was something bad about me. But this woman, whom I didn't know, believed there was something good inside of me. That's what I needed ... someone to believe in me who had no stake in it.

I cried and hugged her with everything in me. She looked at me like she knew my pain, and I guess she did.

"Shugah," she said, "I know it hurts. But you done tried everything else. Nah, why don't you try God?"

Honestly, I didn't know if God was going to do it, but I wanted to smile again. Mrs. Ellie-Mae knew the pain I knew and, if she believed God gave her peace, I thought to myself, *If he did it for her...*

Taking Back Control

I knew it was time I at least tried to get back to some sense of normalcy. My first official effort to getting my life back was to put Damon's house on the market.

Next, I started going to church regularly. Not necessarily because I wanted to ... it was more because I had to. Being in church around other people who were fighting to stay sane made me feel less alone.

Every Sunday, I'd sit quietly next to Mrs. Ellie-Mae like a well-behaved child as the preacher's words scabbed my wounds. I just wanted to be near her; something about her brought me a sense of peace. Mrs. Ellie-Mae treated me like one of her own, she even taught me how to pray. I use to pray the prayer in the Bible ("Our Father who art in heaven ...") then ask God for what I needed. She taught me to give God praise first. Secondly, thank him for what he'd done, then, ask him for what you need. I don't know if that's in the Bible, but it sure sounded good when she prayed it.

She'd pray, "Lord almighty, the beginning and the end, King of Kings, Jehovah-Jireh, Wonderful Counselor, giver of every great and perfect gift, healer, restorer, lover of my heart and my soul, thank ya! Thank ya for waking me up this morning. God, I thank ya that I have breath in my body. Thank ya for the mobility of my limbs. Thank ya that I have a place to lay my head, that I have food on the table. God, I thank ya that the bills are paid. Heavenly Father, I humbly ask that you bless my chil-ren and bless their chil-ren, chil-ren. Provide all dar needs, Lord. Send yo angels to watch ova the babies at school. And guide 'um in dar schoolwork. Father God, bless DeLaina. Mend her brokenness, restore her mind, and keep her in perfect peace. Lord, I'm just asking that you provide all of her needs and after you take care of 'um ... God, won't you bless me? In Jesus name. Amen."

***

Now, I think I'm a reasonably intelligent woman, but to be completely transparent ... I'd go to church, sit in the pew and sing the songs but, honestly,

I didn't know THAT much about God.

After service one Sunday, I caught Ms. Ellie-Mae alone and whispered with child-like curiosity, "Can I ask you something?"

"Sure, baby. You can ask ole' Ellie-Mae any thang." She grabbed my hand. "What's on ya mind, shugah?"

I flashed back to lonely days, tear-stained pillows, and sleepless nights. Almost in a whisper, I said, "I've been through a lot." With tears in my eyes, I said, "God is suppose to be everywhere and all knowing. Why do you think God knowingly let me go through all that pain; was I being punished?"

"Aw, my sweet baby. It's in ya affliction that-chu learn who God is. Can't ya see God has his hand on ya life? Everythang ya going through, everythang ya been through, is a process."

She seemed so sure, but I had to ask, "How do you know?"

"Chile, cause the Word say, 'For those God foreknew, he also predestined to be conformed to the image of his son.' Chile, 'conform' means change—and change, well, honey, there's a process for any thang to change."

"Yeah, I get that, Ms. Ellie-Mae, but why me? Why did I have to go through it?"

With certainty, she said, "So your daughters

won't have to."

Convinced she had me mixed up with someone else, I replied, "I don't have kids."

She patted my leg and smiled as she got up and walked away.

***

After about eight months of attending services and Bible study, I got Saved and joined Paige's church—our church.

Months later, after service one Sunday, while still on an emotional high I asked Paige, "Do you know what your purpose is?"

"I believe so. Why?"

"Because sometimes I feel like I don't know what I'm supposed to do with my life."

"Pray on it. Ask God to make it clear."

I nodded. "I will. Hey, I'm hungry, let's go get something to eat."

"No, I can't."

"My treat ..."

"Today's my goddaughter's birthday. You should come."

"I didn't know you had a—oh no! You're the godmother?"

Bracing herself, she nodded her head. "I'm her friend, too, DeLaina. Do I think she was wrong? Yes, of course, but it's not my place to pass judgment."

"NO! But you could pick a side!"

She took out her wallet. "You should see her." As I pushed the wallet away, she said, "Fine. But realize it's been what ... almost four years ... and you've known Rea longer than you knew Marcus or Damon."

"Whateva! You act like I'm talking about a pair of Donna Karan's she ruined. We're talking about my life. Who knows how long she's been secretly trying to be me?"

Paige continued with her wallet open. "The baby looks just like her father."

My eyes widened as I waited for her to detail that statement.

She finally said, "She has Marcus's dimples."

I let out a sigh of relief like that somehow changed something.

No matter how far it seemed I had come, I would still get caught up in the past from time to time. Although I felt some sense of responsibility some days, others, admittedly, I felt Damon and Marcus got what they deserved. (I'm still working on forgiveness.)

Paige suggested I make peace. The following Sunday after church, she drove me to the cemetery where Marcus was laid to rest. She got out, walked around to my side, and leaned against the hood as she pointed in the direction of his burial plot. As I proceeded through the graveyard, I felt a nervous churning in my stomach. I walked along the path, reading each headstone until I read …

Marcus Elliott Day
Finally At Peace
November 13, 1973 – April 9, 2004

In spite of myself, I hurt for him. I knew oh too well the kind of pain that caused one to think the only way out is a .45 or a handful of pills. I stood there reading and rereading the headstone with my arms folded until finally I said, "Hi." I looked back to Paige for support, but she wasn't there. Looking around the cemetery, I found her sitting across the way on a bench with her eyes closed and Bible clutched to her chest.

Staring at the headstone, I thought to myself, *This seemed like a good idea, but now that I'm here …*

I stood there for a while longer before saying, "I'm sorry I hurt you. I know you came to the house that night to tell me about Damon and Reagan." I knelt down and brushed away the dirt to make a clean place for the lilies I'd brought. "I wonder if you were also going to tell me about you and Reagan. It didn't surprise me that you cheated, but finding out it was with her shattered every good memory I had of us. Marcus, inspite of everything, I never meant to hurt you." I stood up. "I hope you are finally at peace."

Even though Marcus played a major part in my life being in an uproar, it seemed much easier to make peace with the dead than the living.

I'm Not Perfect

Giving up a seven-year relationship with marijuana, a two-year courtship with crack and an on again off again with dark liquor was a piece of cake compared to celibacy.

Living saved was a constant battle. I'd always been in a relationship or had some nameless, faceless person around even while I was going through. So trying to suppress what had become an instinctive nature was a battle.

I'd found that many have the misconception that once you're saved, life is perfect. You no longer have battles with the flesh, sexual urges, or even the desire to curse someone out every now and then. Being saved doesn't completely stop those things; it equips you with the knowledge of how to handle it. It's a choice.

I learned early on in my journey that music was my gateway—the opening to my thoughts—so I had to curtail what I was allowing into my spirit. Listening to love songs caused a ripple effect. I'd remember I didn't have anyone to feel that way about. Then, it was the memory of the last time I had that feeling. Until finally, I was longing for someone to love me, but ended up settling for someone to make love to me.

See, walking the walk of a Christian woman ain't easy. The biggest part of being saved for me was learning what my weaknesses were: alcohol, men, sex, and drugs—not necessarily in that order. Once I realized what my weakness were, I changed my environment and the company I kept. I quickly learned abstinence doesn't mean deliverance. Removing yourself from a certain environment doesn't hide you from the enemy. He will come on your turf.

Case in point … I had been celibate for eleven months and nineteen days. This was the longest I had gone without sex since I lost my virginity in college. In an effort to keep myself busy, it was getting harder to stay focused. My flesh was on the verge of throwing in the towel. I just wanted to feel wanted; I wanted to feel like a woman. With all the fleshly thoughts swarming about, I thought I'd better go to Bible study in an attempt to regain my focus.

As I sat in the second row with my Bible in one hand and my notebook open on my lap, I could feel someone staring. I looked up from my notebook and found the eyes of a man on me. I thought to myself, I've seen him before. When he realized he was caught, he smiled. Suddenly, I remembered seeing him in church with another young lady that I didn't seem to see anymore. As the deacon began teaching, I had trouble maintaining focus. I caught myself drifting off every few minutes, trying to get a glimpse of the attractive man in the third row adjacent.

After service, he came over and introduced himself, saying, "I know this may be inappropriate, but you are the most beautiful woman I've ever seen." I was so flattered that I was lost for words, and that was not an easy feat. As I stood there listening to his spiel about how he'd noticed me for some time, I couldn't help noticing there was something familiar about him. I couldn't put my finger on it. Maybe I should have seen that as a sign.

His name was Raymond Trees III; everyone called him Ray. Though he was a very attractive, saved man, after talking to him a few times on the phone, it seemed he had one foot in the church and one foot out. I'd been warned about people that play church hokey-pokey—doing the things of the world and trying to have a relationship with God at the same time.

I liked Ray ... maybe because we were in similar places. He seemed to have all this love bottled up to give, and I wanted to be loved. I enjoyed being around him, but it seemed the closer he and I became, the less guided I felt. It was rather hard to explain, but I guess it felt like I was cheating ... on God.

The more time he and I spent together, the stronger my urges became. It was getting harder to fight. I didn't want to feel the way I was feeling. I hadn't had a drink, smoked a joint, or snorted in well over a year, but SEX ... some days I struggled like a dope fein.

Ray said and did all the right things. He opened up doors, hung onto my every word, and did all the things I said I wanted a man to do. I forgot the enemy knows what I like.

In time, I asked God for a sign as to if this was meant to be. I was scared that I was quickly growing attached to Ray, and I couldn't deal with anymore heartache, so I prayed, "Lord, if he's not supposed to be in my life, I pray you remove him. Lord, cover my heart that I not love anyone that is not of you. In Jesus' name. Amen."

After dating for several weeks, I didn't know if I genuinely liked him or if in fact it was just that a man was paying me some attention. I began to develop anxiety over the issue and needed to know whether to stop now or proceed with caution. So I prayed, "Lord, please give me a sign. If this is the man I'm supposed to be with, please show me. If not, Lord, please remove him from my life. In Jesus' name. Amen."

One evening after a late dinner, as we stood in the restaurant parking lot talking, he invited me back to his place, but, knowing my flesh was far too weak, I declined. I gave him a light peck on the lips and said, "Good night." I was so proud of myself.

We scheduled another date for the following Friday, but as the days went on, he seemingly couldn't wait. I noticed that he didn't make it to church that night for Bible study, but as I was walking in my door from church, my cell phone rang—it was him.

"I think I'm in your neighborhood," he said. "Can I stop by and get a hug?"

I remember previously telling him the area I lived in, but not the exact community. I was so excited that someone wanted to be around me that I didn't question how he got here so quick. Before I could make it down the hall to change clothes, he was knocking at the door with a single red rose between his teeth. I thought it was cute. We stood at the door talking until I finally invited him in to sit for a while. The boots I had on were killing my feet, so I excused myself and went to my room to take them off. As I plopped down on the bed, there he was standing at my doorway. As I crossed my legs to take off a boot, I asked jokingly, "What are you looking at?"

He didn't respond. He slowly approached, knelt down in front of me, and uncrossed my leg, resting my foot on his upper thigh. He unzipped my boot and wrapped both his hands around my calf, sliding them down slowly to loosen the boot from my skin. He did the same for the other boot. After both were off, he put his arms around my waist and kissed me long and soft. He pushed me back on the bed, then kissed and touched me some more. My mind said, *Make him stop,* but my flesh was like, *Just five more minutes.*

I pushed him off me. "Ray, I'm celibate."

In a failed attempt to make light of the situation, he said, "If you sell a bit, I'll buy a bit."

When he saw I was unmoved, he apologized, saying he didn't mean to offend me and would never try to coax me into anything I didn't want to do. He apologized and kept apologizing. Although I wasn't sure I believed him, I accepted his apology.

We laid there talking and cuddling until we fell asleep. He woke up about 3:00 a.m. and tiptoed out. Later that day, he sent me flowers with a card saying, I'm sorry.

***

As long as I'd lived in that condominium community, I had never seen a bug or anything, outside of the occasional cricket. Late one night, I was resting in my bed after thinking about that man and how good it felt to have a man's arms around me again. I was half asleep when I heard rustling in the paper. I opened my eyes to see MICKEY on the other side of the bed, nibbling at the circular. I ran to the corner and stood on top of the vanity stool as he scurried his little furry behind under the closet door. I grabbed my Timbs by the front door and ran out to the twenty-four-hour store to get rat traps. I bought fifteen sticky traps and laid them all out after I carefully packed a bag. I crashed at Paige's for the next few nights.

I showed up on her doorstep with a tote bag and six words ("I need a place to stay"). As I made myself at home, I told her what happened. I loved her; the anointing on her was so heavy. She was able to see things as a sign or warning that your average person couldn't see. She immediately asked, "How are things going with you and that guy from church?"

Without giving her the details, I said, "Oh, things are good. He seems nice."

In a motherly tone, she said, "Don't sleep with him again."

I quickly responded, "I didn't sleep with him!" Where I come from, sleeping together constitutes having sex with no sleep involved.

"Are you sure? 'Cause I'm trying to understand what it means for you to have been in the bed with a rat."

Admittedly, her words rang out, but I discounted their meaning.

Overindulging in the excitement of having someone new in my life, I took my eyes off God. Praying came second to talking on the phone or texting Ray. I used to rush to church to hear the message from God, but I began rushing to a.m. service to see my boo—God became the bonus.

I wasn't really sure where the relationship was going; I was just glad it was moving.

It was date night: one night a month, a few of his friends would get together at one of their houses and bring a date. Once we arrived, I noticed that the women were very direct with him and a little standoffish toward me, but I didn't let that ruin my night. As I was coming out of the restroom, I overheard him telling his frat brother, "This may be the one." I speculated about the conversation I'd happened upon. All I knew was that I wanted to be someone's *THE ONE.*

If I was honest, there were plenty of signs beyond the fact that he was so touchy-feely or that he still listened to hardcore rap and even the fact that he cursed. But I dismissed it all because, of course, I saw him in church every Sunday. I trusted him, thinking,

He goes to God's house; he wouldn't mistreat me. Therein lies the misconception that a person who's in church has church in them.

At the end of date night, he dropped me back off at home, walked me upstairs, and kissed me on the cheek. I was having such a great time that I didn't want the evening to end. So I invited him in for a cup of coffee. We talked and kissed a little bit. We kissed a little bit more, and it happened—my covenant was broken.

I sat on the side of the bed, sobbing, questioning what had I done. Without a word, he got up, put his clothes back on, and left like a thief in the night. I showered and put some clothes on, but I still felt naked. The guilt riddled me to the point I just wanted to hide my face. I was too embarrassed to pray. What was I gonna say, "Hey, God, remember that dude I met at your house..."?

I felt like I had to get myself together before I went to God—as if he didn't already know.

The next day, I didn't call Ray and he didn't call me, but it didn't matter; I couldn't even deal with me much less with him. I knew I couldn't avoid him at church, so I made up in my mind that I'd speak with him after service on Sunday.

When I woke up Sunday morning, it was a struggle to even get out of bed. I felt this heaviness. I thought I might feel better if I laid on the altar, so I decided to get to church a little early.

When I arrived, the front door wasn't unlocked just yet, so I walked around and went in through the side entrance. As I walked down the main hall with the stained glass windows, I could hear the choir rehearsing. As I neared the sanctuary, I heard Ray's soft, seductive tone. He was talking to the deacon's niece—Mercedes.

He said, "I know this may be inappropriate, but you are the most beautiful woman I've ever seen."

I muttered, "What the ..." before reminding myself where I was. Here I was struggling to even hold my head up, and he was treating the sanctuary like some pickup joint.

Instead of cursing and flipping out—and trust me, there was a part of me that wanted to curse and flip out—I stood in the main hall with my back against the wall, feeling pain and a sense of embarrassment.

Yes, of course, I'd grown to care for him very quickly, but it wasn't like I was in love with him. Reflecting, I realized I was lonely and he was the first "Christian" man I met since I had been saved.

I put up a wall after I found out about Damon and Reagan. I dated people outside of the church from time to time, but I didn't trust anyone enough to let them get close to me. So when Ray came along, he evaded the radar by seemingly, lifting holy hands and praising God.

See, sometimes we put church folk in a separate category and give them special privileges in our lives. So when they disappoint us, it cuts deep. We act as though seeing them agree and nod "Amen" gives them an automatic pass—freedom to romp around in our lives. We give them a waiver and don't make them stand the normal background check we've set in place for everyone else.

I blamed myself for allowing *LONELY* to have a reign over my life that skewed my vision to a dime-sized view. I was looking at all the things he was doing in the now versus looking at the big picture or even the frame that was holding the portrait in place. Like, why was it he could tell me all the things that women did wrong in previous relationships but couldn't tell me one thing he did?

I was so ashamed that I had fallen. With tears in my eyes, I told Paige what happened. Smiling, she took a tissue and wiped the tears running down my face and said, "Look how long you lived an unsaved life. Laina, there's going to be some battles of the flesh, but the fact that you feel guilty says a lot. I venture to say this isn't the last battle, but I pray you remember this feeling so that you can avoid this pain again."

***

For me, typically when a relationship is over,

there are four steps: 1.) Get rid of all relationship paraphernalia; 2.) Delete the name and number(s) from my phone(s)—out of sight, out of mind; 3.) Block his screen name from instant messenger and/or email to ensure I have every quiet opportunity to get past the situation without any setbacks; and 4.) Avoid going anyplace where I think he'd be—out of sight, out of mind.

I detested that this "relationship" didn't afford me the ability to walk away and not look back. Not having that kind of control left me feeling vulnerable, which made going to church every Sunday a task. I thought about going to another church or even not going to church at all, but since neither of those seemed to be a real option, I battled with my flesh and fought the urge to key his car every time I walked passed it in the parking lot. (Pray for me.)

Seeing him in church bothered me to the point that it was hard to hear the sermon over my emotions. I felt used, manipulated, and cast aside. Not to mention embarrassed.

Truthfully, I was afraid of what people thought. He used to walk me to my truck and kiss me on the cheek in front of everyone. Now he was doing the exact same thing with Mercedes.

Knowing the elders on the front row were in everybody's business, I wondered what they were saying. I wondered if they thought it was me, that I did something wrong in the relationship, or even if they questioned my Christianity. At that point, when someone said, "How you doing," I wondered if it was rhetorical or if it was a genuine inquiry?

There I was, wanting to be a good Christian, trying to act fine, smiling wide, speaking on Sundays while bruised Monday through Saturday. So worried about what other people thought that I forgot about the one who truly mattered.

It had been about two months and Ray hadn't spoken to me since we slept together, hadn't parted his lips once. He'd see me in the sanctuary and looked right through me as though I weren't even there, like he never knew me. One afternoon after service, he snickered and spoke to me by name, at which point every curse word I had ever known lined up single-file with hands raised, yelling, "Ooo, pick me, pick me!" I wouldn't give him the satisfaction of not speaking; as hard as it was, I gave him the half smile with no teeth. The fact that it took him that long to acknowledge me hurt.

I kept it together until I made it to my truck. I just sat behind the wheel in tears. Paige was on her way to her car when she noticed me crying.

She jumped in and asked, "What's wrong?"

I was huffing, trying to calm my emotions to explain what happened when Ray and Mercedes walked past my truck hand in hand.

In a soft voice, Paige said, "Forgive him."

"No! He treated me like some random chick."

"Pray for him."

"Nope, nope. Maybe that's the advanced SAVED. Right now, I'm working in remedial. I still wanna slash his tires."

"Laina, the enemy knows your weakness. He's trying to distract you and pull you away from the church, but in spite of the situation, you haven't missed a Sunday."

Finding my way into the sanctuary was not easy while feeling disrespected, rejected, and ignored. While I felt like I was losing ground, it was Paige who reminded me of what I had been through. She told me forthrightly, "This is nothing. If God can heal the pain of death and rebuke suicide, I know he can heal the ache in your chest."

My pastor gave a parable once that will forever stay in my mind. She compared grocery shopping when you're hungry to looking for a mate when you're lonely. The comparison is clear. When you shop hungry, in your mind you want anything that resembles food. When you get home, you find that you've bought ground beef, pork chops, ice cream, bologna, popsicles, and walnut brownies—in spite of you being a lactose-intolerant vegetarian who's allergic to nuts.

Here's the lesson: When you're lonely, you can lose site of the things that aren't good for you. The things that could possibly kill you.

***

I had to learn the hard way that you have to be careful dating in the church. I admit it's nice to know your romantic interest is on good ground and is being feed, but is he digesting or is he bulimic? Church is like a hospital. If that's the case ... that would make the sanctuary the waiting room, and you don't know if you're seated beside someone whose body is riddled with disease or someone who's just there for their weekly checkup.

When you arrive in the ER, you have to be interviewed to determine the nature and severity of your illness. I believe your praise is your interview. It's my belief that your fervent worship pushes you to the front of the list and qualifies you for an immediate appointment with the Great Physician.

Past Hurts

I was still healing. I still cried sometimes, but I was closer to God in my state of despair than I had ever been in my life. In my process, I realized that forgiving Marcus and Damon were only pieces of the puzzle. During the service one Sunday, the pastor seemed to speak directly to me. She leaned over the podium, saying, "Some of you so-called Christians make me sick, sittin' up in here with hate in your hearts right now, holding on to grudges and past hurts. I'm not talking 'bout something that happened last week or even last month. I'm talking about things that happened four and five years ago, but you sittin' up in here with your saved self wanting God to forgive you and you haven't learned how to forgive." She stepped down from the pulpit and walked toward my section. "The Lord forgave you for making that no-good man your god. He forgave you for smoking and drinking instead of fasting and praying."

I was sitting there with a heavy heart, shaking my head, as she called out my issues one by one. I held back the tears until she said, "He even forgave you for the abortion."

I leapt from my seat, screaming, telling all my business. Tears streamed down my face as I flashed back to lying on that cold table as they sucked my baby from my body.

Then the pastor said, "If you're carrying the burdens of your past—past hurts—if you're still hurting from an old relationship and you still haven't been able to let go ... I want you to stand to your feet right now and lift your hands."

With my hands raised, I thought about all the pain I had endured. As I wiped my face, the pastor went on to say, "Call out the name of the person who wronged you and say, 'I forgive you.'"

Raison d'être

Big Momma's House

With every lesson … there's a test. Pencils down.

I had received such a sense of peace that I wanted to bless someone else. So I join the outreach ministry.

The church had adopted a group home on the south side of DC. Big Momma's House was a foster facility where kids were held until a foster home could be established. Members of the "Help Ministry" at the church rotated Saturdays twice a month, organizing educational outings for the kids.

The program director, Olivia, buzzed me into the building when I arrived Saturday morning. Once I reached the top of the stairs, she greeted me with the most beautiful little caramel girl on her hip; she couldn't have been more than four or five. Her perfection rendered me speechless.

I leaned in close and rubbed the tip of my index finger over her fat little leg as I asked, "And who is this angel?"

She giggled and hid her face.

Almost embarrassed, Olivia said, "That's a good question. I was off yesterday. She must have arrived last night or this morning before I checked in."

She handed me the little angel as she looked for the paperwork. I sat down with the pint-sized beauty on my lap and admired the little curly puff ball on the top of her head. Her lashes were so long that they looked like little hands waving when she blinked. She straddled my legs and laid her head on my chest as though she were tired.

There was a familiar sparkle in her eyes; she reminded me of what I'd been asking God for.

As Olivia searched for the papers, she said, "I do know that her mother is at County. I honestly thought someone would have claimed the baby by now. Social services called two nights ago to see if we had space for a toddler, after the police found the mother beaten unconscious." Flipping through the papers on a nearby desk, she said, "The neighbors called the police, but you know, living in the city … they take their sweet time." She got up and walked toward the door. "Excuse me a moment."

I ran the tip of my index finger from her hairline to her nose and tapped it. She had the most beautiful giggle that showed crater-sized dimples when she smiled.

I looked up to see Olivia walking toward me, reviewing the papers. She said, "Her name's A'Neesa DeLaina Day."

My eyes distended as I thought back to when that was to be my name … DeLaina Day. I leaned back, looking for familiar features—and there they were, staring at me this whole time. She had Reagan's hazel eyes. The more I stared, the more I realized that she had Marcus's nose and paper-thin lips.

Olivia said, "The mother's name is …"

In unison, we said, "Reagan Mitchell."

I smiled. "I know this baby." Surprised, I asked, "The grandmother hasn't called?"

"Okay, seriously. Were you listening? I was off yesterday?" Olivia laughed. "I'm just kidding. No, not that I'm aware of."

With baby girl attached to my hip, I paced the floor, fighting the impulse of my flesh to detach myself. "Olivia, call the hospital and see what Reagan's condition is."

"Well, I told you—"

"Please?"

She called the hospital, explaining she was the

director of a foster facility, holding the patient's next of kin. The doctor explained that there was excessive bleeding around the cranial lobe, which had apparently caused her to slip into a coma. After I gave Olivia, Ma Mitchell's phone number I sat falling in love with A'Neesa by the second. As Olivia dialed the number, my stomach tightened. I listening as she told her that Reagan was in the hospital and A'Neesa was being held at a group home. After she explained the situation in its entirety, she got quiet. She sat there nodding her head and saying, "Yes, I understand," for about five minutes. I then heard her say, "And she's the aunt?"

Then she repeated a phone number: "That's 301-555-9873?" The conversation ended with, "Yes, I'll keep you posted."

After she hung up the phone, she repeated the conversation to me, telling me that Ms. Mitchell said that she loved her grandbaby, but her health was deteriorating. She explained that she had cancer and couldn't take adequate care of a toddler.

"What did she say about Reagan?" I asked.

"Nothing useful. How do you know these people?"

As I played with the baby's hair, I explained, "We were friends. Rea and I grew up together."

"I would say very good friends for her to name her child after you. What about the father?"

"He's no longer with us," I said. "If no one comes to claim her, what's gonna happen?"

"Well, she'll go into the system and will be assigned a foster home."

"Can she stay with me? I mean, until Reagan is okay to take care of her?"

"DeLaina, taking care of a child is more than just playing with her. You'd have to find adequate child care, your time would no longer be your own, you'd have to—"

"Please."

Looking at the baby, she said, "I'll see what I can do."

I apologized to Olivia for not being able to stay. I kissed A'Neesa on the forehead and darted out. On my way to the hospital, I called and left Paige a long message explaining what happened.

Forgiveness

I got chills as I rushed through the ER doors the way I had almost five years ago. I asked for Reagan Mitchell's room. My mind slowed as the nurse said, "Family members only." I thought back to the way she use to call me her sister. Although I still felt some residual anger, I couldn't let her go through this alone. I wanted to walk in forgiveness.

"I'm her sister," I said.

As I peeled off the visitor sticker and stuck it to my chest, I questioned myself, What are you going to say?

I stood outside her room, searching the recesses of my mind for the right words to say. I walked into the room, and my heart began pounding as I stared at a woman I hadn't seen or talked to in years. She had lost so much weight. Her cinnamon skin tone was taken over by blacks and blues. With the white bandage wrapped around her head and her eyes swollen shut, it was hard to tell it was her. When I lifted her frail arm to read the wristband, I noticed the scar on her forearm. She got that one when she took a spill trying to pop a wheelie on her Suzuki. I smiled to myself as I remembered she was always determined not to be outdone by the guys. I pulled a chair up beside her bed and stared for about twenty minutes, remembering why I hadn't seen or talked to her in the past few years. Seeing her brought back memories I'd buried ... hurt I thought I was over and memories of the happiness I blamed her for stealing. I sat there with my arms folded as the old me rivaled the new me, asking, *Why did you come here anyway? She ain't your friend; she never was.*

Caught up in a flashback, I stood up and walked out. Pacing the floor with my arms folded, I waited impatiently for the elevator. Once it arrived, I got on, pressed "L" for lobby, and backed into the corner. As the doors began to close, a hand reached in, triggering the sensor to open the doors. A gentlemen stepped on, saying, "I'm not doing this with you."

Two steps behind him, a woman relentlessly reminded him, "You never want to talk about it."

Even after the elevator filled floor by floor, they

continued arguing. I tried not to listen, but their voices drowned my thoughts.

He told her, "You said you forgave me. If you forgive someone, you don't keep throwing it in their face." He yelled, "I made a mistake."

Everyone looked at the numbers across the top of the elevator, watching them slowly decrease and pretending not to hear their voices echo in the shaft of the elevator. Even after the doors finally opened, they continued arguing. I got off the elevator with them and watched as they left the building. Walking through the lobby, he said, "You're such a hypocrite … jumping up and down, shouting in church, but raising hell everywhere else."

I stood in the middle of the lobby, paralyzed as his words penetrated my soul like he was talking to me. I leaned against the wall, regrouping and remembering how God had forgiven me. I got back on the elevator and went back upstairs just as a doctor was going into Reagan's room. I stood in the hallway and watched her press her two fingers against Rea's wrist, checking her vitals. The doctor noticed me standing there and said, "Come on in. I'll just be a minute."

I didn't move. I stood there with my arms folded, contemplating staying or going. I looked up and noticed Paige rushing up the hallway. She hugged me, saying, "I got here as soon as I could. Have you spoken with the doctors yet?"

"No. She's in there now."

The doctor came out, and asked if we were family. Once Paige nodded yes, she introduced herself as Dr. Velasquez and began flipping through her notes before giving the status. "Reagan has progressed to full-blown AIDS."

In a calm tone, I corrected the woman with the medical degree. "No, you've made a mistake." Choosing the lesser of two evils, I said, "She's here because someone beat her."

The doctor nodded. "Yes, there's significant bruising consistent with an assault. However, that's a small part of the problem."

I'd seen Paige frustrated and mad, but I had never seen her scared before that day. In a light voice, she asked, "Are you sure?"

Dr. Velasquez confided that she saw Reagan several months prior, at which point—against her orders—Reagan decided not to take the medicine anymore. She said it was making her tired and weak, and she didn't want that to be her daughter's last memory of her.

"Can't you change her medicine?" Paige asked.

"Yes, I could have. In fact, I offered, but she insisted against it. At this point, all we can do is make her comfortable."

Confronting my fears, I asked, "Where? I mean … do you know when she got it? Or *who* she contracted it from? Has she …" Pacing the floor, I asked, "Does the baby …" There were so many thoughts running through my mind at that moment.

The doctor said, "She gave us a list; however, none of the men or women on the list were infected."

"WOMEN?!"

"Now, that doesn't mean they won't pop positive later," the doctor explained. "As for the baby … she wasn't tested here. Reagan assured me the baby was negative, but I don't know for certain."

I was at a loss for words. With a shallow breath, I asked the doctor, "Where can I get tested?"

After she explained that it would probably be best if I saw my primary care physician, Paige dismissed her, saying, "Thank you, doctor."

I called Olivia and gave her the news. She immediately ordered a full exam for A'Neesa.

As I paced the hallway floor trying to get enough nerve to go back into Reagan's room, every possible thought ran through my mind. I slowly walked toward the bed, staring at her swollen eyes. I forced myself to remember her without the blacks and blues, but I couldn't remember her before the deceit. I increasingly became uneasy and stood there in silence.

Paige whispered, "Talk to her."

"I don't know what to say …"

"Say what you feel."

Confused, I said, "I don't know what I feel!"

I felt a series of emotions that changed by the second. I wanted to be forgiving, but a part of me—a big part—was still upset.

In a *Get over it* tone, Paige said, "Laina, this has gone on long enough. I'd think you'd know better than to take life for granted."

I looked at Paige with confused eyes.

"What if …" Paige said. "What if God held a grudge for our sins and every time you prayed—"

With much conviction, I said, "I MEAN, REALLY, PAIGE! This is real talk. I wouldn't be feeling this animosity had Reagan not slept with Damon, Marcus, and only God knows who else. So forgive me if I'm a little lost for words right now. Maybe if your life was threatened with AIDS, you'd have a little more compassion for what I'm feeling."

My frustration curbed her opinion. She said, "I'm going to talk to the doctor."

"Yeah, you do that!"

I pulled the chair up beside the bed. Rubbing my hands in a nervous motion, I said, "It's DeLaina. I don't know if you can hear me." Searching for words, I said, "I met your little girl this morning. She's absolutely beautiful." I laughed. "Marcus would have been so proud of her."

A tear rolled down my cheek as I sat there reflecting on my life.

"I'm sorry that you're going through this." Then I whispered to her still body, "I promise, your daughter will never want for anything."

Waiting

The next morning, I called the office and told them that I'd be working from home that day and could be reached by cell phone. I called my doctor's office and schedule an emergency appointment. The receptionist insisted they were completely booked but said I could come and wait around to see if the doctor could fit me in. She promised there were no guarantees. I waited in the waiting room for four hours for the doctor to only spend ten minutes with me, then send me off to the lab. They took four tubes of blood and told me the results should be back in about ten days.

Four days later, Paige and I sat beside Rea's bed. Although she remained unresponsive, we were there every day.

"Do the people on her job know?" I asked.

Paige explained that Rea hadn't worked since she had the baby. She's been living off the social security check the baby gets and the little help she gets from social services. "I think she was scared to go back to work," Paige said.

"Scared of what?"

"I don't know."

Mona walked in just then and said, "Scared she wasn't gonna be able to keep her eye on dat nigga she was livin' wit."

I stood up to give Auntie my seat, kissed her on the cheek, and asked, "What are you doing here?"

Defending Rea, Paige said, "You don't know that."

Mona turned around with her hand on her hip. "Ya gonna get enough of dippin' ... diss here grown-folk conversation. Sit ya lil' five-dollar behind down before I make change."

"Auntie?"

"I'm sorry." She laughed, "Chile, dey watchin' *New Jack City* next door. Dat Wesley Snipes somethin' else." As she took off her jacket and got comfortable, she asked, "Lainee, you member dat sweet lil' white lady dat use to live down da hall from me?"

"Yes, ma'am."

"Well, chile, her husband's in intensive care just

a couple doors down." Looking at Paige, she said, "I saw Ms. Thang here comin' down da hall earlier, so I stopped to see if you were here too."

Paige then said, "Someone's going to have to wait in the hall. Rea can only have two visitors at a time."

"Oh, hush, dey always say dat."

"I don't know, Auntie." Trying to explain, I said, "I was here the other day when Mike and Tracey came up. Nurse Wratchet came in and made me leave."

"Chile, you don't know what dat woman's day was like. Imagine if you were wiping grown folks old wrinkly behinds all day. You'd be mad too." Then Mona asked, "What she look like, Lainee?"

"I don't know … she looked like a typical nurse—stocky, older lady with a surly attitude."

"Stocky? Girl, you know big people evil when dey hungry."

Rea's nurse came in to check her vitals. As she placed two fingers on her wrist, she said, "One of you are going to have to leave. Ms. Mitchell is only allowed two visitors at a time."

Paige looked at me and offered to leave, but Mona told her to sit down. Mona asked, "What's ya name, honey?"

"Nurse Williams."

"Well, look here, Ms. Nurse Williams, ma'am …

I just wanna spend time with my three girls. You can understand that … right?"

"I don't make the rules. I'm just here to enforce them."

Mona pulled a king-sized Snickers from her purse, slid it across the eating tray toward Nurse Williams, and winked.

The nurse looked over her glasses. "Excuse me?"

"Look, we both know ya want it. Just take it and we'll pretend dis-here neva happened."

The nurse collected herself and proceeded to leave the room, but not without putting Mona on notice. "If one of you don't leave … in five minutes, I'm calling security."

Paige and I shook our heads in disbelief. I turned to Mona. "Tell me you did not just try to bribe the nurse with a Snickers bar."

"That's why we don't take you anywhere," Paige said. "You don't know how to act."

In an innocent tone, Mona said, "What? She just mean. I thought big people were suppose to be jolly."

***

A couple days later, Olivia called to tell me the baby was negative. To celebrate, Paige and I took A'Neesa to Chuck E. Cheese's. As soon as we got inside, she pulled away from Paige and took off running. I took chase behind her. I loved that little girl. She was the untainted version of the people I loved at one time.

Paige's phone rang. I heard her say, "Okay, we'll be right there." She ended the call and told me, "It was the hospital. Reagan's organs are shutting down."

Once we arrived at the hospital, Paige made all the necessary phone calls as I sat by Rea's bedside, holding her hand for what would be the last time.

Days later, my HIV results showed up in the mail. My stomach tightened as I ran my finger underneath the lip of the envelope. I was negative.

Reagan and I had lived the same life for many years. That very well could have been me lying in that bed. But God ...

Adoption

After the passing, we went back to Rea's apartment and cleaned it out. I took a few keepsake items for the baby, for the day she's all grown up and ask about her mother. I took two photo albums, bronzed baby footprints, and what appeared to be a diary with a little silver lock on it.

A'Neesa was in my foster care, but as the days went by, the more I wanted it to be permanent. Rea's sudden passing caused everyone to come out of the woodworks to state claim to A'Neesa in the name of Marcus. Since his family still blamed me for his death, I knew if they gained custody, I'd never see her again.

One day, Paige asked, "Have you thought about making this permanent … adopting Neesa?"

"Yeah, but she may be better off with her family."

"You are her family. Who better to raise her than you? Who knew Marcus and Regan better than you?"

As the adoption process was underway, people from his family tried to dig up dirt in an effort to discredit me. One evening, as the baby and I were having dinner with Paige, my cell phone rang. Knowing it was the case worker, I excused myself from the dinner table.

She questioned my affiliation with a known drug dealer and ex-con. Even though I explained that he was merely an acquaintance that I hadn't seen or talked to in over three years, she expressed concerns and explained how this could have an effect on my approval. I returned to the table with tears in my eyes and my past mistakes in the forefront of my mind. Paige took the baby out of the booster seat and sent her to play.

In a concerned tone, Paige asked, "Honey, what's wrong? What she say?"

"Basically, that my past may hinder the adoption."

She gave a half smile. "You act surprised. You know the only ammo the enemy has is your past, so he tries to throw that up in your face to make you lose faith."

I knew what she was saying was true, but my flesh got in the way and I worried about a battle that wasn't mine.

"Paige, if they prove me to be an unfit person, they'll come and take her." As I became more emotional, I explained, "I had an abortion that went wrong. There's a possibility I may never have kids of my own. A'Neesa maybe my only chance at a family."

She smiled. "Says man. The thing that people forget most often is that God doesn't do things in our time. He's not on your schedule Laina. Remember Sarah and Abraham? She wanted kids, and the older she got, she thought, 'Well, God hasn't done it by now; he's not gonna do it.' God had plans for her bigger than anything she could imagine. He didn't deny her baring children; he delayed it for the right season.

DeLaina, the Word declares no good thing will the Lord withhold from you. No good thing ... Umh, you can't even spell GOOD without GOD. This adoption is bigger than your past. Though the enemy may try ... he can't stop this."

Ministry

As a leader in the youth ministry, I headed up a program called "The Buck Stops Here." We put together an event for kids aged fifteen to twenty-one to show them they had options. I invited ex-convicts, stockbrokers, reformed drug addicts, professors, reformed street walkers, and our very own Assistant Pastor, Daniel Waters. Their only job was to speak openly to kids about their lives and the choices they made or should have made.

I closed out the segment, saying, "This night was all about you guys. You're getting older and you need to understand that there's going to be pressure to do things to fit in, but I want you to know that you don't have to fit into someone else's mold. Remember when Officer Wallace explained that, when a crime is committed, an office comes and dusts for fingerprints? Well, he's able to do that because God created you so uniquely. He created you so special that even the tips of your fingers are different from anyone else. You're fearfully and wonderfully made, just as God intended you to be." After I closed out the night, one of the parents, Sista Jergens—Alex's mom—approached me. "You did an awesome job," she said. "I would like to talk to you about coming to speak to my twelfth grade class?"

A little taken back, I thought to myself, *I'm just doing this for the church.*

"Let me back up a minute," she said. "I'm the assistant principal at Alexandra High School. Sista DeLaina, they all have such potential. I feel, if you could just put together an event of this magnitude, it would mean so much. Something like a scared straight tactic."

I told her I could put her in contact with someone who could do it, but she insisted she wanted me to head it up. I told her that I'd pray on it and get back to her.

A month later, I found myself organizing a motivational seminar titled "You Make the Difference." Excited and on my way to the school, one of the speakers called and said she had a family emergency. I didn't sweat it because the other speaker was strong enough to carry the event all on his own. I was standing in the main office talking to Sista Jergens about the format when my cell phone rang. I stepped out to take it. It was Bobby MacArthur, the other speaker. He said he had a meeting that was running late and didn't think he would make it in time. I freaked out. I went back into the main office and asked Sista Jergens if we could talk privately. She led me into her office, where I explained the situation.

"Okay, what's the problem?"

In a panic, I explained, "Ok, let me say this another way ... we don't have a speaker."

"Yes, we do. Why can't you do it?"

"Because I'm not prepared. I came to facilitate ... not speak."

"DeLaina, the senior class consists of 158 kids. Out of that 158, forty-seven of them have at least one child."

"I'm not prepared; I'd be winging it."

She closed the door. "Well, then, let's pray that the Lord puts the words on your lips."

"But I—"

She took my hands. "Lord, in the name of Jesus, I come before you this morning, thanking you for this appointed time. I'm standing on your Word. You said when two or more are gathered in your name, there you are also. Lord, as DeLaina prepares to speak to your children, I pray you give her the words. Stand up in her that she may rest in you. Lord God, just move DeLaina out of the way. I pray that you remove any agendas and use her, Lord. Speak through her. Allow the words from her mouth and the meditation of her heart to be exceptional in your sight. In Jesus' name we pray. Amen."

How could I not feel confident? I looked down at my watch, noting the seminar was due to start in forty-five minutes. I excused myself to get my thoughts together and pray alone. I stood there, unsure of what to say or how to say it, remembering if I quoted the Scripture too much, I'd lose them. I had to find a way to reach them, but nothing was coming to me. Before I knew it, my time was up. The auditorium began to fill with sixteen- to eighteen-year-olds.

As I took the podium, I said, "My name is DeLaina Richards. Does anyone know why I'm here today?"

A voice from the back of the room said, "You're here to talk about us having sex."

"No, I'm here to talk about you having choices." I walked to the edge of the stage. "I remember being your age and having trouble believing adults use to be my age, but it's true. So as I talk to you today, I want you to understand that I'm not talking to you just as an adult but as someone who knows what it's like to want to fit in … to have pressure from your peers to do things you may not want to do—and I'm not just talking about sex."

They sat there attentively.

"Let's talk about choices. First, stand up if you have a child."

Only a few stood.

"Come on. Let's be honest. How would you feel if your parents denied you?"

Twenty more or so stood.

"Okay, now let's do this … The boys standing, you come down to the front of the stage and face me. Now, girls, I want you to sit down if your father lives in your house." No one moved. "Or you talk to him or see him at least twice a week." Still, no one moved. "Okay, now the girls standing, I want you to come down and stand behind a boy. I see there's more girls than boys, so two girls can stand behind one boy if you need to."

Once the girls were in place, I told the boys to turn around.

"Guys, the girl you're looking at could be your daughter in fifteen or sixteen years if you don't give her the foundation she needs now. You're her first introduction to a man, so you have to remember that you set the standard. If you don't tell her she's beautiful, she's smart, or even that you love her, she'll start looking for someone else to tell her, to validate her worth. She'll start looking for you in the arms of some knucklehead boy."

The pregnant girl on the end began crying.

"Girls, the boy you're looking at could very well be your son one day if you don't instill the right values in him. See, when you have a different boy coming to your house every week—going in mommy's room—guess what? He's going to grow up to think that's what a man is supposed to do. You all have to understand you can't undo what's been done. The babies are here. All you can do is set a good example. If you want your kids to be better than you, you have to set the stage by being a better you."

I dismissed them back to their seats.

By this time, Mr. MacArthur had arrived, and we decided to break them off into two groups. I hopped down off the stage and told all the girls to follow me. It was a nice spring day, so I took the girls out to the football field.

"Okay, girls, so lets talk. I know some of you are dealing with insecurities with your bodies and hormones changing, unfortunately it comes with teenage territory. But if it brings you any comfort you're not alone. See, when I was younger I had a self-esteem deficiency-"

A girl in the back interrupted. "What does that mean?"

"It means I had low self-esteem."

A girl on the front row asked, "How? You're so pretty."

"What's your name, baby?"

"Alecia."

"Alecia, thank you. But beauty isn't what people think of you. Beauty is what you think of yourself. And the truth is, I didn't think I was pretty. I had been told that, but I thought people were just being nice. See, what people think of you doesn't change who you are. Your self-esteem is your own self-assessment of you, and your value."

Looking at the girls sitting clustered together, I asked, "Have you ever tried to be friends with a girl or boy, and they didn't want to be friends with you?" They nodded yes. "How did that make you feel?"

A little fair-skinned girl with a ponytail said, "It made me want to punch him in his nose."

I said, "Okay, somebody give lil' Laila Ali a hug."

Everyone laughed.

"But seriously, whether it's a boy or a girl, being rejected can be a difficult feeling, but you have to remember, it's their loss. They're missing out on the opportunity to be friends with the likes of you; they should be so lucky."

Acknowledging a dark-skinned girl with her

hand raised, I said, "Yes, what's your name?"

"Shaquita."

"Go ahead, Shaquita."

In a somewhat confident tone, she said, "Well, that sounds good, Ms. DeLaina, but for real, some people don't like me cuz of my complexion, like it's contagious. The boys run from me like they gonna catch Wesley Snipes disease or something."

The girls and I laughed.

"Shaquita, you have a strong personality. I like that. Girls, here's what I want you to do. Look at the differences between the young lady on your left and on your right. Some of you have long hair, short hair. Some of you get A's, some B's, some C's."

The back row looked at me like *Keep going*.

I laughed. "The rest of y'all, I'm praying for you." I continued, "God made us all different, every one of us. So when you come up against someone who doesn't like you and doesn't even know you, more than likely it's not about you. They see the joy in you and can't understand how it is that you don't have what they have, but you're happier than they are. If you don't remember anything else, remember that you never, ever have to be jealous of what someone else has, 'cause the good news is… if God did it for them, he can do it for you.

And moms … serious business, listen, don't let

your burdens be your babies' burdens. Don't weigh them down with your issues. Love them ... and tell them you love them over and over again. And just a little secret ... buying them toys and games doesn't make up for not spending time with them. Make them your priority. I promise you, the club is going to be there ... the party is going to be there ... that guy is going to be there ... and if not, you don't want anyone who doesn't think your child should come first. You understand?"

Heads nodded in agreement.

"As for you girls without kids ... this is real talk, having a baby doesn't keep a man. Ask any one of these moms. You all have to protect yourselves, because this day in time, getting pregnant is the least of your worries. You can catch something a prescription won't cure. Although abstinence and celibacy is the key, if you are having sex, please be smart enough to use protection. The protection isn't about anyone but you. I don't care what he says about 'It doesn't feel the same' ... or 'Baby, I ain't sleepin' wit no body else' ... protect yourself. Because, understand that he doesn't have to be sleeping with them now to be infected. It can take an upwards of ten years for HIV to show up in your body."

They all seemed a bit overwhelmed.

"Does anyone have any questions?"

No one said a word.

I comforted them, saying, "If you don't want to talk in this forum, you can come talk to me one on one afterwards."

One girl raised her hand.

"Yes?" I said. "You in the red shirt."

"You said you went through a hard time with your parents not being around, but you seem okay."

"Everybody repeat after me … I'm blessed and highly favored!"

"I'm blessed and highly favored!" they said.

"My yesterday didn't dictate that I'd be here... I was suicidal at one point, homicidal at another. I was a drug addict and an alcoholic. But Baby, once I stopped running from God and started running to him my life changed. Listen, I just want to leave you with this … whatever you're going thru at home, at school, with a boy, or whateva, just remember, trouble don't last always."

After I answered all the questions, I dismissed them back to class.

Deacon Stubbs

At this point in my life, I had never knowingly heard God speak. I heard people say, "God said" or "God told me." I was embarrassed that I was saved and wasn't hearing from God like everyone else claimed. I wondered if I was doing something wrong. So the next time Paige started a statement with "I was talking to God and ..." I cut her off and asked, "What does he sound like?" I imagined he'd sound strong like Ving Rhames or gentle like Delroy Lindo.

"Sometimes he speaks to my heart," Paige said. "While other times, it's like a voice in my ear. It's God. He speaks in many different ways."

"How do you know it's God?"

"The Word says 'My sheep will know my voice.'"

Although I couldn't heard God, sometimes I could hear lonely clearly. When I felt lonely trying to creep in to suffocate me, I'd just throw myself into my work. The Bible says that God didn't create us to be alone, but I have to admit there were times it didn't feel that way.

One Saturday afternoon, I pulled up in front of the church to meet Sista Agnes, the choir director, to pick up the Girl Scout cookies I'd ordered from her daughter. I was a little early. I sat in my car killing time when I saw Sista Kandis being dropped off by her new husband. My eyes filled as I watched them kiss and trade "I love you's."

As I remembered what that felt like, I thought about all the ones I'd loved and lost. Even the ones I loved that didn't love me back. I thought to myself, *I miss hearing "I love you."*

That's when a voice responded, *I love you.*

I cried out, *God, I want to love again, but I'm scared because… I've loved people that didn't love me back. I gave so much of myself. I gave and gave, and they just took and took.*

As soon as I said it, I felt God must be saying, How do you think I feel?

I prayed, *God, show me how to love you. Show me*

how to love you the way I loved them. Lord, show me how to pour all my heart and my soul into you. Be my one and only, God, until you see fit to release me to another. Show me how to be faithful and loyal to you. In Jesus' name. AMEN!

***

When I was younger, I had certain standards for men. After you've been through some things, all you care about is if he's saved … not just on Sundays but Monday through Saturday, too.

In walked Nathan—Deacon Stubbs—a systems engineer and Sunday school teacher. The fellowship hall usually smelled like him, and it left my nose with the same excitement I'd get walking into Auntie Mona's house, smelling the essence of sweet potato pie. He smelled good.

There's something so very appealing about a man who's seeking God's face. So, every Sunday, when I'd drop off A'Neesa, he'd strike up conversation.

"Good morning, Sista Richards."

I nodded. "Good morning."

One Sunday, as the other mothers were leaving, he leaned in. "I've been meaning to tell you about the programs we have for preschoolers. Maybe we could talk about it over dinner?"

I thought to myself, *Over dinner*? I looked around the room and said, "We can't talk about it here?"

He smiled. "Well, we have to eat, so I thought

we could do it together."

I wasn't sure if he was asking me out or just being friendly. Remembering what happened last time somebody in church was smiling my way … I passed.

We went on as usual for the next seven or eight Sundays: we'd speak, smile, joke, and end it with a holy hug. After several more weeks of this, something jolted and I found myself looking forward to seeing Deacon Stubbs. I found myself stopping by the ladies' room after service to check my hair and makeup before heading downstairs to pick up the baby, something I hadn't done before. As I walked into the room, Neesa ran and jumped into my arms. I looked around the room to find the good deacon engaged in conversation with Sista Evelyn's daughter, Candice. She hung onto his every word as I stood there watching, thinking, I like words. He looked up and caught me staring. Embarrassed, I told Neesa, "Go grab your coat. Hurry, hurry, hurry."

I couldn't believe I was feeling jealous. When Neesa came back with her coat on, I grabbed her hand and practically ran for the steps.

"Sista Richards," Deacon Stubbs called out. "Do you have a second?"

With one foot on the step, I exhaled, put on my game face, and turned around. "Sure, Deacon. What can I do for you?"

He smiled. "You look pretty today. Not that you

don't look pretty every day ..."

I laughed. "Thank you."

"I want you to meet someone."

I thought to myself, *Oh, I know who Candice is.*

He called out. "Come here, Ashley." Then he picked up a beautiful little brown girl and said, "This is A'Neesa's mommy. Say hi to Ms. DeLaina."

She smiled and put her head in his chest. He laughed and told her to take A'Neesa to go play for a few minutes.

As the girls ran away, he explained, "Ashley's mom, my sister had an emergency C-section."

"Oh my goodness!"

He laughed. "No, no. She's an anesthesiologist."

"Oh." I smiled. "So do you have any kids, Deacon?" As he shook his head no, I inquired, "Why hasn't some woman tied you down?"

He laughed. "I'm saved. I ain't into all that kinky stuff."

I stuttered, "No, I, uh, I meant—"

"Relax. I'm just joking. I know what you meant. I don't know. It just hasn't happened for me. If you don't mind me inquiring ... what happened with you and A'Neesa's dad?"

"Excuse me? Oh, no! Oh, I'm in the process of adopting A'Neesa."

"WOW! That's big! You ever been married?"

"Uhh, no."

"Why not? I see the men waiting in line to get your attention. Why haven't you given any of them your time?"

"Uh, well, truth of the matter is I spend a lot of time here. So if it doesn't work out, it could make for an uncomfortable situation."

"Yeah, I guess you're right. Hey, I'm going to take Miss Ashley to Chuck E. Cheese's. Would you and A'Neesa like to join us?"

I laughed. "As long as it's not a date."

"No, conceited, it's not a date."

That was the beginning.

Over the next several months, we spent a lot of time together, ending each evening with a holy hug and a peck on the cheek. Over time, the hugs became a little less holy. One evening while I was at his house, waiting for him to finish cooking dinner, his brother called. I couldn't hear the other side of the conversation, but Nathan said, "A'ight, look here, I have company so I'm gonna make this quick. Valentine's Day isn't about you; it's about her. She doesn't want to hear about what you bought her for Christmas in February. For real, stop listening to your boys. It's a real holiday … ask any woman. I'll call you tomorrow, but trust me, man, if you don't get her something, you will regret it."

He called me into the kitchen to taste the mashed potatoes he'd made. He grabbed a teaspoon from the drawer and scooped a sample from the pot. As the spoon neared my face, I leaned in and opened my mouth. "Umm, this is good."

With a sly grin, he said, "Yeah, it is."

The smile on his face said we weren't talking about the potatoes anymore.

After about four months of spending time together, I'd begun to want more than a peck on the cheek or a kiss on the forehead. I wanted to feel his lips pressed against mine. I didn't want to break any rules … I just wanted to bend them a little bit.

So, one night after dinner at my house, I was in the kitchen loading up the dishwasher when I made up in my mind that I was going to kiss him; I was going to plant one on his lips. I was wiping down the counter and trying to get my thoughts together when he walked in. I dried my hands on the dish towel while the butterflies with wings the size of vultures flapped around in my belly.

I took a deep breath, walked toward him, and said, "There's something I've been wanting to do."

As I got closer, he took a step back and said, "Pray about it. God can give you the strength and wisdom to do anything."

Wasn't quit the response I was looking for.

Trying to get my mind right, I agreed, "Um, yeah, I know that's right."

Flustered, I went into the dining room, pretending to fix the table by moving the placemats and adjusting the center piece.

As I headed toward the sofa, he asked, "What have you been wanting to do?"

"Uhh, scuba diving." I thought, *Lord, forgive me.*

"I thought you couldn't swim."

"Yeah, see the dilemma." I felt like an idiot.

A couple of weeks passed before I got up the nerve to confront him.

I showed up at his house after work one afternoon, burst through the door, and asked point blank, "What are we doing?"

In a state of confusion, he looked around and responded, "That's a good question. You first." Then, laughing, he asked, "Where is this coming from?"

"I'm serious. Are we friends ... are we more than friends? What are we?"

He smiled. "I thought we were more than friends."

In a frustrated tone, I asked, "Then why haven't you tried to kiss me in the past four months?" I traipsed back and forth. "Are you attracted to me?"

He laughed out loud like I was doing stand-up. I pointed at my face. "Notice I'm not laughing."

He continued laughing. "Women say they want a saved man, but when they get one, they don't know how to act."

I stood in his living room feeling like an idiot as he curtailed my fleshly thoughts, confessing that God was his number one priority.

"Yes, I'm attracted to you." He laughed. "I haven't kissed you because I'm afraid I'm not going to want to stop." He grabbed my hand and led me to the couch. "You know I haven't always been saved." He paused as if he were reflecting on another time. "I've met a number of extraordinary women in my life. I always thought I may have missed out on something good because I was … being a man. Laina, I've been saved and celibate for three years, and I promised God if he sent me another angel…" He kissed the back of my hand. "I promised I'd do right this time."

A couple of months later, after service, Nathan pulled out the grill and had a few people over. When I went inside to get more ice for the cooler, Nate and his brother, Carlos, were standing by the freezer talking, and as I got closer, their voices dropped to a whisper. Noting he was tied up, I went back outside and took over the grill. Several minutes later, when he and his brother returned, I overheard him tell Carlos, "Walk by faith and not by the flesh. Dude, this is real talk … if you trust in God, you will never have to chase another woman. God will show you if she's the one."

As the day went on, I went back inside to get his kitchen in order. As I stood at the double sink washing dishes, I turned around to see him standing in the doorway staring at me.

"What?" I asked.

He just shook his head. "I love you."

I instinctively wanted to respond the way you do when someone sneezes, but I couldn't form the words. I just smiled. Because of the man that he was, he didn't pressure me to reciprocate. He just went back to the cookout like nothing ever happened.

By this point, I had spent most of my adult life chasing after love and allowing someone else's definition of love to define me. Although past relationships left me broken and bruised, I did want to be in love. I wanted to love like I'd never been hurt—uninhabited.

I can say this relationship was vastly different from any other; I was different.

For the first time, I knew that, no matter what happened, I would be okay.

Ruling

The ruling on the adoption was to be heard at 10:45 a.m. on August 8. I sat on the right with my attorney, Ms. Wakefield, and Melissa sat on the left with hers, Mr. Ryder. As the family court judge took the stand, Paige tiptoed in and sat behind me, beside Nathan.

Judge Yahmeen explained that he'd read the case.

"I do have questions for both parties," he said. "Ms. Richards, I understand that you had a battle with alcoholism and drugs abuse several years ago. Did you join a support group?"

I moved closer to the microphone. "In a manner

of speaking, Your Honor, I did."

"Was it AA?"

"No, Your Honor. It was G-O-D."

"I see. So outside of the church, there was no other counseling?"

Ms. Wakefield intervened on my behalf, stating, "Your Honor, my client witnessed the suicide of the father of the child in question, which triggered the lapse in judgment."

"I understand that, counselor. I read the file. My concern is that the support group teaches you how to deal with traumas in the future without turning to a substance for a temporary fix. Ms. Richards, how long have you been sober and clean?"

"For three years, Your Honor."

The judge then turned to Melissa. "Ms. Jones, who currently lives at your residency?"

"Me and my three kids."

"How many bedrooms?"

"Two, Your Honor, but I'm looking for a bigger place."

"Okay, I'll take that into consideration. Counselors, either of you have anything else to add?"

They both said, "No, Your Honor."

"We will take a fifteen-minute recess and I will return with my decision."

While court was in recess, I walked over to

Melissa's table and whispered to her, "Whatever happens today, I think it's imperative that A'Neesa remains in contact with all of her family. We just have to find a happy medium."

"Whateva, DeLaina!" Rolling her eyes, she said, "You're just saying that 'cause you know you're gonna lose."

"This isn't about you or me!"

"It ain't gonna have anything to do with you at all when I get custody."

The judge returned. "Upon reviewing the case, I feel both parties would provide adequate care for the child in question. However, I do believe one would provide slightly more stability than the other. I'm ruling in favor of DeLaina Richards, contingent on a court-ordered drug test."

Melissa blurted out, "Dis heffa killed a Chia Pet and you're gonna give her a child?"

The judge said, "Thank you, Ms. Jones. That brings me to the second clause of the ruling. Ms. Richards, I am also ordering you to take a forty-hour parenting course."

He banged the gavel to seal his judgment.

Wisdom

As we welcomed in the first frost of the year, the ministry's schedule for feeding the homeless changed from once a month to twice a month. In order to facilitate the need and cut church cost, members of the ministry offered to open up their homes for preparation. This month, we were using Sista Goodman's house. When Paige and I arrived, there was food all over the table and countertops. As the members arrived one by one, she put them to work immediately. My job was to prepare the spiritual food. Sista Goodman printed Scripture excerpts and a message from the pastor that needed to be collated, folded, and stapled. I was sitting at the table, preparing the packets when one of the elders asked Sista Goodman how her granddaughter, Kania, was doing.

"Dat chile's at her sista's house, licking her wounds."

"What happened?"

In a thick Southern drawl, she said, "Hun-ney! She met some lil' nappy-headed boy, and the next thing I knew she was talkin' bout she loved him."

The elder replied, "These young-uns quick to fall in love, ain't dey? Well, wha-chu tell her?"

"I told her she ain't know nuffin 'bout him. She was just infatuated but ..."

Sista Ann said, "Well, you know how these kids are ..."

"She round here mad at me like it's my fault," Sista Goodman said. "But God knows I was just trying to break the cycle. I wanted to keep her from goin' through what her mother went through. Shoot, I was tryin' to stop her from the hell I went through." She laughed. "Between her moma and me, we've been married seven times. It took dat dar last divorce for me to realize the problem was me. Yeah, I divorced them, but chile, they all divorced me."

She turned to me and asked if I knew who the "Representative" was. Thinking she was referring to the ministry, I answered, "Sista Mosby, I think."

She laughed. "No, hun-ney. I mean the person ya meet when ya start spending time wit a gentleman caller. Ya not really meeting him, ya meeting the Representative. The one dat's paving the road for the person he really is."

Much like Sista Goodman, I'd always been in love with love so it was nothing for me to trade "I love you's" in the first month.

She continued, "In the first thirty to ninety days, hun-ney, the Rep will open doors, send flowers, buy gifts, and call just to say hi. After ninety days, you lucky to get a petal much less the whole rose."
Sista Ann interrupted, "Some men!"

"Most men!" Sista Goodman said. "Men naturally have an animalistic nature; they hunters. They disguise themselves in order to lure ya in. He can't tell ya up front dat he has bad credit, his ex got a restraining order against him, or dat he had four jobs in the last three months."

She wiped her hands on the dish towel and asked the girl on the end, rhetorically, "What happens when ya fall in love wit the Representative? Ya spend the life of the relationship tryin' to coax, prod, trick, and manipulate him into doing what he use to … the things the Representative did to make ya fall in love wit him in the first place."

One of the elders interjected, "When da fella stops responding the way he use ta and doing the thangs he use ta … ya begin ta question ya-self … I do somethin' wrong? When all along, the truth is ... it ain't-chu; da Rep done left the building."

Sista Goodman said, "So when ya ask him, 'Baby, what's wrong? Why things changed?' ... he's baffled. But here's why: some men don't even realize the standards the Representative set."

One of the young girls asked, "Hold up, wait, wait ... So you sayin' when the woman's mad cuz he ain't doing what he use to, he thinks she trippin'?"

"Yes, chile. It's a chain reaction. He reacting to her reaction to the new person," Sista Goodman replied.

Sista Goodman's new husband, Mr. Earl, passed through the kitchen with a word of insight. "If women spent half as much time listening as they do talking, they'd know what they were getting into. You have to listen to what a man is sayin and not sayin."

"Aww, go on, get outta here, Earl!"

He poured himself a cup of coffee. "Shoot, dees lil' young thangs move too fast. A man like a chase. Take that away from him and he'll lose interest quick."

I sat on the edge of my chair, listening to wisdom spoken in volumes. It all made sense; it was as though they clarified the complexity of the theory of relativity. Explaining the construct of eighty percent of my past relationships.

In a quiet tone, one of the volunteers asked,

"Mrs. Goodman, can I ask you a question?"

As she washed her hands preparing to delve back into work, she said, "Sure. What's ya name, hun-ney?"

"Oh, my name's Vicky. See, my husband, Carl, and I are coming up on our one-year anniversary, but something's going on with him. All of a sudden, it seems when we go out he's breaking his neck looking at other women. Not just any woman … these little petite women."

One of the women interrupted. "Would you feel better if he were looking at full-figured women?"

Confused, she responded, "No … maybe. Well, at least I could compete. I can't compete wit these lil' Barbie girls." Her tone changed as she said, "Carl could have anyone he wants. I don't know what he would want with someone my size anyway."

Sista Armstrong, a friend of Vicky's family, moved in closer. "Wait a minute, Vicky. Whateva you and Carl are goin' through in your marriage, it's not about your size. Let me tell you something: God had to create you big as a symbol of the gift in you. He had to make you big enough to carry the weight of your family. You were born into a family of addicts … everybody is addicted to one thing or another, but you … you're the first woman in your family to go to college, the first homeowner, and you did all that under your family's stigma. Anyone else would probably have crumbled under the pressure, but God built you to carry it."

The elders looked at one another and simultaneously let out an, "Um!"

Sista Goodman wiped her hands on her apron and said, "Hun-ney, the first thang ya need to know is, if ya trying to compete with another woman, ya gonna always lose. There's always gonna be somebody taller, prettier, and smarter, but there's only gonna be one you, and can't nobody beat you at being you."

"Well, what am I suppose to do?" Vicky asked. One of the other ladies inquired, "What did he say?"

"He said there was nothing wrong with him. He just keeps saying that I'm nagging him."

One of the younger girls said, "If I was you, I'd tell him to get it together or get out."

Sista Goodman nodded but cleared up the statement, saying, "Marriage is work all day every day … 24/7. Listen, men don't like to be told what to do. But, hun-ney, ya have to be clear and direct about what-chu will and will not tolerate. Men will only do what-chu allow them to do. Ya understand? Tell him that ya love him, but let him know how the man ya love is making you feel."

The ladies nodded in agreement.

Sista Goodman continued, "Baby, I understand how this could mess wit ya self-esteem. But ya don't deserve to be made to feel *less than*. So when ya tell him ya deserve better, ya have to say it like ya believe it. Ya hear me?"

As Vicky smiled and hugged Sista Goodman, there was a knock at the door. Assuming it was more ladies from the church, Sista Goodman yelled over Vicky's shoulder, "Come on in."

A frightened, battered young girl came into the kitchen with her clothes torn and bloody. As she noticed all the people, she backed out. "I'm sorry, Mrs. Goodman, I didn't know you had company."

Looking her up and down, Sista Goodman grabbed her. "Hun-ney, what happened to ya?"

I recognized the fear in her eyes. She had been beaten by someone she trusted.

Trying to escape the prying eyes, the girl said, "No, nothing, I'm fine. I'll come back later."

"No, ya won't neither." Sista Goodman took off her apron and told Paige to take the girl into the den. Moments later, after they left the room one of the ladies began sharing a story about her abused coworker. She said, "Girl, the guy she was dating …"

Just then, I noticed Paige standing in the hallway, motioning for me.

Without question, I followed her. As we slid the den's double doors open, Sista Goodman was walking the floor with a Bible close to her bosom. She opened it, placed it on the young girl's lap, then pointed to a passage and said, "Read it out loud."

The girl began reading. "The LORD is my light and my salvation—whom shall I fear? The LORD is the stronghold of my life—of whom shall I be afraid?"

Sista Goodman stopped her, then said, "Declare it again!"

As the girl repeated the verse, Sista Goodman paced the floor. The girl continued reading, "When evil men advance against me to devour my flesh, when my enemies and my foes attack me, they will stumble and fall."

She stopped her once more and said, "Declare it again!"

As the girl continued to read, Paige and I joined in intercessory prayer, tearing down strongholds. Something fell over me. Sista Goodman paced the floor and declared, "Satan, you are already defeated. The blood of Jesus is against you."

Sista Goodman poured oil into her aged hands, rubbed them together, and whispered a prayer only she and God could hear. Much to my surprise, she told me to lift my hands. As I did, she placed her palms against mine and said, "Go and speak healing and life into her."

It took only moments for my mind to catch up with what was happening. I stared at the girl and began to weep as I saw flashes of me—the me that God covered and saved when prayer and church were the farthest things from my mind. I went to the girl and told her to lift her hands. With her trembling hands in the air and tears flowing from her eyes, I placed both hands on her head.

"By the authority of the King ... Devil, you're already defeated. I command you to flee. Release her mind in the name of Jesus. I'm transferring everything that's in me ... into you. I'm believing by faith that every door the Lord opened for me is being opened for you. Every door he shut on my behalf, I'm believing he'll shut for you, in the name of Jesus. Lord, renew her mind and give her the strength to walk away. I bind the spirit of insecurity, the spirit of insanity, and the spirit of complacency ... in the name of Jesus. You are the head and not the tail. I speak healing and restoration over your life. I pray the Lord gives you the faith of Daniel ... the strength of David ... and the wisdom of Solomon, in the name of Jesus. By the blood of the Lamb, you shall live and you shall not die. We declare and decree that it is already done. In Jesus' name. AMEN!"

From bouts with suicide to intercessory prayer. I never would have thought ...

The following month, Paige held a book club meeting at her home. I couldn't find a sitter initially, so I ended up arriving later than expected. Once I got there, they were already done discussing the book and were just talking about life ... and love.

I walked in as LaDawn—Paige's next-door neighbor—said, "I don't know what's wrong. We go to church every Sunday."

Not knowing the content of the conversation, I said, "Well, maybe you need to go Friday and Saturday, too."

Everyone snickered except her. After I explained that I was just joking, she asked desperately what she should do. After several of the other women gave their opinions, Paige reiterated LaDawn's situation, explaining her husband's sexual addictions.

I said, "I think it's great that he goes to church with you, but going to church doesn't keep the Lord's decrees. I know who Bill Gates is, but I don't know him personally. Knowing who God is and having a relationship with him is completely different."

Someone declared, "A'ight, preach."

"Your husband has to want to do right," I said. "The spirit of perversion is strong." Then, with the raspy voice of my great aunt, I said, "But if he wants to change, he need only ask. In the book of Matthew, there was an unclean man. The Bible doesn't tell us much about him, but I'm inclined to believe that he'd been through some things. Somebody say, 'It takes one to know one.'"

The women laughed and repeated, "It takes one to know one."

"I've been places and done things that would categorize me as being unclean, unholy, unsaved."

One of the women confessed, "Me, too."

I went on. "Even unclean, the man was a smart man. Knowing the mess he was in, he had enough sense to fall to his knees, and in no uncertain terms, he said, 'Lord, if you are willing, you can make me clean.' He was saying, 'Lord, I don't want to be like this anymore. I'm willing to change if you're willing to change me.' I WAS THAT MAN in Matthew, but by the grace of God …"

I think it was that night that I came to the realization, I'm not the woman I use to be.

In Love

I woke up one day and realized that I was in love with Nathan. I didn't think I'd ever love again with my whole heart, yet there I was. I think I had always known, but it was apparent to me the one evening I met him at his house after work. We were going to a basketball game in DC. Both running late, we pulled into his driveway about the same time. I got out and grabbed my backpack off the backseat with my change of clothes. When we got in the house, he threw his laptop bag on the couch and said, "I have to take a quick shower. You know where everything is. Go ahead and do what you need to do."

When I went upstairs to the guest room to change, I heard him mumbling. I thought he was on the phone. But, as I passed his room on my way back downstairs, I could see him kneeling down at the foot of his bed, thanking God.

He had box seats to see LA whoop up on Washington—and a woman in his house—but he was down on his knees.

He made me want to be better woman, a better servant.

A few weeks later, Nathan invited A'Neesa and me on a day trip to his family reunion in Connecticut. We got up early Saturday morning and drove five hours to Hartford. We went directly to his aunt and uncle's house, where his mom and dad were staying for the weekend, and then drove to the reunion from there. The day was filled with, Nice to meet you too's. About six o'clock or so, he cornered his parents and said, "Hey, we have to get ready to head back."

His mother hugged A'Neesa. "It was a pleasure meeting you, young lady." Neesa smiled.

I then overheard Nate's father whispering to him, "It's all set up. The rest is up to you," just before they hugged.

After his mother hugged me, she said, "I'm sorry we didn't get a chance to spend more time together, but I look forward to seeing you again soon." Everyone was so warm and welcoming that I hated to leave.

We left the park and got on the main highway.

Fifteen minutes and two exits later, Nathan pulled off.

"You stopping for gas?" I asked.

"No, I want to check out this house that my dad and I were talking about."

We drove through the suburban two-car garage neighborhood until we reached a house with a Sold sign in the front yard. I sat in the car and marveled at the cobblestone driveway of the brick-front, single-family home.

He said, "Come on, ladies. Let's go take a look."

"I don't know, Nate, a black couple in a white neighborhood? They probably called the police when we got off the exit."

He laughed. "Baby, its fine." He got out the car and headed up the walkway with A'Neesa running behind him, yelling, "Wait for me!"

I got out of the car and looked around at all the huge, single family homes. Just beyond the house at the end of the cul-de-sac was a lake. Even from where I was standing, it was beautiful.

As I walked up the walkway and into the house, I immediately noticed how the light bounced off the eggshell colored walls. Wondering how it seemed almost brighter inside than out, I looked up to see the skylight in the cathedral ceiling of the entrance way. I wandered through the first floor of the empty house, noticing the library with the built-in bookcase, the huge kitchen with all new appliances, and the glassed-in sunroom overlooking the pool on the backside of the house.

Nate yelled out, "Hey, come check out the upstairs."

As I walked up the circular staircase, I called out, "Where are you?"

A'Neesa replied, "In here, Mommy." Her voice came from the closed double doors at the end of the hallway.

Walking toward the doors, I thought to myself, this house is amazing.

As I turned the knob of the door, I asked, "Nate, whose house is this?"

The door opened, and there he was in a room filled with red roses. "It's yours if you want it." He knelt down on one knee with an open ring box. "Will you marry me?"

Without any thought, I exclaimed, "Yes!"

He hugged me and kissed me on the lips for the first time.

As A'Neesa stood there, seemingly a little confused, he knelt down and asked her, "Are you okay with all of this?"

She looked down for a moment before she responded. "Um, will I get to call you 'Daddy'?"

"If you want to."

She smiled. "I'm okay with it."

Four months later, we had a little ceremony in our backyard in Connecticut with family and a few of our closest friends. I wore a beautiful ankle length, spaghetti-strap, cream-colored satin dress while Nathan wore a matching colored suit. My little A'Neesa never looked more beautiful than she did walking down the aisle in the miniature version of my dress, dropping red and white rose petals.

Not the wedding I dreamed about as a little girl. But I would have married Nathan in some sweatpants in a junkyard.

***

Eighteen months from that day, I did what the doctors said I wouldn't be able to do. Nathan and I gave A'Neesa a little sister: Sarai LaNee. When I held her in my arms for the first time, I realized Mrs. Ellie-Mae was prophesying when she said I was carrying the burdens for my daughters—the little women I had no idea I'd have. God rest her soul.

The next few years flew right on by between family, work, and the ministry. Now, as I look at my family, I realize just how much God has changed and healed me. When God changes you, there's a shift in the atmosphere that changes everything around you.

One night after I had gone through the

normal weeknight ritual—shower, iron clothes, and pack lunches—I went to tuck the girls in. As I opened A'Neesa's door, I found myself overcome with joy as I listened to her praying.

It sounded more like she was having a conversation. She said, "And thank you for not letting Mommy get mad at Daddy when he said he broke the glass, when it was really me. I didn't mean to. Sometimes I'm just clumsy … like when I knocked the lamp over last week. Thank you for letting me get an A on my spelling test. It was rigorous—R-I-G-O-R-O-U-S … rigorous. Oh yeah, one more thing … Sarai keeps having nightmares. God, if it's the Devil, make him stop messing with her. She comes and gets in my bed and steals all the covers. Love you! Amen."

The joy I felt hearing my daughter earnestly talk to God was incomparable. Before that night, I think I thought of my restoration as God having mercy upon me … that he changed me for me. But I now know it wasn't only for me—he changed me because the foundation had to be laid for those little girls.

After that night, I felt a call to fully commit in my ministry, to talk to young girls who may be struggling. When I told people I was quitting the firm where I was about to make "Principal," they looked at me crazy. The looks worsened when I talked about the vision of going school to school. Many tried to plant doubt, saying, "You have a family to take care of. Why would you leave a sure thing and not even have a contract or funding lined up?" Though it wasn't easy, I held on. I was turned away by the public and private schools. I was sure Christian-based schools would jump at the idea, but they weren't interested either. After months of hearing, "I don't think it's the right fit for our students," my faith got shaky. It's in those times that you see the strength of your mate. Nate came home one evening and saw doubt and disappointment covering my face like a new brand of foundation and asked, "Honey, what's wrong?"

After I explained that none of the schools were interested in a youth program, he said, "Baby, sometimes to get where you're trying to go, you have to do something you've never done. If God called you to do this, then we have to fast and pray until something happens."

Did you hear him? He said "we."

Several months later, Sista Jergens moved to Connecticut to become school superintendent. As she settled into her new role, she contacted me to kick off a statewide program geared toward teens, which opened up other opportunities. Won't he make a make a way.

***

One evening while I was home cooking, I received a call from the doctor confirming my 2:00

a.m. brownie cravings. On October 28, I gave birth to an eight-pound, nine-ounce baby boy: Ezell Corneal, named after my daddy. He looked just like Sarai when she was born … reddish colored skin, pouty lips, and a full head of hair that laid down perfectly into a little wrap. He was the most perfect little boy I had ever seen. Nathan and Ezell were inseparable. Nate loves his girls, but that boy … oh, there's something special about a father and son.

I tried to talk Paige into coming to stay for a little while after the baby was born, but she wasn't able to make it. Nathan's mother was insistent upon staying the first couple weeks, the way she'd done with Sarai. I love Mother Stubbs, mostly when she's not in my house. After Sarai was born, let's just say she took my prayer life to a whole 'nother level. Nathan took off the first two weeks and talked his mom into coming after he went back to work.

Ain't he sweet? I got to have Mother Stubbs all to myself during the day … all to myself … just me and Mother Stubbs … us.

The Diary

I looked up and it was Ezell's fifth birthday. Sarai was eight, and A'Neesa had just turned fifteen. It was Saturday morning, and the guests were due to start arriving about 2:00 p.m.—and the basement was nowhere near ready. Paige's flight arrived late the night before, but I knew, as soon as she got up, I could count on her to take over and make this party a success. With that in mind, I went downstairs to my office to check my emails. Once Paige came downstairs and the gang began gathering in the kitchen, the jobs were assigned.

A'Neesa had, had a funky little attitude the past couple days. Although I remembered how hard it was being a teenager, I almost snatched a knot in her, twice.

I was trying to give her some time to work through her emotions, but if she snapped at me one more time …

I told Sarai, "Go wake up your sister."

"Mommy, she's up. She's reading a book."

Nathan and I laughed. "On purpose?"

"Well, tell her to come downstairs," I said.

Nathan's job was to keep Ezell entertained while we cleaned and decorated. Sarai was on goodie bag duty, I was a one-woman cleaning crew, Paige was in charge of decorations, and A'Neesa was assigned to balloon duty.

Neesa came downstairs and sat at the kitchen table with her arms folded.

"How's my beautiful goddaughter?" Paige asked.

Neesa gave a half smile. "I'm fine, Auntee."

It was more than adolescence—her hostility was directed toward me, and I didn't know why. After breakfast, Neesa went to the basement, put up a few balloons, and left. I called her back downstairs to finish what she started. That's when she told me, "You do it!"

I put the dust mop down and charged toward her. "Oh, I'm gonna do it alright." Paige stood in my way, giving A'Neesa time to get back upstairs.

"Get your little red behind back down here!" I yelled.

Nathan came to the top of the stairs with the birthday boy on his shoulders. "What's all the yelling about?" he asked.

Neesa brushed past him to her bedroom and slammed the door.

"What's going on?" he asked me.

"Nothing, honey." I took off my earrings, squatted, stretched my legs, and said, "I got this." I proceeded toward the steps.

Paige grabbed my arm. "What are you doing?"

"Oh, I'm bout to beat her down."

"You gonna go to jail."

"Oh, don't worry. She ain't gonna make it to the phone."

Paige laughed. "Let me talk to her."

Once upstairs, Paige asked her, "What's wrong, baby?"

"Nothing."

"I'm your auntee! If you don't talk to me, who are you going to talk to?"

She sat on the side of the bed with her arms folded and lips sealed tight, just as stubborn as Reagan.

Paige said, "Fine, you don't have to talk to me. But you better go apologize to Laina before she come up here and go crouching tiger, hidden dragon on you."

"She's a hypocrite, auntee!"

Confused, Paige asked, "What happen?"

She blurted out, "Mommy was having an affair with my father."

"With Nathan?"

A'Neesa pulled a little diary with a silver lock from underneath her pillow. "No. DeLaina was sleeping with Marcus behind my mother's back."

Confused by the allegations, Paige stared at A'Neesa before taking the diary into her hands. Paige flipped through the pages, skimming through the confusion and hell that we survived, until she got to the entry with a folded picture of Marcus and me, kissing outside the club. The entry read …

The last time Marcus came ova here, he asked me do I ever feel guilty. I told him of course I do, but the truth is, I don't. I just want to be happy. She ain't eva had problems finding a man. Men look at me and wanna sleep with me. They look at her and wanna build a life. Why can't those same eyes see life in me?

Paige sighed. "Oh my goodness." As she continued flipping through the pages, she asked A'Neesa, "Did you read the whole book?"

She nodded her head yes.

The next entry read …

Marcus came ova last night. He think he's slick … he waited till afterwards to tell me he was gonna ask her to marry him cuz he know if he had told me before … who am I kiddin'? I still would have given him some.

I know we were just having a little fun and no feelings were suppose to be involved, but I had to ask. I told him, you and I make more sense that you and her … why her; why not me?

I mean, I expect him to do wrong and she expects him to do right. He just laughed and said after they got married, he and I couldn't sleep together anymore. That's what his lips say.

Paige skimmed the next couple of pages and quickly closed the diary, saying, "Oh my!" With a firm grip on it, she asked A'Neesa, "Where did you get this?"

"Sarai found it in a box in the attic."

Uncomfortable, Paige said, "You need to talk to Laina."

"NO!"

Gripping the diary in one hand, Paige said, "Honey, this is not what you think it is."

"Then what is it?"

"You're too young to understand."

"No, I'm not."

"Yes, you are!"

"I understand that DeLaina was screwing my father."

"You watch your mouth."

"It's the truth!"

"No, it isn't!" Paige laid the diary on the bed between

them. As she shook her head, she explained, "This isn't DeLaina's diary."

"Yes, it is."

Staring at the little tan book, Paige said, "Darling, this diary belonged to Reagan."

"No, it's DeLaina's."

"I'm your auntee. I will never lie to you." She put her hand on top of A'Neesa's. "I was there. These aren't DeLaina's words … these are Regan's."

"My mother?" There was a short pause before she attempted to interpret "But it said … Then who was the woman engaged to my father?"

"DeLaina."

In a faint voice, she said, "Mommy?" In a state of confusion, she said, "But he … with Reagan and … Does she know he cheated on her?"

Paige nodded yes.

As A'Neesa sat there overwhelmed, trying to digest the situation, Paige explained, "DeLaina and Reagan were best friends at one point. Rea was a good person who made some very bad decisions."

Although Paige tried to comfort A'Neesa, she withdrew. She sat in her window seat with her knees pulled in close to her chest, thinking.

Leaving Neesa to sort out her emotions, Paige came back downstairs to help me get ready for the party, only telling me that my little girl was growing up. I asked her if she was able to find out what was going on with her, but she only said, "She's a teenager. You know how they are. I'm sure she'll tell you when she's ready."

After a few days, Neesa still seemed a little distance, but I could feel her coming around.

Gonna Party Like It's My Birthday!

Over the course of my life, there were many times I didn't think I would make it to the next moment much less the next day, yet there I was, by the grace of God, on my forty-seventh birthday.

Nathan sent me to the spa for a day of pampering. When I got back, no one was home. Relaxed, I slowly climbed the staircase. When I reached the top, there was a note taped to my bedroom door that said, *Be ready at 7*. I smiled to myself like a little kid on Christmas Eve counting down the hours. I love surprises. When I entered my bedroom, there was a long garment bag lying on the bed with a note that said, *Wear me.*

I pinned up my hair and shimmied into the red and black form-fitting, strapless evening gown. No sooner than I slipped my feet into the three-inch open toed sandals, the door bell rang.

It was Nathan, standing there with three dozen red roses.

"WOW!" he said. "Baby, you look amazing."

Behind him was a man in a black derby and a tuxedo, holding open the door to a stretch Hummer.

"You rented a limo?"

"Tonight is your night!"

We sat in the back, cuddled up like teenagers enjoying every moment. I kept asking, "Where are we going?" But he just insisted that it was a surprise.

When the driver finally stopped, I looked out the window to see we were at the largest hotel in Connecticut. Jokingly, I said, "Baby, you gonna give me some for my birthday?"

"I'm-a pray for you!"

As my husband proudly escorted me in, we walked through the restaurant to a private dimly lit area where everyone jumped out and yelled, "SURPRISE!!"

"OH MY GOODNESS!"

Looking around the room, I noted that everyone was there: members of the church, members from my old church in Annapolis, friends, neighbors, Mike and his wife Tracey, Paige, and the kids. There had to be over two hundred people there. As I moved through the room, thanking people for coming and accepting well-wishes, an older woman with long silky silver hair stopped me, kissed me on the cheek, and said, "Happy birthday, Lainee."

I stood there frozen as my heart pounded rapidly, attempting to catch up with my mind. As I stood in the middle of the floor, baffled, Nathan took the microphone and asked everyone to take their seat. I turned around and caught a final glimpse of the woman I believed to be my mother just as she walked under the exit sign.

Nathan insisted, "Baby, that means you, too."

Several people stood up and recalled their favorite DeLaina moments, but I must admit my focus tittered as my mind raced through emotions, shifting from *what is she doing here*? to *where did she go*? A few more people spoke, then my husband took the microphone.

"You guys have no idea how incredible this woman really is. Ya know, sometimes I hear her praying in the morning or late at night for these kids and every area of my life. I think she prays for us more than she prays for herself." He smiled. "Baby, you're my good when everything seems bad. You inspire me.

You're my best friend and I love you. Happy birthday, baby!"

I blew him a kiss.

"The kids have something to say," he said.

The three of them lined up side by side, youngest to oldest. Ezell took the microphone and said, "Happy birthday, Mommy! I made you a surprise but I left it on my bed. I'll give you a hint … it's a picture of me and you on Mommy and Son Day." Everyone laughed at his innocence.

Sarai then took the microphone. "You are my favorite mommy."

I laughed. "I'm your only mommy!"

With her quick wit, she said, "Don't sell yourself short. You're still the best!"

Everyone laughed, thinking that was rehearsed, but that was just a part of her personality.

She handed the microphone to A'Neesa. "You are the most amazing woman I know. I just want to take a moment to say thank you for all the times you never heard it. Thank you! Thank you! Thank you!"

As she continued saying thank you, Sarai pointed her microphone at Ezell and he said, "Thank you for happy-face pancakes on Saturdays."

Sarai said, "Thank you for loving me even when I make a mistake."

A'Neesa added, "Thank you for being patient

and understanding."

The guests stood and clapped as Ezell and Sarai walked away from the podium.

A'Neesa looked at me. "There's something else I want to say. Something's been on my mind for the past week, and I think I just figured it out." She looked out into the crowd. "I'm sure most of you didn't know I was adopted."

Ezell whispered with innocence, "What's adopted?"

Sarai, always thinking she's his mother, whispered back, "I'll tell you when you get older."

A'Neesa continued, "Last week at teen Bible study, Deacon Chase said God saw our unformed bodies and all our days before one existed." With a tear in her eye, she said, "You always taught us that God would supply all our needs." Her tears dropped one by one. "Now I get it. He knew who I was in my mother's belly but knew she couldn't give me everything that I needed, but because he's a supplier ..."

I stood up to acknowledge the wisdom spouting from my child's lips. I always thought of her as my little girl, but there was something so grown up about what she said.

"Mommy, he made a way for me to have exactly what I needed ... in you."

I don't think she understood the impact of her

words. There wasn't a dry eye in the room. As if she hadn't said enough, she began to sing a cappella, "Did you ever know that you're my hero?"

I covered my mouth in amazement. I had never so much as heard her hum much less sing.

"You're everything I would like to be."

She had a mature, jazzy, Jill Scott sound to her voice.

"I can fly higher than an eagle … 'cause you are the wind beneath my wings."

To Contact The Author

Tammi L. Jackson
P.O. Box 1289
Ellicott City, MD 21041

tam@tammijackson.com

TO ORDER MORE BOOKS:

www.tammijackson.com